CRIMINAL PROCEDURE

2020 Case and Statutory Supplement

CRIMINAL PROCEDURE

2020 Case and Statutory Supplement

Erwin Chemerinsky

Dean and Jesse H. Choper Distinguished Professor of Law
University of California, Berkeley School of Law

Laurie L. Levenson

Professor of Law and
David W. Burcham Chair in Ethical Advocacy
Loyola Law School

SUSTAINABLE FORESTRY INITIATIVE
Certified Chain of Custody
At Least 10% Certified Forest Content
www.sfiprogram.org
SFI-01028

About Wolters Kluwer Legal & Regulatory U.S.

Wolters Kluwer Legal & Regulatory U.S. delivers expert content and solutions in the areas of law, corporate compliance, health compliance, reimbursement, and legal education. Its practical solutions help customers successfully navigate the demands of a changing environment to drive their daily activities, enhance decision quality and inspire confident outcomes.

Serving customers worldwide, its legal and regulatory portfolio includes products under the Aspen Publishers, CCH Incorporated, Kluwer Law International, ftwilliam.com and MediRegs names. They are regarded as exceptional and trusted resources for general legal and practice-specific knowledge, compliance and risk management, dynamic workflow solutions, and expert commentary.

CONTENTS

Contents

Contents

PREFACE

The third edition of the casebook was published in 2018 and includes cases decided by June 28, 2017. This Supplement is needed for a few reasons. First, it covers cases decided since publication of the third edition. Second, we have included new material in this Supplement on police excessive force and on civil remedies for Fourth Amendment violations. Finally, it is a statutory supplement providing statutory material related to each of the chapters.

We plan to do a supplement each year. Each will include the cases decided since the latest edition of the casebook was published, as well as the most recent version of this statutory material. We welcome comments and suggestions from the professors and students using our book.

Erwin Chemerinsky
Laurie Levenson

July 2020

CRIMINAL PROCEDURE

2020 Case and Statutory Supplement

Chapter 1

INTRODUCTION TO CRIMINAL PROCEDURE

E. The Application of the Bill of Rights to the States

3. The Current Law as to What's Incorporated (casebook p. 24)

Although almost all of the Bill of Rights has been deemed incorporated and thus to apply to state and local governments, the Court never had ruled on whether the Eighth Amendment's excessive fines clause applies to state and local governments. The Court addressed and resolved that issue in *Timbs v. Indiana*.

Timbs v. Indiana
139 S. Ct. 682 (2019)

Justice GINSBURG delivered the opinion of the Court.

Tyson Timbs pleaded guilty in Indiana state court to dealing in a controlled substance and conspiracy to commit theft. The trial court sentenced him to one year of home detention and five years of probation, which included a court-supervised addiction-treatment program. The sentence also required Timbs to pay fees and costs totaling $1,203. At the time of Timbs's arrest, the police seized his vehicle, a Land Rover SUV Timbs had purchased for about $42,000. Timbs paid for the vehicle with money he received from an insurance policy when his father died.

The State engaged a private law firm to bring a civil suit for forfeiture of Timbs's Land Rover, charging that the vehicle had been used to transport heroin. After Timbs's guilty plea in the criminal case, the trial court held a hearing on the forfeiture demand. Although finding that Timbs's vehicle had been used to facilitate violation of a criminal statute, the court denied the requested forfeiture, observing that Timbs had recently purchased the vehicle for $42,000, more than four times the maximum $10,000 monetary fine assessable against him for his drug conviction. Forfeiture of the Land Rover, the court determined, would be grossly disproportionate to the gravity of Timbs's offense, hence unconstitutional under the Eighth Amendment's Excessive Fines Clause. The Court of Appeals of Indiana affirmed that determination, but the Indiana Supreme Court reversed.

The question presented: Is the Eighth Amendment's Excessive Fines Clause an "incorporated" protection applicable to the States under the Fourteenth

Amendment's Due Process Clause? Like the Eighth Amendment's proscriptions of "cruel and unusual punishment" and "[e]xcessive bail," the protection against excessive fines guards against abuses of government's punitive or criminal-law-enforcement authority. This safeguard, we hold, is "fundamental to our scheme of ordered liberty," with "dee[p] root[s] in *687 [our] history and tradition." The Excessive Fines Clause is therefore incorporated by the Due Process Clause of the Fourteenth Amendment.

I

When ratified in 1791, the Bill of Rights applied only to the Federal Government. *Barron ex rel. Tiernan v. Mayor of Baltimore* (1833). "The con-stitutional Amendments adopted in the aftermath of the Civil War," however, "fundamentally altered our country's federal system." With only "a handful" of exceptions, this Court has held that the Fourteenth Amendment's Due Process Clause incorporates the protections contained in the Bill of Rights, rendering them applicable to the States. A Bill of Rights protection is incorporated, we have explained, if it is "fundamental to our scheme of ordered liberty," or "deeply rooted in this Nation's history and tradition."

Incorporated Bill of Rights guarantees are "enforced against the States under the Fourteenth Amendment according to the same standards that protect those personal rights against federal encroachment." Thus, if a Bill of Rights protection is incorporated, there is no daylight between the federal and state conduct it prohibits or requires.

Under the Eighth Amendment, "[e]xcessive bail shall not be required, nor excessive fines imposed, nor cruel and unusual punishments inflicted." Taken together, these Clauses place "parallel limitations" on "the power of those entrusted with the criminal-law function of government." Directly at issue here is the phrase "nor excessive fines imposed," which "limits the government's power to extract payments, whether in cash or in kind, 'as punishment for some offense.'" The Fourteenth Amendment, we hold, incorporates this protection.

The Excessive Fines Clause traces its venerable lineage back to at least 1215, when Magna Carta guaranteed that "[a] Free-man shall not be amerced for a small fault, but after the manner of the fault; and for a great fault after the great-ness thereof, saving to him his contenement . . . ." As relevant here, Magna Carta required that economic sanctions "be proportioned to the wrong" and "not be so large as to deprive [an offender] of his livelihood."

Despite Magna Carta, imposition of excessive fines persisted. The 17th century Stuart kings, in particular, were criticized for using large fines to raise reve-nue, harass their political foes, and indefinitely detain those unable to pay. When James II was overthrown in the Glorious Revolution, the attendant English Bill of Rights reaffirmed Magna Carta's guarantee by providing that "excessive Bail ought not to be required, nor excessive Fines imposed; nor cruel and unusual Punishments inflicted."

1. Introduction to Criminal Procedure

Across the Atlantic, this familiar language was adopted almost verbatim, first in the Virginia Declaration of Rights, then in the Eighth Amendment, which states: "Excessive bail shall not be required, nor excessive fines imposed, nor cruel and unusual punishments inflicted."

Adoption of the Excessive Fines Clause was in tune not only with English law; the Clause resonated as well with similar colonial-era provisions.

An even broader consensus obtained in 1868 upon ratification of the Fourteenth Amendment. By then, the constitutions of 35 of the 37 States—accounting for over 90% of the U.S. population—expressly prohibited excessive fines. Today, acknowledgment of the right's fundamental nature remains widespread. As Indiana itself reports, all 50 States have a constitutional provision prohibiting the imposition of excessive fines either directly or by requiring proportionality.

For good reason, the protection against excessive fines has been a constant shield throughout Anglo-American history: Exorbitant tolls undermine other constitutional liberties. Excessive fines can be used, for example, to retaliate against or chill the speech of political enemies, as the Stuarts' critics learned several centuries ago. Even absent a political motive, fines may be employed "in a measure out of accord with the penal goals of retribution and deterrence," for "fines are a source of revenue," while other forms of punishment "cost a State money."

In short, the historical and logical case for concluding that the Fourteenth Amendment incorporates the Excessive Fines Clause is overwhelming. Protection against excessive punitive economic sanctions secured by the Clause is, to repeat, both "fundamental to our scheme of ordered liberty" and "deeply rooted in this Nation's history and tradition."

II

The State of Indiana does not meaningfully challenge the case for incorporating the Excessive Fines Clause as a general matter. Instead, the State argues that the Clause does not apply to its use of civil *in rem* forfeitures because, the State says, the Clause's specific application to such forfeitures is neither fundamental nor deeply rooted.

In *Austin v. United States* (1993), however, this Court held that civil *in rem* forfeitures fall within the Clause's protection when they are at least partially punitive. *Austin* arose in the federal context. But when a Bill of Rights protection is incorporated, the protection applies "identically to both the Federal Government and the States."

Justice GORSUCH, concurring.

The majority faithfully applies our precedent and, based on a wealth of historical evidence, concludes that the Fourteenth Amendment incorporates the Eighth Amendment's Excessive Fines Clause against the States. I agree with that conclusion. As an original matter, I acknowledge, the appropriate vehicle for incorporation may well be the Fourteenth Amendment's Privileges or Immunities Clause, rather than, as this Court has long assumed, the Due Process Clause. But nothing in this case turns on that question, and, regardless of the precise vehicle, there can be no serious doubt that the Fourteenth Amendment requires the States to respect the freedom from excessive fines enshrined in the Eighth Amendment.

Justice THOMAS, concurring in the judgment.

I agree with the Court that the Fourteenth Amendment makes the Eighth Amendment's prohibition on excessive fines fully applicable to the States. But I cannot agree with the route the Court takes to reach this conclusion. Instead of reading the Fourteenth Amendment's Due Process Clause to encompass a substantive right that has nothing to do with "process," I would hold that the right to be free from excessive fines is one of the "privileges or immunities of citizens of the United States" protected by the Fourteenth Amendment.

The right against excessive fines traces its lineage back in English law nearly a millennium, and from the founding of our country, it has been consistently recognized as a core right worthy of constitutional protection. As a constitutionally enumerated right understood to be a privilege of American citizenship, the Eighth Amendment's prohibition on excessive fines applies in full to the States.

Chapter 2

SEARCHES AND SEIZURES

B. What Is a Search?

5. Observation and Monitoring of Public Behavior (casebook p. 81)

In *United States v. Jones* (casebook p. 38), the Supreme Court held that it is a violation of the Fourth Amendment for the police to put a GPS device on someone's car without a valid warrant. But what if the police track someone through cellular location information? Does it matter that the cellular company has the information and under *Maryland v. Smith* (casebook p. 89) is that enough to eliminate a reasonable expectation of privacy? That is the issue in *Carpenter v. United States*.

Carpenter v. United States
138 S. Ct. 2206 (2018)

Chief Justice ROBERTS delivered the opinion of the Court.

This case presents the question whether the Government conducts a search under the Fourth Amendment when it accesses historical cell phone records that provide a comprehensive chronicle of the user's past movements.

I

There are 396 million cell phone service accounts in the United States—for a Nation of 326 million people. Cell phones perform their wide and growing variety of functions by connecting to a set of radio antennas called "cell sites." Although cell sites are usually mounted on a tower, they can also be found on light posts, flagpoles, church steeples, or the sides of buildings. Cell sites typically have several directional antennas that divide the covered area into sectors.

Cell phones continuously scan their environment looking for the best signal, which generally comes from the closest cell site. Most modern devices, such as smartphones, tap into the wireless network several times a minute whenever their signal is on, even if the owner is not using one of the phone's features. Each time the phone connects to a cell site, it generates a time-stamped record known as cell-site location information (CSLI). The precision of this information depends on the size of the geographic area covered by the cell site. The greater the concentration of cell sites, the smaller the coverage area. As data usage from cell phones has increased, wireless carriers have installed more cell sites to handle the traffic. That has led to increasingly compact coverage areas, especially in urban areas.

Wireless carriers collect and store CSLI for their own business purposes, including finding weak spots in their network and applying "roaming" charges when another carrier routes data through their cell sites. In addition, wireless carriers often sell aggregated location records to data brokers, without individual identifying information of the sort at issue here. While carriers have long retained CSLI for the start and end of incoming calls, in recent years phone companies have also collected location information from the transmission of text messages and routine data connections. Accordingly, modern cell phones generate increasingly vast amounts of increasingly precise CSLI.

In 2011, police officers arrested four men suspected of robbing a series of Radio Shack and (ironically enough) T-Mobile stores in Detroit. One of the men confessed that, over the previous four months, the group (along with a rotating cast of getaway drivers and lookouts) had robbed nine different stores in Michigan and Ohio. The suspect identified 15 accomplices who had participated in the heists and gave the FBI some of their cell phone numbers; the FBI then reviewed his call records to identify additional numbers that he had called around the time of the robberies.

Based on that information, the prosecutors applied for court orders under the Stored Communications Act to obtain cell phone records for petitioner Timothy Carpenter and several other suspects. That statute, as amended in 1994, permits the Government to compel the disclosure of certain telecommunications records when it "offers specific and articulable facts showing that there are reasonable grounds to believe" that the records sought "are relevant and material to an ongoing criminal investigation." Federal Magistrate Judges issued two orders directing Carpenter's wireless carriers—MetroPCS and Sprint—to disclose "cell/site sector [information] for [Carpenter's] telephone[ ] at call origination and at call termination for incoming and outgoing calls" during the four-month period when the string of robberies occurred. The first order sought 152 days of cell-site records from MetroPCS, which produced records spanning 127 days. The second order requested seven days of CSLI from Sprint, which produced two days of records covering the period when Carpenter's phone was "roaming" in northeastern Ohio. Altogether the Government obtained 12,898 location points cataloging Carpenter's movements—an average of 101 data points per day.

Carpenter was charged with six counts of robbery and an additional six counts of carrying a firearm during a federal crime of violence. Prior to trial, Carpenter moved to suppress the cell-site data provided by the wireless carriers. He argued that the Government's seizure of the records violated the Fourth Amendment because they had been obtained without a warrant supported by probable cause. The District Court denied the motion.

2. Searches and Seizures

At trial, seven of Carpenter's confederates pegged him as the leader of the operation. In addition, FBI agent Christopher Hess offered expert testimony about the cell-site data. Hess explained that each time a cell phone taps into the wireless network, the carrier logs a time-stamped record of the cell site and particular sector that were used. With this information, Hess produced maps that placed Carpenter's phone near four of the charged robberies. In the Government's view, the location records clinched the case: They confirmed that Carpenter was "right where the . . . robbery was at the exact time of the robbery." Carpenter was convicted on all but one of the firearm counts and sentenced to more than 100 years in prison.

The Court of Appeals for the Sixth Circuit affirmed. The court held that Carpenter lacked a reasonable expectation of privacy in the location information collected by the FBI because he had shared that information with his wireless carriers.

II

For much of our history, Fourth Amendment search doctrine was "tied to common-law trespass" and focused on whether the Government "obtains information by physically intruding on a constitutionally protected area." More recently, the Court has recognized that "property rights are not the sole measure of Fourth Amendment violations." In *Katz v. United States* (1967), we established that "the Fourth Amendment protects people, not places," and expanded our conception of the Amendment to protect certain expectations of privacy as well.

Although no single rubric definitively resolves which expectations of privacy are entitled to protection, the analysis is informed by historical understandings "of what was deemed an unreasonable search and seizure when [the Fourth Amendment] was adopted." On this score, our cases have recognized some basic guideposts. First, that the Amendment seeks to secure "the privacies of life" against "arbitrary power." Second, and relatedly, that a central aim of the Framers was "to place obstacles in the way of a too permeating police surveillance."

We have kept this attention to Founding-era understandings in mind when applying the Fourth Amendment to innovations in surveillance tools. As technology has enhanced the Government's capacity to encroach upon areas normally guarded from inquisitive eyes, this Court has sought to "assure [ ] preservation of that degree of privacy against government that existed when the Fourth Amendment was adopted." *Kyllo v. United States* (2001). For that reason, we rejected in *Kyllo* a "mechanical interpretation" of the Fourth Amendment and held that use of a thermal imager to detect heat radiating from the side of the defendant's home was a search. Because any other conclusion would leave homeowners "at the mercy of advancing technology," we determined that the Government—absent a warrant—could not capitalize on such new sense-enhancing technology to explore what was happening within the home.

The case before us involves the Government's acquisition of wireless carrier cell-site records revealing the location of Carpenter's cell phone whenever it made or received calls. This sort of digital data—personal location information maintained by a third party—does not fit neatly under existing precedents. Instead, requests for cell-site records lie at the intersection of two lines of cases, both of which inform our understanding of the privacy interests at stake.

The first set of cases addresses a person's expectation of privacy in his physical location and movements. In a second set of decisions, the Court has drawn a line between what a person keeps to himself and what he shares with others. [*Smith v. Maryland* (1979)] We have previously held that "a person has no legitimate expectation of privacy in information he voluntarily turns over to third parties." That remains true "even if the information is revealed on the assumption that it will be used only for a limited purpose." *United States v. Miller* (1976). As a result, the Government is typically free to obtain such information from the recipient without triggering Fourth Amendment protections.

III

The question we confront today is how to apply the Fourth Amendment to a new phenomenon: the ability to chronicle a person's past movements through the record of his cell phone signals. Such tracking partakes of many of the qualities of the GPS monitoring we considered in *Jones*. Much like GPS tracking of a vehicle, cell phone location information is detailed, encyclopedic, and effortlessly compiled.

At the same time, the fact that the individual continuously reveals his location to his wireless carrier implicates the third-party principle of *Smith* and *Miller*. But while the third-party doctrine applies to telephone numbers and bank records, it is not clear whether its logic extends to the qualitatively different category of cell-site records. After all, when *Smith* was decided in 1979, few could have imagined a society in which a phone goes wherever its owner goes, conveying to the wireless carrier not just dialed digits, but a detailed and comprehensive record of the person's movements.

We decline to extend *Smith* and *Miller* to cover these novel circumstances. Given the unique nature of cell phone location records, the fact that the information is held by a third party does not by itself overcome the user's claim to Fourth Amendment protection. [W]e hold that an individual maintains a legitimate expectation of privacy in the record of his physical movements as captured through CSLI. The location information obtained from Carpenter's wireless carriers was the product of a search.

A person does not surrender all Fourth Amendment protection by venturing into the public sphere. To the contrary, "what [one] seeks to preserve as private, even in an area accessible to the public, may be constitutionally protected." A majority of this Court has already recognized that individuals have a reasonable expectation of privacy in the whole of their physical movements. Prior to the digital age, law enforcement might have pursued a suspect for a brief stretch, but doing so "for any extended period of time was difficult and costly and therefore rarely undertaken." For that reason, "society's expectation has been that law enforcement agents and others would not—and indeed, in the main, simply could not—secretly monitor and catalogue every single movement of an individual's car for a very long period."

Allowing government access to cell-site records contravenes that expectation. Although such records are generated for commercial purposes, that distinction does not negate Carpenter's anticipation of privacy in his physical location. Mapping a cell phone's location over the course of 127 days provides an all-encompassing record of the holder's whereabouts. As with GPS information, the time-stamped data provides an intimate window into a person's life, revealing not only his particular movements, but through them his "familial, political, professional, religious, and sexual associations." These location records "hold for many Americans the 'privacies of life.'" And like GPS monitoring, cell phone tracking is remarkably easy, cheap, and efficient compared to traditional investigative tools. With just the click of a button, the Government can access each carrier's deep repository of historical location information at practically no expense.

In fact, historical cell-site records present even greater privacy concerns than the GPS monitoring of a vehicle we considered in *Jones* [*v. United States.*]" [A] cell phone—almost a "feature of human anatomy," tracks nearly exactly the movements of its owner. While individuals regularly leave their vehicles, they compulsively carry cell phones with them all the time. A cell phone faithfully follows its owner beyond public thoroughfares and into private residences, doctor's offices, political headquarters, and other potentially revealing locales.

Moreover, the retrospective quality of the data here gives police access to a category of information otherwise unknowable. In the past, attempts to reconstruct a person's movements were limited by a dearth of records and the frailties of recollection. With access to CSLI, the Government can now travel back in time to retrace a person's whereabouts, subject only to the retention polices of the wireless carriers, which currently maintain records for up to five years. Critically, because location information is continually logged for all of the 400 million devices in the United States—not just those belonging to persons who might happen to come under investigation—this newfound tracking capacity runs against everyone. Unlike with the GPS device in *Jones*, police need not even know in advance whether they want to follow a particular individual, or when.

Whoever the suspect turns out to be, he has effectively been tailed every moment of every day for five years, and the police may—in the Government's view—call upon the results of that surveillance without regard to the constraints of the Fourth Amendment. Only the few without cell phones could escape this tireless and absolute surveillance. Accordingly, when the Government accessed CSLI from the wireless carriers, it invaded Carpenter's reasonable expectation of privacy in the whole of his physical movements.

The Government's primary contention to the contrary is that the third-party doctrine governs this case. In its view, cell-site records are fair game because they are "business records" created and maintained by the wireless carriers. The Government's position fails to contend with the seismic shifts in digital technology that made possible the tracking of not only Carpenter's location but also everyone else's, not for a short period but for years and years. Sprint Corporation and its competitors are not your typical witnesses. Unlike the nosy neighbor who keeps an eye on comings and goings, they are ever alert, and their memory is nearly infallible. There is a world of difference between the limited types of personal information addressed in *Smith* and *Miller* and the exhaustive chronicle of location information casually collected by wireless carriers today. The Government thus is not asking for a straightforward application of the third-party doctrine, but instead a significant extension of it to a distinct category of information.

The third-party doctrine partly stems from the notion that an individual has a reduced expectation of privacy in information knowingly shared with another. But the fact of "diminished privacy interests does not mean that the Fourth Amendment falls out of the picture entirely." [T]his case is not about "using a phone" or a person's movement at a particular time. It is about a detailed chronicle of a person's physical presence compiled every day, every moment, over several years. Such a chronicle implicates privacy concerns far beyond those considered in *Smith* and *Miller*.

Neither does the second rationale underlying the third-party doctrine — voluntary exposure — hold up when it comes to CSLI. Cell phone location information is not truly "shared" as one normally understands the term. In the first place, cell phones and the services they provide are "such a pervasive and insistent part of daily life" that carrying one is indispensable to participation in modern society. Second, a cell phone logs a cell-site record by dint of its operation, without any affirmative act on the part of the user beyond powering up. Virtually any activity on the phone generates CSLI, including incoming calls, texts, or e-mails and countless other data connections that a phone automatically makes when checking for news, weather, or social media updates. Apart from disconnecting the phone from the network, there is no way to avoid leaving behind a trail of location data. As a result, in no meaningful sense does the user voluntarily "assume[ ] the risk" of turning over a comprehensive dossier of his physical movements.

We therefore decline to extend *Smith* and *Miller* to the collection of CSLI. Given the unique nature of cell phone location information, the fact that the Government obtained the information from a third party does not overcome Carpenter's claim to Fourth Amendment protection. The Government's acquisition of the cell-site records was a search within the meaning of the Fourth Amendment.

Our decision today is a narrow one. We do not express a view on matters not before us: real-time CSLI or "tower dumps" (a download of information on all the devices that connected to a particular cell site during a particular interval).

2. Searches and Seizures

We do not disturb the application of *Smith* and *Miller* or call into question conventional surveillance techniques and tools, such as security cameras. Nor do we address other business records that might incidentally reveal location information. Further, our opinion does not consider other collection techniques involving foreign affairs or national security. As Justice Frankfurter noted when considering new innovations in airplanes and radios, the Court must tread carefully in such cases, to ensure that we do not "embarrass the future."

IV

Having found that the acquisition of Carpenter's CSLI was a search, we also conclude that the Government must generally obtain a warrant supported by probable cause before acquiring such records. Although the "ultimate measure of the constitutionality of a governmental search is 'reasonableness,'" our cases establish that warrantless searches are typically unreasonable where "a search is undertaken by law enforcement officials to discover evidence of criminal wrongdoing." Thus, "[i]n the absence of a warrant, a search is reasonable only if it falls within a specific exception to the warrant requirement."

The Government acquired the cell-site records pursuant to a court order issued under the Stored Communications Act, which required the Government to show "reasonable grounds" for believing that the records were "relevant and material to an ongoing investigation." That showing falls well short of the probable cause required for a warrant. The Court usually requires "some quantum of individualized suspicion" before a search or seizure may take place. Under the standard in the Stored Communications Act, however, law enforcement need only show that the cell-site evidence might be pertinent to an ongoing investigation—a "gigantic" departure from the probable cause rule, as the Government explained below. Before compelling a wireless carrier to turn over a subscriber's CSLI, the Government's obligation is a familiar one—get a warrant.

As Justice Brandeis explained in his famous dissent, the Court is obligated—as "[s]ubtler and more far-reaching means of invading privacy have become available to the Government"—to ensure that the "progress of science" does not erode Fourth Amendment protections. Here the progress of science has afforded law enforcement a powerful new tool to carry out its important responsibilities. At the same time, this tool risks Government encroachment of the sort the Framers, "after consulting the lessons of history," drafted the Fourth Amendment to prevent.

We decline to grant the state unrestricted access to a wireless carrier's database of physical location information. In light of the deeply revealing nature of CSLI, its depth, breadth, and comprehensive reach, and the inescapable and automatic nature of its collection, the fact that such information is gathered by a third party does not make it any less deserving of Fourth Amendment protection. The Government's acquisition of the cell-site records here was a search under that Amendment.

Justice KENNEDY, with whom Justice THOMAS and Justice ALITO join dissenting.

This case involves new technology, but the Court's stark departure from relevant Fourth Amendment precedents and principles is, in my submission, unnecessary and incorrect, requiring this respectful dissent.

The new rule the Court seems to formulate puts needed, reasonable, accepted, lawful, and congressionally authorized criminal investigations at serious risk in serious cases, often when law enforcement seeks to prevent the threat of violent crimes. And it places undue restrictions on the lawful and necessary enforcement powers exercised not only by the Federal Government, but also by law enforcement in every State and locality throughout the Nation. Adherence to this Court's longstanding precedents and analytic framework would have been the proper and prudent way to resolve this case.

The Court has twice held that individuals have no Fourth Amendment interests in business records which are possessed, owned, and controlled by a third party. *United States v. Miller* (1976); *Smith v. Maryland* (1979). This is true even when the records contain personal and sensitive information. So when the Government uses a subpoena to obtain, for example, bank records, telephone records, and credit card statements from the businesses that create and keep these records, the Government does not engage in a search of the business's customers within the meaning of the Fourth Amendment.

In this case petitioner challenges the Government's right to use compulsory process to obtain a now-common kind of business record: cell-site records held by cell phone service providers. The Government acquired the records through an investigative process enacted by Congress. Upon approval by a neutral magistrate, and based on the Government's duty to show reasonable necessity, it authorizes the disclosure of records and information that are under the control and ownership of the cell phone service provider, not its customer. Petitioner acknowledges that the Government may obtain a wide variety of business records using compulsory process, and he does not ask the Court to revisit its precedents. Yet he argues that, under those same precedents, the Government searched his records when it used court-approved compulsory process to obtain the cell-site information at issue here.

Cell-site records, however, are no different from the many other kinds of business records the Government has a lawful right to obtain by compulsory process. Customers like petitioner do not own, possess, control, or use the records, and for that reason have no reasonable expectation that they cannot be disclosed pursuant to lawful compulsory process.

The Court today disagrees. It holds for the first time that by using compulsory process to obtain records of a business entity, the Government has not just engaged in an impermissible action, but has conducted a search of the business's customer. The Court further concludes that the search in this case was unreasonable and the Government needed to get a warrant to obtain more than six days of cell-site records.

In concluding that the Government engaged in a search, the Court unhinges Fourth Amendment doctrine from the property-based concepts that have long grounded the analytic framework that pertains in these cases. In doing so it draws an unprincipled and unworkable line between cell-site records on the one hand and financial and telephonic records on the other. According to today's majority opinion, the Government can acquire a record of every credit card purchase and phone call a person makes over months or years without upsetting a legitimate expectation of privacy. But, in the Court's view, the Government crosses a constitutional line when it obtains a court's approval to issue a subpoena for more than six days of cell-site records in order to determine whether a person was within several hundred city blocks of a crime scene. That distinction is illogical and will frustrate principled application of the Fourth Amendment in many routine yet vital law enforcement operations.

It is true that the Cyber Age has vast potential both to expand and restrict individual freedoms in dimensions not contemplated in earlier times. [H]owever, there is simply no basis here for concluding that the Government interfered with information that the cell phone customer, either from a legal or commonsense standpoint, should have thought the law would deem owned or controlled by him.

Justice THOMAS, dissenting.

This case should not turn on "whether" a search occurred. It should turn, instead, on *whose* property was searched. The Fourth Amendment guarantees individuals the right to be secure from unreasonable searches of "*their* persons, houses, papers, and effects." In other words, "*each* person has the right to be secure against unreasonable searches . . . in *his own* person, house, papers, and effects." By obtaining the cell-site records of MetroPCS and Sprint, the Government did not search Carpenter's property. He did not create the records, he does not maintain them, he cannot control them, and he cannot destroy them. Neither the terms of his contracts nor any provision of law makes the records his. The records belong to MetroPCS and Sprint.

The Court concludes that, although the records are not Carpenter's, the Government must get a warrant because Carpenter had a reasonable "expectation of privacy" in the location information that they reveal. The more fundamental problem with the Court's opinion, however, is its use of the "reasonable expectation of privacy" test, which was first articulated by Justice Harlan in *Katz v. United States* (1967) (concurring opinion). The *Katz* test has no basis in the text or history of the Fourth Amendment. And, it invites courts to make judgments about policy, not law. Until we confront the problems with this test, *Katz* will continue to distort Fourth Amendment jurisprudence.

Under the *Katz* test, a "search" occurs whenever "government officers violate a person's 'reasonable expectation of privacy.'" The most glaring problem with this test is that it has "no plausible foundation in the text of the Fourth Amendment." The Fourth Amendment, as relevant here, protects "[t]he right of the people to be secure in their persons, houses, papers, and effects, against unreasonable searches." By defining "search" to mean "any violation of a reasonable expectation of privacy," the *Katz* test misconstrues virtually every one of these words.

That the *Katz* test departs so far from the text of the Fourth Amendment is reason enough to reject it. But the *Katz* test also has proved unworkable in practice. Jurists and commentators tasked with deciphering our jurisprudence have described the *Katz* regime as "an unpredictable jumble," "a mass of contradictions and obscurities," "all over the map," "riddled with inconsistency and incoherence," "a series of inconsistent and bizarre results that [the Court] has left entirely undefended," "unstable," "chameleon-like," "notoriously unhelpful,'" "a conclusion rather than a starting point for analysis," "distressingly unmanageable," "a dismal failure," "flawed to the core," "unadorned fiat," and "inspired by the kind of logic that produced Rube Goldberg's bizarre contraptions."[10] Even Justice Harlan, four years after penning his concurrence in *Katz*, confessed that the test encouraged "the substitution of words for analysis."

Because the *Katz* test is a failed experiment, this Court is dutybound to reconsider it. Until it does, I agree with my dissenting colleagues' reading of our precedents.

Justice ALITO, with whom Justice THOMAS, joins dissenting.

I share the Court's concern about the effect of new technology on personal privacy, but I fear that today's decision will do far more harm than good. The Court's reasoning fractures two fundamental pillars of Fourth Amendment law, and in doing so, it guarantees a blizzard of litigation while threatening many legitimate and valuable investigative practices upon which law enforcement has rightfully come to rely.

First, the Court ignores the basic distinction between an actual search (dispatching law enforcement officers to enter private premises and root through private papers and effects) and an order merely requiring a party to look through its own records and produce specified documents. The former, which intrudes on personal privacy far more deeply, requires probable cause; the latter does not. Treating an order to produce like an actual search, as today's decision does, is revolutionary. It violates both the original understanding of the Fourth Amendment and more than a century of Supreme Court precedent. Unless it is somehow restricted to the particular situation in the present case, the Court's move will cause upheaval. Must every grand jury subpoena *duces tecum* be supported by probable cause? If so, investigations of terrorism, political corruption, white-collar crime, and many other offenses will be stymied. And what about subpoenas and other document-production orders issued by administrative agencies?

Second, the Court allows a defendant to object to the search of a third party's property. This also is revolutionary. The Fourth Amendment protects "[t]he right of the people to be secure in *their* persons, houses, papers, and effects" not the persons, houses, papers, and effects of others. Until today, we have been careful to heed this fundamental feature of the Amendment's text. This was true when the Fourth Amendment was tied to property law, and it remained true after *Katz v. United States* (1967), broadened the Amendment's reach.

By departing dramatically from these fundamental principles, the Court destabilizes long-established Fourth Amendment doctrine. We will be making repairs—or picking up the pieces—for a long time to come.

Justice GORSUCH, dissenting.

In the late 1960s this Court suggested for the first time that a search triggering the Fourth Amendment occurs when the government violates an "expectation of privacy" that "society is prepared to recognize as 'reasonable.'" Then, in a pair of decisions in the 1970s applying the *Katz* test, the Court held that a "reasonable expectation of privacy" *doesn't* attach to information shared with "third parties." By these steps, the Court came to conclude, the Constitution does nothing to limit investigators from searching records you've entrusted to your bank, accountant, and maybe even your doctor.

What's left of the Fourth Amendment? Today we use the Internet to do most everything. Smartphones make it easy to keep a calendar, correspond with friends, make calls, conduct banking, and even watch the game. Countless Internet companies maintain records about us and, increasingly, *for* us. Even our most private documents—those that, in other eras, we would have locked safely in a desk drawer or destroyed—now reside on third party servers. *Smith* and *Miller* teach that the police can review all of this material, on the theory that no one reasonably expects any of it will be kept private. But no one believes that, if they ever did.

Deciding what privacy interests *should be* recognized often calls for a pure policy choice, many times between incommensurable goods—between the value of privacy in a particular setting and society's interest in combating crime. Answering questions like that calls for the exercise of raw political will belonging to legislatures, not the legal judgment proper to courts. When judges abandon legal judgment for political will we not only risk decisions where "reasonable expectations of privacy" come to bear "an uncanny resemblance to those expectations of privacy" shared by Members of this Court. We also risk undermining public confidence in the courts themselves.

What does all this mean for the case before us? To start, I cannot fault the Sixth Circuit for holding that *Smith* and *Miller* extinguish any *Katz*-based Fourth Amendment interest in third party cell-site data. That is the plain effect of their categorical holdings. Nor can I fault the Court today for its implicit but unmistakable conclusion that the rationale of *Smith* and *Miller* is wrong; indeed, I agree with that. The Sixth Circuit was powerless to say so, but this Court can and should. At the same time, I do not agree with the Court's decision today to keep *Smith* and *Miller* on life support and supplement them with a new and multilayered inquiry that seems to be only *Katz*-squared. Returning there, I worry, promises more trouble than help. Instead, I would look to a more traditional Fourth Amendment approach. Even if *Katz* may still supply one way to prove a Fourth Amendment interest, it has never been the only way. Neglecting more traditional approaches may mean failing to vindicate the full protections of the Fourth Amendment.

Our case offers a cautionary example. It seems to me entirely possible a person's cell-site data could qualify as *his* papers or effects under existing law. Yes, the telephone carrier holds the information. . . . Plainly, customers have substantial legal interests in this information, including at least some right to include, exclude, and control its use. Those interests might even rise to the level of a property right.

The problem is that we do not know anything more. Before the district court and court of appeals, Mr. Carpenter pursued only a *Katz* "reasonable expectations" argument. He did not invoke the law of property or any analogies to the common law, either there or in his petition for certiorari. Even in his merits brief before this Court, Mr. Carpenter's discussion of his positive law rights in cell-site data was cursory. In these circumstances, I cannot help but conclude—reluctantly—that Mr. Carpenter forfeited perhaps his most promising line of argument.

E. Exceptions to the Warrant Requirement

1. Exigent Circumstances

d. *Limits on Exigent Circumstances* (casebook p. 175)

In *Missouri v. McNeely*, the Court rejected the argument that there are always exigent circumstances wen there is an arrest for driving under the influence. The Court said that absent exigent circumstances which prevent being able to obtain a warrant, the police must obtain one before taking blood from a person. In *Birchfield v. North Dakota*, the Court held that a state may require a person to submit to a breath test, but not a blood test when there is suspicion of driving under the influence.

In its most recent case, *Mitchell v. Wisconsin*, the Court considered whether exigent circumstances permit police to draw blood from an unconscious person who is suspected of driving under the influence.

Mitchell v. Wisconsin
139 S. Ct. 2525 (2019)

Justice ALITO announced the judgment of the Court and delivered an opinion in which THE CHIEF JUSTICE, Justice BREYER, and Justice KAVANAUGH join.

In this case, we return to a topic that we have addressed twice in recent years: the circumstances under which a police officer may administer a warrantless blood alcohol concentration (BAC) test to a motorist who appears to have been driving under the influence of alcohol. We have previously addressed what officers may do in two broad categories of cases. First, an officer may conduct a BAC test if the facts of a particular case bring it within the exigent-circumstances exception to the Fourth Amendment's general requirement of a warrant. Second, if an officer has probable cause to arrest a motorist for drunk driving, the officer may conduct a breath test (but not a blood test) under the rule allowing warrant-less searches of a person incident to arrest.

Today, we consider what police officers may do in a narrow but important category of cases: those in which the driver is unconscious and therefore cannot be given a breath test. In such cases, we hold, the exigent-circumstances rule almost always permits a blood test without a warrant. When a breath test is impossible, enforcement of the drunk-driving laws depends upon the administration of a blood test. And when a police officer encounters an unconscious driver, it is very likely that the driver would be taken to an emergency room and that his blood would be drawn for diagnostic purposes even if the police were not seeking BAC information. In addition, police officers most frequently come upon unconscious drivers when they report to the scene of an accident, and under those circumstances, the officers' many responsibilities—such as attending to other injured drivers or passengers and preventing further accidents—may be incompatible with the procedures that would be required to obtain a warrant. Thus, when a driver is unconscious, the general rule is that a warrant is not needed.

I

In *Birchfield v. North Dakota* (2016), we recounted the country's efforts over the years to address the terrible problem of drunk driving. Today, "all States have laws that prohibit motorists from driving with a [BAC] that exceeds a specified level." And to help enforce BAC limits, every State has passed what are popularly called implied-consent laws. As "a condition of the privilege of" using the public roads, these laws require that drivers submit to BAC testing "when there is sufficient reason to believe they are violating the State's drunk-driving laws."

Wisconsin's implied-consent law is much like those of the other 49 States and the District of Columbia. It deems drivers to have consented to breath or blood tests if an officer has reason to believe they have committed one of several drug- or alcohol-related offenses. Officers seeking to conduct a BAC test must read aloud a statement declaring their intent to administer the test and advising drivers of their options and the implications of their choice. If a driver's BAC level proves too high, his license will be suspended; but if he refuses testing, his license will be *revoked* and his refusal may be used against him in court. No test will be administered if a driver refuses—or, as the State would put it, "withdraws" his statutorily presumed consent. But "[a] person who is unconscious or otherwise not capable of withdrawing consent is presumed not to have" withdrawn it. More than half the States have provisions like this one regarding unconscious drivers.

The sequence of events that gave rise to this case began when Officer Alexander Jaeger of the Sheboygan Police Department received a report that petitioner Gerald Mitchell, appearing to be very drunk, had climbed into a van and driven off. Jaeger soon found Mitchell wandering near a lake. Stumbling and slurring his words, Mitchell could hardly stand without the support of two officers. Jaeger judged a field sobriety test hopeless, if not dangerous, and gave Mitchell a preliminary breath test. It registered a BAC level of 0.24%, triple the legal limit for driving in Wisconsin. Jaeger arrested Mitchell for operating a vehicle while intoxicated and, as is standard practice, drove him to a police station for a more reliable breath test using better equipment.

On the way, Mitchell's condition continued to deteriorate—so much so that by the time the squad car had reached the station, he was too lethargic even for a breath test. Jaeger therefore drove Mitchell to a nearby hospital for a blood test; Mitchell lost consciousness on the ride over and had to be wheeled in. Even so, Jaeger read aloud to a slumped Mitchell the standard statement giving drivers a chance to refuse BAC testing. Hearing no response, Jaeger asked hospital staff to draw a blood sample. Mitchell remained unconscious while the sample was taken, and analysis of his blood showed that his BAC, about 90 minutes after his arrest, was 0.222%.

Mitchell was charged with violating two related drunk-driving provisions. He moved to suppress the results of the blood test on the ground that it violated his Fourth Amendment right against "unreasonable searches" because it was conducted without a warrant.

II

We have also reviewed BAC tests under the "exigent circumstances" exception—which, as noted, allows warrantless searches "to prevent the imminent destruction of evidence." *Missouri v. McNeely* (2013). In *McNeely*, we were asked if this exception covers BAC testing of drunk-driving suspects in light of the fact that blood-alcohol evidence is always dissipating due to "natural metabolic processes." We answered that the fleeting quality of BAC evidence alone is not enough. But in *Schmerber* it *did* justify a blood test of a drunk driver who had gotten into a car accident that gave police other pressing duties, for then the "*further* delay" caused by a warrant application really "*would* have threatened the destruction of evidence."

Like *Schmerber*, this case sits much higher than *McNeely* on the exigency spectrum. *McNeely* was about the minimum degree of urgency common to all drunk-driving cases. In *Schmerber*, a car accident heightened that urgency. And here Mitchell's medical condition did just the same.

Mitchell's stupor and eventual unconsciousness also deprived officials of a reasonable opportunity to administer a breath test. To be sure, Officer Jaeger managed to conduct "a preliminary breath test" using a portable machine when he first encountered Mitchell at the lake. But he had no reasonable opportunity to give Mitchell a breath test using "evidence-grade breath testing machinery." As a result, it was reasonable for Jaeger to seek a better breath test at the station; he acted with reasonable dispatch to procure one; and when Mitchell's condition got in the way, it was reasonable for Jaeger to pursue a blood test.

III

A blood draw is a search of the person, so we must determine if its administration here without a warrant was reasonable. Though we have held that a warrant is normally required, we have also "made it clear that there are exceptions to the warrant requirement." And under the exception for exigent circumstances, a warrantless search is allowed when "'there is compelling need for official action and no time to secure a warrant.'" In *McNeely*, we considered how the exigent-circumstances exception applies to the broad category of cases in which a police officer has probable cause to believe that a motorist was driving under the influence of alcohol, and we do not revisit that question. Nor do we settle whether the exigent-circumstances exception covers the specific facts of this case. Instead, we address how the exception bears on the category of cases encompassed by the question on which we granted certiorari — those involving unconscious drivers. In those cases, the need for a blood test is compelling, and an officer's duty to attend to more pressing needs may leave no time to seek a warrant.

The importance of the needs served by BAC testing is hard to overstate. The bottom line is that BAC tests are needed for enforcing laws that save lives. The specifics, in short, are these: Highway safety is critical; it is served by laws that criminalize driving with a certain BAC level; and enforcing these legal BAC limits requires efficient testing to obtain BAC evidence, which naturally dissipates. So BAC tests are crucial links in a chain on which vital interests hang. And when a breath test is unavailable to advance those aims, a blood test becomes essential.

For these reasons, there clearly is a "compelling need" for a blood test of drunk-driving suspects whose condition deprives officials of a reasonable opportunity to conduct a breath test. The only question left, under our exigency doctrine, is whether this compelling need justifies a warrantless search because there is, furthermore, "'no time to secure a warrant.'"

We held that there was no time to secure a warrant before a blood test of a drunk-driving suspect in *Schmerber* because the officer there could "reasonably have believed that he was confronted with an emergency, in which the delay necessary to obtain a warrant, under the circumstances, threatened the destruction of evidence." So even if the constant dissipation of BAC evidence *alone* does not create an exigency, *Schmerber* shows that it does so when combined with other pressing needs:

Mitchell objects that a warrantless search is unnecessary in cases involving unconscious drivers because warrants these days can be obtained faster and more easily. But even in our age of rapid communication, "[w]arrants inevitably take some time for police officers or prosecutors to complete and for magistrate judges to review. Telephonic and electronic warrants may still require officers to follow time-consuming formalities designed to create an adequate record, such as preparing a duplicate warrant before calling the magistrate judge. . . . And improvements in communications technology do not guarantee that a magistrate judge will be available when an officer needs a warrant after making a late-night arrest."

In other words, with better technology, the time required has shrunk, but it has not disappeared. In the emergency scenarios created by unconscious drivers, forcing police to put off other tasks for even a relatively short period of time may have terrible collateral costs. That is just what it means for these situations to *be* emergencies.

IV

When police have probable cause to believe a person has committed a drunk-driving offense and the driver's unconsciousness or stupor requires him to be taken to the hospital or similar facility before police have a reasonable opportunity to administer a standard evidentiary breath test, they may almost always order a warrantless blood test to measure the driver's BAC without offending the Fourth Amendment. We do not rule out the possibility that in an unusual case a defendant would be able to show that his blood would not have been drawn if police had not been seeking BAC information, and that police could not have reasonably judged that a warrant application would interfere with other pressing needs or duties. Because Mitchell did not have a chance to attempt to make that showing, a remand for that purpose is necessary.

Justice THOMAS, concurring in the judgment.

Today, the plurality adopts a difficult-to-administer rule: Exigent circumstances are generally present when police encounter a person suspected of drunk driving—except when they aren't. The plurality's presumption will rarely be rebutted, but it will nevertheless burden both officers and courts who must attempt to apply it. "The better (and far simpler) way to resolve" this case is to apply "the *per se* rule" I proposed in *Missouri v. McNeely* (2013) (dissenting opinion); *Birchfield v. North Dakota* (2016) (Thomas, J., concurring in judgment in part and dissenting in part). Under that rule, the natural metabolization of alcohol in the blood stream "'creates an exigency once police have probable cause to believe the driver is drunk,'" regardless of whether the driver is conscious.

Justice SOTOMAYOR, with whom Justice GINSBURG, and Justice KAGAN join, dissenting.

The plurality's decision rests on the false premise that today's holding is necessary to spare law enforcement from a choice between attending to emergency situations and securing evidence used to enforce state drunk-driving laws. Not so. To be sure, drunk driving poses significant dangers that Wisconsin and other

States must be able to curb. But the question here is narrow: What must police do before ordering a blood draw of a person suspected of drunk driving who has become unconscious? Under the Fourth Amendment, the answer is clear: If there is time, get a warrant.

The State of Wisconsin conceded in the state courts that it had time to get a warrant to draw Gerald Mitchell's blood, and that should be the end of the matter. Because the plurality needlessly casts aside the established protections of the warrant requirement in favor of a brand new presumption of exigent circumstances that Wisconsin does not urge, that the state courts did not consider, and that contravenes this Court's precedent, I respectfully dissent.

When the aim of a search is to uncover evidence of a crime, the Fourth Amendment generally requires police to obtain a warrant. The warrant requirement is not a mere formality; it ensures that necessary judgment calls are made "'by a neutral and detached magistrate,'" not "'by the officer engaged in the often competitive enterprise of ferreting out crime.'" A warrant thus serves as a check against searches that violate the Fourth Amendment by ensuring that a police officer is not made the sole interpreter of the Constitution's protections. Accordingly, a search conducted without a warrant is *per se* unreasonable under the Fourth Amendment—subject only to a few specifically established and well-delineated exceptions."

Blood draws are "searches" under the Fourth Amendment. The act of drawing a person's blood, whether or not he is unconscious, "involve[s] a compelled physical intrusion beneath [the] skin and into [a person's] veins," all for the purpose of extracting evidence for a criminal investigation. The blood draw also "places in the hands of law enforcement authorities a sample that can be preserved and from which it is possible to extract information beyond a simple BAC reading," such as whether a person is pregnant, is taking certain medications, or suffers from an illness. That "invasion of bodily integrity" disturbs "an individual's 'most personal and deep-rooted expectations of privacy.'"

Schmerber and *McNeely* establish that there is no categorical exigency exception for blood draws, although exigent circumstances might justify a warrantless blood draw on the facts of a particular case. And from *Birchfield*, we know that warrantless blood draws cannot be justified as searches incident to arrest. The lesson is straightforward: Unless there is too little time to do so, police officers must get a warrant before ordering a blood draw.

Rather than simply applying this Court's precedents to address—and reject—Wisconsin's implied-consent theory, the plurality today takes the extraordinary step of relying on an issue, exigency, that Wisconsin has affirmatively waived. Wisconsin has not once, in any of its briefing before this Court or the state courts, argued that exigent circumstances were present here. In fact, in the state proceedings, Wisconsin "conceded" that the exigency exception does not justify the warrantless blood draw in this case. Accordingly, the state courts proceeded on the acknowledgment that no exigency is at issue here. As the Wisconsin Court of Appeals put it:

"In particular, this case is not susceptible to resolution on the ground of exigent circumstances. No testimony was received that would support the conclusion that exigent circumstances justified the warrantless blood draw. [The officer] expressed agnosticism as to how long it would have taken to obtain a warrant, and he never once testified (or even implied) that there was no time to get a warrant."

The exigency issue is therefore waived—that is, knowingly and intentionally abandoned—and the Court should not have considered it.

IV

There are good reasons why Wisconsin never asked any court to consider applying any version of the exigency exception here: This Court's precedents foreclose it. According to the plurality, when the police attempt to obtain a blood sample from a person suspected of drunk driving, there will "almost always" be exigent circumstances if the person falls unconscious. As this case demonstrates, however, the fact that a suspect fell unconscious at some point before the blood draw does not mean that there was insufficient time to get a warrant. And if the police have time to secure a warrant before the blood draw, "the Fourth Amendment mandates that they do so."

The exigent-circumstances exception to the Fourth Amendment warrant requirement applies if the State can demonstrate a "compelling need for official action and no time to secure a warrant."

The reasons the Court gave for rejecting a categorical exigency exception in *McNeely* apply with full force when the suspected drunk driver is (or becomes) unconscious.

In these cases, there is still a period of delay during which a police officer might take steps to secure a warrant. Indeed, as the plurality observes, that delay is guaranteed because an unconscious person will need to be transported to the hospital for medical attention. Such a delay occurred in Mitchell's case, even more so than it did in McNeely's. All told, the mere fact that a person is unconscious does not materially change the calculation that the Court made in *McNeely* when it rejected a categorical exigency exception for blood draws. In many cases, even when the suspect falls unconscious, police officers will have sufficient time to secure a warrant—meaning that the Fourth Amendment requires that they do so.

V

The Fourth Amendment, as interpreted by our precedents, requires police officers seeking to draw blood from a person suspected of drunk driving to get a warrant if possible. That rule should resolve this case. The plurality misguidedly departs from this rule, setting forth its own convoluted counterpresumption instead. But the Fourth Amendment is not as pliable as the plurality suggests. The warrant requirement safeguards privacy and physical autonomy by "assuring citizens" that searches "are not the random or arbitrary acts of government agents."

There is no doubt that drunk drivers create grave danger on our roads. It is, however, "[p]recisely because the need for action . . . is manifest" in such cases that "the need for vigilance against unconstitutional excess is great." "Requiring a warrant whenever practicable helps ensure that when blood draws occur, they are indeed justified." For that reason, "the police bear a heavy burden" to justify a warrantless search like the one here based on "urgent need."

The plurality today carries that burden for a State that never asked it to do so, not only here but also in a scattershot mass of future cases. Acting entirely on its own freewheeling instincts—with no briefing or decision below on the question—the plurality permits officers to order a blood draw of an unconscious person in all but the rarest cases, even when there is ample time to obtain a warrant. The plurality may believe it is helping to ameliorate the scourge of drunk driving, but what it really does is to strike another needless blow at the protections guaranteed by the Fourth Amendment. With respect, I dissent.

Justice GORSUCH, dissenting.

We took this case to decide whether Wisconsin drivers impliedly consent to blood alcohol tests thanks to a state statute. That law says that anyone driving in Wisconsin agrees—by the very act of driving—to testing under certain circumstances. But the Court today declines to answer the question presented. Instead, it upholds Wisconsin's law on an entirely different ground—citing the exigent circumstances doctrine. While I do not doubt that the Court may affirm for any reason supported by the record, the application of the exigent circumstances doctrine in this area poses complex and difficult questions that neither the parties nor the courts below discussed. Rather than proceeding solely by self-direction, I would have dismissed this case as improvidently granted and waited for a case presenting the exigent circumstances question.

3. The Automobile Exception

a. *The Exception and Its Rationale* (casebook p. 201)

In *Collins v. Virginia*, the Court considered whether the automobile exception applies to a vehicle that is parked on a person's property. In doing so, the Court discussed the underlying purposes of the automobile exception.

Collins v. Virginia
138 S. Ct. 1663 (2018)

Justice SOTOMAYOR delivered the opinion of the Court.

This case presents the question whether the automobile exception to the Fourth Amendment permits a police officer, uninvited and without a warrant, to enter the curtilage of a home in order to search a vehicle parked therein. It does not.

I

Officer Matthew McCall of the Albemarle County Police Department in Virginia saw the driver of an orange and black motorcycle with an extended frame commit a traffic infraction. The driver eluded Officer McCall's attempt to stop the motorcycle. A few weeks later, Officer David Rhodes of the same department saw an orange and black motorcycle traveling well over the speed limit, but the driver got away from him, too. The officers compared notes and concluded that the two incidents involved the same motorcyclist.

Upon further investigation, the officers learned that the motorcycle likely was stolen and in the possession of petitioner Ryan Collins. After discovering photographs on Collins' Facebook profile that featured an orange and black motorcycle parked at the top of the driveway of a house, Officer Rhodes tracked down the address of the house, drove there, and parked on the street. It was later established that Collins' girlfriend lived in the house and that Collins stayed there a few nights per week.

From his parked position on the street, Officer Rhodes saw what appeared to be a motorcycle with an extended frame covered with a white tarp, parked at the same angle and in the same location on the driveway as in the Facebook photograph. Officer Rhodes, who did not have a warrant, exited his car and walked toward the house. He stopped to take a photograph of the covered motorcycle from the sidewalk, and then walked onto the residential property and up to the top of the driveway to where the motorcycle was parked. In order "to investigate further," Officer Rhodes pulled off the tarp, revealing a motorcycle that looked like the one from the speeding incident. He then ran a search of the license plate and vehicle identification numbers, which confirmed that the motorcycle was stolen. After gathering this information, Officer Rhodes took a photograph of the uncovered motorcycle, put the tarp back on, left the property, and returned to his car to wait for Collins.

Shortly thereafter, Collins returned home. Officer Rhodes walked up to the front door of the house and knocked. Collins answered, agreed to speak with Officer Rhodes, and admitted that the motorcycle was his and that he had bought it without title. Officer Rhodes then arrested Collins.

Collins was indicted by a Virginia grand jury for receiving stolen property. He filed a pretrial motion to suppress the evidence that Officer Rhodes had obtained as a result of the warrantless search of the motorcycle. Collins argued that Officer Rhodes had trespassed on the curtilage of the house to conduct an investigation in violation of the Fourth Amendment. The trial court denied the motion and Collins was convicted.

The Supreme Court of Virginia affirmed [and] explained that the case was most properly resolved with reference to the Fourth Amendment's automobile exception. Under that framework, it held that Officer Rhodes had probable cause to believe that the motorcycle was contraband, and that the warrantless search therefore was justified.

II

This case arises at the intersection of two components of the Court's Fourth Amendment jurisprudence: the automobile exception to the warrant requirement and the protection extended to the curtilage of a home.

A

The Court has held that the search of an automobile can be reasonable without a warrant. The "ready mobility" of vehicles served as the core justification for the automobile exception for many years.) Later cases then introduced an additional rationale based on "the pervasive regulation of vehicles capable of traveling on the public highways." In announcing each of these two justifications, the Court took care to emphasize that the rationales applied only to automobiles and not to houses, and therefore supported "treating automobiles differently from houses" as a constitutional matter. When these justifications for the automobile exception "come into play," officers may search an automobile without having obtained a warrant so long as they have probable cause to do so.

Like the automobile exception, the Fourth Amendment's protection of curtilage has long been black letter law. "[W]hen it comes to the Fourth Amendment, the home is first among equals." "At the Amendment's 'very core' stands 'the right of a man to retreat into his own home and there be free from unreasonable governmental intrusion.'" To give full practical effect to that right, the Court considers curtilage — "the area 'immediately surrounding and associated with the home'" — to be "'part of the home itself for Fourth Amendment purposes.'" "The protection afforded the curtilage is essentially a protection of families and personal privacy in an area intimately linked to the home, both physically and psychologically, where privacy expectations are most heightened."

When a law enforcement officer physically intrudes on the curtilage to gather evidence, a search within the meaning of the Fourth Amendment has occurred. Such conduct thus is presumptively unreasonable absent a warrant.

B

With this background in mind, we turn to the application of these doctrines in the instant case. As an initial matter, we decide whether the part of the driveway where Collins' motorcycle was parked and subsequently searched is curtilage.

According to photographs in the record, the driveway runs alongside the front lawn and up a few yards past the front perimeter of the house. The top portion of the driveway that sits behind the front perimeter of the house is enclosed on two sides by a brick wall about the height of a car and on a third side by the house. A side door provides direct access between this partially enclosed section of the driveway and the house. A visitor endeavoring to reach the front door of the house would have to walk partway up the driveway, but would turn off before entering the enclosure and instead proceed up a set of steps leading to the front porch. When Officer Rhodes searched the motorcycle, it was parked inside this partially enclosed top portion of the driveway that abuts the house.

The "'conception defining the curtilage' is . . . familiar enough that it is 'easily understood from our daily experience.'" Just like the front porch, side garden, or area "outside the front window," the driveway enclosure where Officer Rhodes searched the motorcycle constitutes "an area adjacent to the home and 'to which the activity of home life extends,'" and so is properly considered curtilage.

In physically intruding on the curtilage of Collins' home to search the motorcycle, Officer Rhodes not only invaded Collins' Fourth Amendment interest in the item searched, *i.e.*, the motorcycle, but also invaded Collins' Fourth Amendment interest in the curtilage of his home. The question before the Court is whether the automobile exception justifies the invasion of the curtilage. The answer is no.

Applying the relevant legal principles to a slightly different factual scenario confirms that this is an easy case. Imagine a motorcycle parked inside the living room of a house, visible through a window to a passerby on the street. Imagine further that an officer has probable cause to believe that the motorcycle was involved in a traffic infraction. Can the officer, acting without a warrant, enter the house to search the motorcycle and confirm whether it is the right one? Surely not.

The reason is that the scope of the automobile exception extends no further than the automobile itself. Virginia asks the Court to expand the scope of the automobile exception to permit police to invade any space outside an automobile even if the Fourth Amendment protects that space. Nothing in our case law, however, suggests that the automobile exception gives an officer the right to enter a home or its curtilage to access a vehicle without a warrant. Expanding the scope of the automobile exception in this way would both undervalue the core Fourth Amendment protection afforded to the home and its curtilage and "untether" the automobile exception "from the justifications underlying" it.

The Court already has declined to expand the scope of other exceptions to the warrant requirement to permit warrantless entry into the home. The reasoning behind those decisions applies equally well in this context. For instance, under the plain-view doctrine, "any valid warrantless seizure of incriminating evidence" requires that the officer "have a lawful right of access to the object itself." Had Officer Rhodes seen illegal drugs through the window of Collins' house, for example, assuming no other warrant exception applied, he could not have entered the house to seize them without first obtaining a warrant.

Just as an officer must have a lawful right of access to any contraband he discovers in plain view in order to seize it without a warrant, and just as an officer must have a lawful right of access in order to arrest a person in his home, so, too, an officer must have a lawful right of access to a vehicle in order to search it pursuant to the automobile exception. The automobile exception does not afford the necessary lawful right of access to search a vehicle parked within a home or its curtilage because it does not justify an intrusion on a person's separate and substantial Fourth Amendment interest in his home and curtilage.

Given the centrality of the Fourth Amendment interest in the home and its curtilage and the disconnect between that interest and the justifications behind the automobile exception, we decline Virginia's invitation to extend the automobile exception to permit a warrantless intrusion on a home or its curtilage.

For the foregoing reasons, we conclude that the automobile exception does not permit an officer without a warrant to enter a home or its curtilage in order to search a vehicle therein. We leave for resolution on remand whether Officer Rhodes' warrantless intrusion on the curtilage of Collins' house may have been reasonable on a different basis, such as the exigent circumstances exception to the warrant requirement.

Justice THOMAS concurring.

I join the Court's opinion because it correctly resolves the Fourth Amendment question in this case. I write separately because I have serious doubts about this Court's authority to impose that rule on the States. The assumption that state courts must apply the federal exclusionary rule is legally dubious, and many jurists have complained that it encourages "distort[ions]" in substantive Fourth Amendment law.

While those who ratified the Fourth and Fourteenth Amendments would agree that a constitutional violation occurred here, they would be deeply confused about the posture of this case and the remedy that Collins is seeking. Historically, the only remedies for unconstitutional searches and seizures were "tort suits" and "self-help." The exclusionary rule—the practice of deterring illegal searches and seizures by suppressing evidence at criminal trials—did not exist. No such rule existed in "Roman Law, Napoleonic Law or even the Common Law of England." And this Court did not adopt the federal exclusionary rule until the 20th century. See *Weeks v. United States* (1914). As late as 1949, nearly two-thirds of the States did not have an exclusionary rule.

The Founders would not have understood the logic of the exclusionary rule either. Historically, if evidence was relevant and reliable, its admissibility did not "depend upon the lawfulness or unlawfulness of the mode, by which it [was] obtained." And the common law sometimes reflected the inverse of the exclusionary rule: The fact that someone turned out to be guilty could *justify* an illegal seizure.

Despite this history, the Court concluded in *Mapp v. Ohio* (1961) that the States must apply the federal exclusionary rule in their own courts. *Mapp* suggested that the exclusionary rule was required by the Constitution itself. But that suggestion could not withstand even the slightest scrutiny. The exclusionary rule appears nowhere in the Constitution, postdates the founding by more than a century, and contradicts several longstanding principles of the common law.

Recognizing this, the Court has since rejected *Mapp*'s "[e]xpansive dicta" and clarified that the exclusionary rule is not required by the Constitution. Although the exclusionary rule is not part of the Constitution, this Court has continued to describe it as "federal law" and assume that it applies to the States. Yet the Court has never attempted to justify this assumption. If the exclusionary rule is federal law, but is not grounded in the Constitution or a federal statute, then it must be federal common law. As federal common law, however, the exclusionary rule cannot bind the States.

In sum, I am skeptical of this Court's authority to impose the exclusionary rule on the States. We have not yet revisited that question in light of our modern precedents, which reject *Mapp*'s essential premise that the exclusionary rule is required by the Constitution. We should do so.

Justice ALITO dissenting.

The Fourth Amendment prohibits "unreasonable" searches. What the police did in this case was entirely reasonable. The Court's decision is not.

If the motorcycle had been parked at the curb, instead of in the driveway, it is undisputed that Rhodes could have searched it without obtaining a warrant. Nearly a century ago, this Court held that officers with probable cause may search a motor vehicle without obtaining a warrant. The principal rationale for this so-called automobile or motor-vehicle exception to the warrant requirement is the risk that the vehicle will be moved during the time it takes to obtain a warrant. We have also observed that the owner of an automobile has a diminished expectation of privacy in its contents.

So why does the Court come to the conclusion that Officer Rhodes needed a warrant in this case? Because, in order to reach the motorcycle, he had to walk 30 feet or so up the driveway of the house rented by petitioner's girlfriend, and by doing that, Rhodes invaded the home's "curtilage." The Court does not dispute that the motorcycle, when parked in the driveway, was just as mobile as it would have been had it been parked at the curb. Nor does the Court claim that Officer Rhodes's short walk up the driveway did petitioner or his girlfriend any harm. Rhodes did not damage any property or observe anything along the way that he could not have seen from the street. But, the Court insists, Rhodes could not enter the driveway without a warrant, and therefore his search of the motorcycle was unreasonable and the evidence obtained in that search must be suppressed.

An ordinary person of common sense would react to the Court's decision the way Mr. Bumble famously responded when told about a legal rule that did not comport with the reality of everyday life. If that is the law, he exclaimed, "the law is a ass—a idiot." C. Dickens, Oliver Twist 277 (1867).

The Fourth Amendment is neither an "ass" nor an "idiot." Its hallmark is reasonableness, and the Court's strikingly unreasonable decision is based on a misunderstanding of Fourth Amendment basics.

The question before us is not whether there was a Fourth Amendment search but whether the search was reasonable. And the only possible argument as to why it might not be reasonable concerns the need for a warrant. For nearly a century, however, it has been well established that officers do not need a warrant to search a motor vehicle on public streets so long as they have probable cause. Thus, the issue here is whether there is any good reason why this same rule should not apply when the vehicle is parked in plain view in a driveway just a few feet from the street.

In considering that question, we should ask whether the reasons for the "automobile exception" are any less valid in this new situation. Is the vehicle parked in the driveway any less mobile? Are any greater privacy interests at stake? If the answer to those questions is "no," then the automobile exception should apply. And here, the answer to each question is emphatically "no." The tarp-covered motorcycle parked in the driveway could have been uncovered and ridden away in a matter of seconds. And Officer Rhodes's brief walk up the driveway impaired no real privacy interests.

This does not mean, however, that a warrant is never needed when officers have probable cause to search a motor vehicle, no matter where the vehicle is located. While a case-specific inquiry regarding *exigency* would be inconsistent with the rationale of the motor-vehicle exception, a case-specific inquiry regarding *the degree of intrusion on privacy* is entirely appropriate when the motor vehicle to be searched is located on private property. After all, the ultimate inquiry under the Fourth Amendment is whether a search is reasonable, and that inquiry often turns on the degree of the intrusion on privacy. Thus, contrary to the opinion of the Court, an affirmance in this case would not mean that officers could perform a warrantless search if a motorcycle were located inside a house. In that situation, the intrusion on privacy would be far greater than in the present case, where the real effect, if any, is negligible.

G. Stop and Frisk

4. What Is Sufficient for Reasonable Suspicion?

a. *Reasonable Suspicion: General Principles* (casebook p. 409)

Kansas v. Glover

140 S. Ct. 1183 (2020)

Justice THOMAS delivered the opinion of the Court.

This case presents the question whether a police officer violates the Fourth Amendment by initiating an investigative traffic stop after running a vehicle's license plate and learning that the registered owner has a revoked driver's license. We hold that when the officer lacks information negating an inference that the owner is the driver of the vehicle, the stop is reasonable.

I

Kansas charged respondent Charles Glover, Jr., with driving as a habitual violator after a traffic stop revealed that he was driving with a revoked license. Glover filed a motion to suppress all evidence seized during the stop, claiming that the officer lacked reasonable suspicion. Neither Glover nor the police officer testified at the suppression hearing. Instead, the parties stipulated to the following facts:

"1. Deputy Mark Mehrer is a certified law enforcement officer employed by the Douglas County Kansas Sheriff's Office.

2. On April 28, 2016, Deputy Mehrer was on routine patrol in Douglas County when he observed a 1995 Chevrolet 1500 pickup truck with Kansas plate 295ATJ.

3. Deputy Mehrer ran Kansas plate 295ATJ through the Kansas Department of Revenue's file service. The registration came back to a 1995 Chevrolet 1500 pickup truck.

4. Kansas Department of Revenue files indicated the truck was registered to Charles Glover Jr. The files also indicated that Mr. Glover had a revoked driver's license in the State of Kansas.

5. Deputy Mehrer assumed the registered owner of the truck was also the driver, Charles Glover Jr.

6. Deputy Mehrer did not observe any traffic infractions, and did not attempt to identify the driver [of] the truck. Based solely on the information that the registered owner of the truck was revoked, Deputy Mehrer initiated a traffic stop.

7. The driver of the truck was identified as the defendant, Charles Glover Jr."

The Kansas Supreme Court [ruled that] Deputy Mehrer did not have reasonable suspicion because his inference that Glover was behind the wheel amounted to "only a hunch" that Glover was engaging in criminal activity. The court further explained that Deputy Mehrer's "hunch" involved "applying and stacking unstated assumptions that are unreasonable without further factual basis," namely, that "the registered owner was likely the primary driver of the vehicle" and that "the owner will likely disregard the suspension or revocation order and continue to drive."

II

Under this Court's precedents, the Fourth Amendment permits an officer to initiate a brief investigative traffic stop when he has "a particularized and objective basis for suspecting the particular person stopped of criminal activity." "Although a mere 'hunch' does not create reasonable suspicion, the level of suspicion the standard requires is considerably less than proof of wrongdoing by a preponderance of the evidence, and obviously less than is necessary for probable cause."

Because it is a "less demanding" standard, "reasonable suspicion can be established with information that is different in quantity or content than that required to establish probable cause." The standard "depends on the factual and practical considerations of everyday life on which *reasonable and prudent men*, not legal technicians, act." Courts "cannot reasonably demand scientific certainty . . . where none exists." Rather, they must permit officers to make "commonsense judgments and inferences about human behavior."

III

We have previously recognized that States have a "vital interest in ensuring that only those qualified to do so are permitted to operate motor vehicles [and] that licensing, registration, and vehicle inspection requirements are being observed." With this in mind, we turn to whether the facts known to Deputy Mehrer at the time of the stop gave rise to reasonable suspicion. We conclude that they did.

Before initiating the stop, Deputy Mehrer observed an individual operating a 1995 Chevrolet 1500 pickup truck with Kansas plate 295ATJ. He also knew that the registered owner of the truck had a revoked license and that the model of the truck matched the observed vehicle. From these three facts, Deputy Mehrer drew the commonsense inference that Glover was likely the driver of the vehicle, which provided more than reasonable suspicion to initiate the stop.

The fact that the registered owner of a vehicle is not always the driver of the vehicle does not negate the reasonableness of Deputy Mehrer's inference. Such is the case with all reasonable inferences. The reasonable suspicion inquiry "falls considerably short" of 51% accuracy, for, as we have explained, "[t]o be reasonable is not to be perfect."

Glover's revoked license does not render Deputy Mehrer's inference unreasonable either. Empirical studies demonstrate what common experience readily reveals: Drivers with revoked licenses frequently continue to drive and therefore to pose safety risks to other motorists and pedestrians. Although common sense suffices to justify this inference, Kansas law reinforces that it is reasonable to infer that an individual with a revoked license may continue driving.

IV

Glover and the dissent respond with two arguments as to why Deputy Mehrer lacked reasonable suspicion. Neither is persuasive.

First, Glover and the dissent argue that Deputy Mehrer's inference was unreasonable because it was not grounded in his law enforcement training or experience. Nothing in our Fourth Amendment precedent supports the notion that, in determining whether reasonable suspicion exists, an officer can draw inferences based on knowledge gained only through law enforcement training and experience. We have repeatedly recognized the opposite. The inference that the driver of a car is its registered owner does not require any specialized training; rather, it is a reasonable inference made by ordinary people on a daily basis.

In reaching this conclusion, we in no way minimize the significant role that specialized training and experience routinely play in law enforcement investigations. We simply hold that such experience is not *required* in every instance.

Glover and the dissent also contend that adopting Kansas' view would eviscerate the need for officers to base reasonable suspicion on "specific and articulable facts" particularized to the individual, because police could instead rely exclusively on probabilities. Their argument carries little force.

As an initial matter, we have previously stated that officers, like jurors, may rely on probabilities in the reasonable suspicion context. Moreover, as explained above, Deputy Mehrer did not rely exclusively on probabilities. He knew that the license plate was linked to a truck matching the observed vehicle and that the registered owner of the vehicle had a revoked license. Based on these minimal facts, he used common sense to form a reasonable suspicion that a specific individual was potentially engaged in specific criminal activity—driving with a revoked license. Traffic stops of this nature do not delegate to officers "broad and unlimited discretion" to stop drivers at random. Nor do they allow officers to stop drivers whose conduct is no different from any other driver's. Accordingly, combining database information and commonsense judgments in this context is fully consonant with this Court's Fourth Amendment precedents.

V

This Court's precedents have repeatedly affirmed that "the ultimate touchstone of the Fourth Amendment is 'reasonableness.'" Under the totality of the circumstances of this case, Deputy Mehrer drew an entirely reasonable inference that Glover was driving while his license was revoked.

Justice KAGAN, with whom Justice GINSBURG joins, concurring.

When you see a car coming down the street, your common sense tells you that the registered owner may well be behind the wheel. Not always, of course. Families share cars; friends borrow them. Still, a person often buys a vehicle to drive it himself. So your suspicion that the owner is driving would be perfectly reasonable.

Now, though, consider a wrinkle: Suppose you knew that the registered owner of the vehicle no longer had a valid driver's license. That added fact raises a new question. What are the odds that someone who has lost his license would continue to drive? The answer is by no means obvious. You might think that a person told not to drive on pain of criminal penalty would obey the order—so that if his car was on the road, someone else (a family member, a friend) must be doing the driving. Or you might have the opposite intuition—that a person's reasons for driving would overcome his worries about violating the law, no matter the possible punishment. But most likely (let's be honest), you just wouldn't know. Especially if you've not had your own license taken away, your everyday experience has given you little basis to assess the probabilities. Your common sense can therefore no longer guide you.

2. Searches and Seizures

Even so, Deputy Mark Mehrer had reasonable suspicion to stop the truck in this case, and I join the Court's opinion holding as much. Crucially for me, Mehrer knew yet one more thing about the vehicle's registered owner, and it related to his proclivity for breaking driving laws. As the Court recounts, Mehrer learned from a state database that Charles Glover, the truck's owner, had had his license revoked under Kansas law. And Kansas almost never revokes a license except for serious or repeated driving offenses. Crimes like vehicular homicide and manslaughter, or vehicular flight from a police officer, provoke a license revocation; so too do multiple convictions for moving traffic violations within a short time. In other words, a person with a revoked license has already shown a willingness to flout driving restrictions. That fact, as the Court states, provides a "reason[ ] to infer" that such a person will drive without a license—at least often enough to warrant an investigatory stop. And there is nothing else here to call that inference into question. That is because the parties' unusually austere stipulation confined the case to the facts stated above—*i.e.,* that Mehrer stopped Glover's truck because he knew that Kansas had revoked Glover's license.

But as already suggested, I would find this a different case if Kansas had barred Glover from driving on a ground that provided no similar evidence of his penchant for ignoring driving laws.

In this strange case, contested on a barebones stipulation, the record contains no evidence of these kinds. There is but a single, simple fact: A police officer learned from a state database that a car on the road belonged to a person with a revoked license. Given that revocations in Kansas nearly always stem from serious or repeated driving violations, I agree with the Court about the reasonableness of the officer's inference that the owner, "Glover[,] was driving while his license was revoked." And because Glover offered no rebuttal, there the matter stands. But that does not mean cases with more complete records will all wind up in the same place. A defendant like Glover may still be able to show that his case is different—that the "presence of additional facts" and circumstances "dispel[s] reasonable suspicion." Which is to say that in more fully litigated cases, the license-revocation alert does not (as it did here) end the inquiry. It is but the first, though no doubt an important, step in assessing the reasonableness of the officer's suspicion.

Justice SOTOMAYOR, dissenting.

In upholding routine stops of vehicles whose owners have revoked licenses, the Court ignores key foundations of our reasonable-suspicion jurisprudence and impermissibly and unnecessarily reduces the State's burden of proof. I therefore dissent.

The stop at issue here, however, rests on just one key fact: that the vehicle was owned by someone with a revoked license. The majority concludes—erroneously, in my view—that seizing this vehicle was constitutional on the record below because drivers with revoked licenses (as opposed to suspended licenses) in Kansas "have already demonstrated a disregard for the law or are categorically unfit to drive." This analysis breaks from settled doctrine and dramatically alters both the quantum and nature of evidence a State may rely on to prove suspicion.

The State bears the burden of justifying a seizure. This requires the government to articulate factors supporting its reasonable suspicion, usually through a trained agent. While the Court has not dictated precisely what evidence a government must produce, it has stressed that an officer must at least "articulate more than an 'inchoate and unparticularized suspicion or "hunch"' of criminal activity." That articulation must include both facts and an officer's "rational inferences from those facts." A logical "gap as to any one matter" in this analysis may be overcome by "'a strong showing'" regarding "'other indicia of reliability.'" But gaps may not go unfilled.

Additionally, reasonable suspicion eschews judicial common sense, in favor of the perspectives and inferences of a reasonable officer viewing "the facts through the lens of his police experience and expertise." It is the reasonable officer's assessment, not the ordinary person's—or judge's—judgment, that matters.

Finally, a stop must be individualized—that is, based on "a suspicion that the particular [subject] being stopped is engaged in wrongdoing." This does not mean that the officer must know the driver's identity. But a seizure must rest on more than the "likelihood that [a] given person" or particular vehicle is engaged in wrongdoing. The inquiry ordinarily involves some observation or report about the target's behavior—not merely the class to which he belongs.

Faithful adherence to these precepts would yield a significantly different analysis and outcome than that offered by the majority. For starters, the majority flips the burden of proof. It permits Kansas police officers to effectuate roadside stops whenever they lack "information negating an inference" that a vehicle's unlicensed owner is its driver. This has it backwards: The State shoulders the burden to supply the key inference that tethers observation to suspicion. The majority repeatedly attributes such an inference to Deputy Mehrer. But that is an after-the-fact gloss on a seven-paragraph stipulation. Nowhere in his terse submission did Deputy Mehrer indicate that he had any informed belief about the propensity of unlicensed drivers to operate motor vehicles in the area—let alone that he relied on such a belief in seizing Glover.

The consequence of the majority's approach is to absolve officers from any responsibility to investigate the identity of a driver where feasible. But that is precisely what officers ought to do—and are more than capable of doing. Of course, some circumstances may not warrant an officer approaching a car to take a closer look at its occupants. But there are countless other instances where officers have been able to ascertain the identity of a driver from a distance and make out their approximate age and gender. Indeed, our cases are rife with examples of officers who have perceived more than just basic driver demographics. The majority underestimates officers' capabilities and instead gives them free rein to stop a vehicle involved in no suspicious activity simply because it is registered to an unlicensed person. That stop is based merely on a guess or a "hunch" about the driver's identity.

With no basis in the record to presume that unlicensed drivers routinely continue driving, the majority endeavors to fill the gap with its own "common sense." But simply labeling an inference "common sense" does not make it so, no matter how many times the majority repeats it. Whether the driver of a vehicle is likely to be its unlicensed owner is "by no means obvious."

Contrary to the majority's claims, the reasonable-suspicion inquiry does not accommodate the average person's intuition. Rather, it permits reliance on a particular type of common sense—that of the reasonable officer, developed through her experiences in law enforcement. This approach acknowledges that what may be "common sense" to a layperson may not be relevant (or correct) in a law enforcement context. Indeed, this case presents the type of geographically localized inquiry where an officer's "inferences and deductions that might well elude an untrained person" would come in handy. By relying on judicial inferences instead, the majority promotes broad, inflexible rules that overlook regional differences.

Allowing judges to offer their own brand of common sense where the State's proffered justifications for a search come up short also shifts police work to the judiciary. Our cases—including those the majority cites—have looked to officer sensibility to establish inferences about human behavior, even though they just as easily could have relied on the inferences "made by ordinary people on a daily basis."

The majority's justifications for this new approach have no foundation in fact or logic. In fact, it is the majority's approach that makes scant policy sense. If the State need not set forth all the information its officers considered before forming suspicion, what conceivable evidence could be used to mount an effective challenge to a vehicle stop, as the concurrence imagines?

Vehicle stops "interfere with freedom of movement, are inconvenient, and consume time." Worse still, they "may create substantial anxiety" through an "unsettling show of authority." Before subjecting motorists to this type of investigation, the State must possess articulable facts and officer inferences to form suspicion. The State below left unexplained key components of the reasonable-suspicion inquiry. In an effort to uphold the conviction, the Court destroys Fourth Amendment jurisprudence that requires individualized suspicion. I respectfully dissent.

I. Excessive Police Force (new; casebook p. 450)

The killing of George Floyd by police officers in Minneapolis in May 2020 has again focused attention on the problem of excessive police force. The Supreme Court has held that excessive force by the police violates the Fourth Amendment. The following cases hold this and articulate the legal standard for when excessive force violates the Constitution.

Tennessee v. Garner
471 U.S. 1 (1985)

Justice WHITE delivered the opinion of the Court.

This case requires us to determine the constitutionality of the use of deadly force to prevent the escape of an apparently unarmed suspected felon. We conclude that such force may not be used unless it is necessary to prevent the escape and the officer has probable cause to believe that the suspect poses a significant threat of death or serious physical injury to the officer or others.

I

At about 10:45 P.M. on October 3, 1974, Memphis Police Officers Elton Hymon and Leslie Wright were dispatched to answer a "prowler inside call." Upon arriving at the scene they saw a woman standing on her porch and gesturing toward the adjacent house. She told them she had heard glass breaking and that "they" or "someone" was breaking in next door. While Wright radioed the dispatcher to say that they were on the scene, Hymon went behind the house. He heard a door slam and saw someone run across the backyard. The fleeing suspect, who was appellee-respondent's decedent, Edward Garner, stopped at a 6-feet-high chain link fence at the edge of the yard. With the aid of a flashlight, Hymon was able to see Garner's face and hands. He saw no sign of a weapon, and, though not certain, was "reasonably sure" and "figured" that Garner was unarmed. He thought Garner was 17 or 18 years old and about 5'5" or 5'7" tall. While Garner was crouched at the base of the fence, Hymon called out "police, halt" and took a few steps toward him. Garner then began to climb over the fence. Convinced that if Garner made it over the fence he would elude capture, Hymon shot him. The bullet hit Garner in the back of the head. Garner was taken by ambulance to a hospital, where he died on the operating table. Ten dollars and a purse taken from the house were found on his body.

In using deadly force to prevent the escape, Hymon was acting under the authority of a Tennessee statute and pursuant to Police Department policy. The statute provides that "[i]f, after notice of the intention to arrest the defendant, he either flee or forcibly resist, the officer may use all the necessary means to effect the arrest." The Department policy was slightly more restrictive than the statute, but still allowed the use of deadly force in cases of burglary. The incident was reviewed by the Memphis Police Firearm's Review Board and presented to a grand jury. Neither took any action.

Garner's father then brought this action in the Federal District Court for the Western District of Tennessee, seeking damages under 42 U.S.C. §1983 for asserted violations of Garner's constitutional rights. The complaint alleged that the shooting violated the Fourth, Fifth, Sixth, Eighth, and Fourteenth Amendments of the United States Constitution. It named as defendants Officer Hymon, the Police Department, its Director, and the Mayor and city of Memphis. After a

2. Searches and Seizures

3-day bench trial, the District Court entered judgment for all defendants. [The Sixth Circuit ultimately reversed.]

II

Whenever an officer restrains the freedom of a person to walk away, he has seized that person. While it is not always clear just when minimal police interference becomes a seizure, see *United States v. Mendenhall* (1980), there can be no question that apprehension by the use of deadly force is a seizure subject to the reasonableness requirement of the Fourth Amendment.

A police officer may arrest a person if he has probable cause to believe that person committed a crime. Petitioners and appellant argue that if this requirement is satisfied the Fourth Amendment has nothing to say about *how* that seizure is made. This submission ignores the many cases in which this Court, by balancing the extent of the intrusion against the need for it, has examined the reasonableness of the manner in which a search or seizure is conducted. To determine the constitutionality of a seizure "[w]e must balance the nature and quality of the intrusion on the individual's Fourth Amendment interests against the importance of the governmental interests alleged to justify the intrusion." We have described "the balancing of competing interests" as "the key principle of the Fourth Amendment." Because one of the factors is the extent of the intrusion, it is plain that reasonableness depends on not only when a seizure is made, but also how it is carried out.

The same balancing process demonstrates that, notwithstanding probable cause to seize a suspect, an officer may not always do so by killing him. The intrusiveness of a seizure by means of deadly force is unmatched. The suspect's fundamental interest in his own life need not be elaborated upon. The use of deadly force also frustrates the interest of the individual, and of society, in judicial determination of guilt and punishment. Against these interests are ranged governmental interests in effective law enforcement. It is argued that overall violence will be reduced by encouraging the peaceful submission of suspects who know that they may be shot if they flee. Effectiveness in making arrests requires the resort to deadly force, or at least the meaningful threat thereof. "Being able to arrest such individuals is a condition precedent to the state's entire system of law enforcement."

Without in any way disparaging the importance of these goals, we are not convinced that the use of deadly force is a sufficiently productive means of accomplishing them to justify the killing of nonviolent suspects. The use of deadly force is a self-defeating way of apprehending a suspect and so setting the criminal justice mechanism in motion. If successful, it guarantees that that mechanism will not be set in motion. And while the meaningful threat of deadly force might be thought to lead to the arrest of more live suspects by discouraging escape attempts, the presently available evidence does not support this thesis. The fact is that a majority of police departments in this country have forbidden the use of deadly force against nonviolent suspects. If those charged with the enforcement of the criminal law have abjured the use of deadly force in arresting nondangerous felons, there is a substantial basis for doubting that the use of such force is an essential attribute of the arrest power in all felony cases. Petitioners and appellant have not persuaded us that shooting nondangerous fleeing suspects is so vital as to outweigh the suspect's interest in his own life.

The use of deadly force to prevent the escape of all felony suspects, whatever the circumstances, is constitutionally unreasonable. It is not better that all felony suspects die than that they escape. Where the suspect poses no immediate threat to the officer and no threat to others, the harm resulting from failing to apprehend him does not justify the use of deadly force to do so. It is no doubt unfortunate when a suspect who is in sight escapes, but the fact that the police arrive a little late or are a little slower afoot does not always justify killing the suspect. A police officer may not seize an unarmed, nondangerous suspect by shooting him dead. The Tennessee statute is unconstitutional insofar as it authorizes the use of deadly force against such fleeing suspects.

It is not, however, unconstitutional on its face. Where the officer has probable cause to believe that the suspect poses a threat of serious physical harm, either to the officer or to others, it is not constitutionally unreasonable to prevent escape by using deadly force. Thus, if the suspect threatens the officer with a weapon or there is probable cause to believe that he has committed a crime involving the infliction or threatened infliction of serious physical harm, deadly force may be used if necessary to prevent escape, and if, where feasible, some warning has been given. As applied in such circumstances, the Tennessee statute would pass constitutional muster.

III

It is insisted that the Fourth Amendment must be construed in light of the common-law rule, which allowed the use of whatever force was necessary to effect the arrest of a fleeing felon, though not a misdemeanant. The State and city argue that because this was the prevailing rule at the time of the adoption of the Fourth Amendment and for some time thereafter, and is still in force in some States, use of deadly force against a fleeing felon must be "reasonable." It is true that this Court has often looked to the common law in evaluating the reasonableness, for Fourth Amendment purposes, of police activity. On the other hand, it "has not simply frozen into constitutional law those law enforcement practices that existed at the time of the Fourth Amendment's passage." Because of sweeping change in the legal and technological context, reliance on the common-law rule in this case would be a mistaken literalism that ignores the purposes of a historical inquiry.

It has been pointed out many times that the common-law rule is best understood in light of the fact that it arose at a time when virtually all felonies were punishable by death. Almost all crimes formerly punishable by death no longer are or can be. These changes have undermined the concept, which was questionable to begin with, that use of deadly force against a fleeing felon is merely a speedier execution of someone who has already forfeited his life. They have also made the assumption that a "felon" is more dangerous than a misdemeanant untenable. Indeed, numerous misdemeanors involve conduct more dangerous than many felonies.

There is an additional reason why the common-law rule cannot be directly translated to the present day. The common-law rule developed at a time when weapons were rudimentary. Deadly force could be inflicted almost solely in a hand-to-hand struggle during which, necessarily, the safety of the arresting officer was at risk. Handguns were not carried by police officers until the latter half of the last century. Only then did it become possible to use deadly force from a distance as a means of apprehension. As a practical matter, the use of deadly force under the standard articulation of the common-law rule has an altogether different meaning—and harsher consequences—now than in past centuries.

IV

The dissent argues that the shooting was justified by the fact that Officer Hymon had probable cause to believe that Garner had committed a nighttime burglary. While we agree that burglary is a serious crime, we cannot agree that it is so dangerous as automatically to justify the use of deadly force. The FBI classifies burglary as a "property" rather than a "violent" crime. See Federal Bureau of Investigation, Uniform Crime Reports, Crime in the United States 1 (1984). Although the armed burglar would present a different situation, the fact that an unarmed suspect has broken into a dwelling at night does not automatically mean he is physically dangerous. This case demonstrates as much. In fact, the available statistics demonstrate that burglaries only rarely involve physical violence. During the 10-year period from 1973-1982, only 3.8% of all burglaries involved violent crime.

Justice O'CONNOR, with whom CHIEF JUSTICE BURGER and Justice REHNQUIST join, dissenting.

The Court today holds that the Fourth Amendment prohibits a police officer from using deadly force as a last resort to apprehend a criminal suspect who refuses to halt when fleeing the scene of a nighttime burglary. This conclusion rests on the majority's balancing of the interests of the suspect and the public interest in effective law enforcement. Notwithstanding the venerable common-law rule authorizing the use of deadly force if necessary to apprehend a fleeing felon, and continued acceptance of this rule by nearly half the States, the majority concludes that Tennessee's statute is unconstitutional inasmuch as it allows the use of such force to apprehend a burglary suspect who is not obviously armed or otherwise dangerous. Although the circumstances of this case are unquestionably tragic and unfortunate, our constitutional holdings must be sensitive both to the history of the Fourth Amendment and to the general implications of the Court's reasoning.

By disregarding the serious and dangerous nature of residential burglaries and the longstanding practice of many States, the Court effectively creates a Fourth Amendment right allowing a burglary suspect to flee unimpeded from a police officer who has probable cause to arrest, who has ordered the suspect to halt, and who has no means short of firing his weapon to prevent escape. I do not believe that the Fourth Amendment supports such a right, and I accordingly dissent.

II

For purposes of Fourth Amendment analysis, I agree with the Court that Officer Hymon "seized" Garner by shooting him. Whether that seizure was reasonable and therefore permitted by the Fourth Amendment requires a careful balancing of the important public interest in crime prevention and detection and the nature and quality of the intrusion upon legitimate interests of the individual. In striking this balance here, it is crucial to acknowledge that police use of deadly force to apprehend a fleeing criminal suspect falls within the "rubric of police conduct . . . necessarily [involving] swift action predicated upon the on-the-spot observations of the officer on the beat." The clarity of hindsight cannot provide the standard for judging the reasonableness of police decisions made in uncertain and often dangerous circumstances. Moreover, I am far more reluctant than is the Court to conclude that the Fourth Amendment proscribes a police practice that was accepted at the time of the adoption of the Bill of Rights and has continued to receive the support of many state legislatures. Although the Court has recognized that the requirements of the Fourth Amendment must respond to the reality of social and technological change, fidelity to the notion of *constitutional*—as opposed to purely judicial—limits on governmental action requires us to impose a heavy burden on those who claim that practices accepted when the Fourth Amendment was adopted are now constitutionally impermissible.

The public interest involved in the use of deadly force as a last resort to apprehend a fleeing burglary suspect relates primarily to the serious nature of the crime. Household burglaries not only represent the illegal entry into a person's home, but also "pos[e] real risk of serious harm to others. According to recent Department of Justice statistics, "[t]hree-fifths of all rapes in the home, three-fifths of all home robberies, and about a third of home aggravated and simple assaults are committed by burglars." 2.8 million such violent crimes were committed in the course of burglaries. Victims of a forcible intrusion into their home by a nighttime prowler will find little consolation in the majority's confident assertion that "burglaries only rarely involve physical violence." Moreover, even if a particular burglary, when viewed in retrospect, does not involve physical harm to others, the "harsh potentialities for violence" inherent in the forced entry into a home preclude characterization of the crime as "innocuous, inconsequential, minor, or 'nonviolent.'"

Because burglary is a serious and dangerous felony, the public interest in the prevention and detection of the crime is of compelling importance. Where a police officer has probable cause to arrest a suspected burglar, the use of deadly force as a last resort might well be the only means of apprehending the suspect. With respect to a particular burglary, subsequent investigation simply cannot represent a substitute for immediate apprehension of the criminal suspect at the scene.

Against the strong public interests justifying the conduct at issue here must be weighed the individual interests implicated in the use of deadly force by police officers. The majority declares that "[t]he suspect's fundamental interest in his own life need not be elaborated upon." This blithe assertion hardly provides an adequate substitute for the majority's failure to acknowledge the distinctive manner in which the suspect's interest in his life is even exposed to risk. For purposes of this case, we must recall that the police officer, in the course of investigating a nighttime burglary, had reasonable cause to arrest the suspect and ordered him to halt. The officer's use of force resulted because the suspected burglar refused to heed this command and the officer reasonably believed that there was no means short of firing his weapon to apprehend the suspect. Without questioning the importance of a person's interest in his life, I do not think this interest encompasses a right to flee unimpeded from the scene of a burglary. The legitimate interests of the suspect in these circumstances are adequately accommodated by the Tennessee statute: to avoid the use of deadly force and the consequent risk to his life, the suspect need merely obey the valid order to halt.

A proper balancing of the interests involved suggests that use of deadly force as a last resort to apprehend a criminal suspect fleeing from the scene of a nighttime burglary is not unreasonable within the meaning of the Fourth Amendment. Admittedly, the events giving rise to this case are in retrospect deeply regrettable. No one can view the death of an unarmed and apparently nonviolent 15-year-old without sorrow, much less disapproval. Nonetheless, the reasonableness of Officer Hymon's conduct for purposes of the Fourth Amendment cannot be evaluated by what later appears to have been a preferable course of police action. The officer pursued a suspect in the darkened backyard of a house that from all indications had just been burglarized. The police officer was not certain whether the suspect was alone or unarmed; nor did he know what had transpired inside the house. He ordered the suspect to halt, and when the suspect refused to obey and attempted to flee into the night, the officer fired his weapon to prevent escape. The reasonableness of this action for purposes of the Fourth Amendment is not determined by the unfortunate nature of this particular case; instead, the question is whether it is constitutionally impermissible for police officers, as a last resort, to shoot a burglary suspect fleeing the scene of the crime.

III

Even if I agreed that the Fourth Amendment was violated under the circumstances of this case, I would be unable to join the Court's opinion. The Court holds that deadly force may be used only if the suspect "threatens the officer with a weapon or there is probable cause to believe that he has committed a crime involving the infliction or threatened infliction of serious physical harm." The Court ignores the more general implications of its reasoning. Relying on the Fourth Amendment, the majority asserts that it is constitutionally unreasonable to *use* deadly force against fleeing criminal suspects who do not appear to pose a threat of serious physical harm to others. By declining to limit its holding to the use of firearms, the Court unnecessarily implies that the Fourth Amendment constrains the use of any police practice that is potentially lethal, no matter how remote the risk.

IV

The Court's opinion sweeps broadly to adopt an entirely new standard for the constitutionality of the use of deadly force to apprehend fleeing felons. Thus, the Court "lightly brushe[s] aside," a long-standing police practice that predates the Fourth Amendment and continues to receive the approval of nearly half of the state legislatures. I cannot accept the majority's creation of a constitutional right to flight for burglary suspects seeking to avoid capture at the scene of the crime. Whatever the constitutional limits on police use of deadly force in order to apprehend a fleeing felon, I do not believe they are exceeded in a case in which a police officer has probable cause to arrest a suspect at the scene of a residential burglary, orders the suspect to halt, and then fires his weapon as a last resort to prevent the suspect's escape into the night. I respectfully dissent.

Graham v. Connor
490 U.S. 386 (1989)

CHIEF JUSTICE REHNQUIST delivered the opinion of the Court.

This case requires us to decide what constitutional standard governs a free citizen's claim that law enforcement officials used excessive force in the course of making an arrest, investigatory stop, or other "seizure" of his person. We hold that such claims are properly analyzed under the Fourth Amendment's "objective reasonableness" standard, rather than under a substantive due process standard.

In this action under 42 U.S.C. §1983, petitioner Dethorne Graham seeks to recover damages for injuries allegedly sustained when law enforcement officers used physical force against him during the course of an investigatory stop. Because the case comes to us from a decision of the Court of Appeals affirming the entry of a directed verdict for respondents, we take the evidence hereafter noted in the light most favorable to petitioner. On November 12, 1984, Graham, a diabetic, felt the onset of an insulin reaction. He asked a friend, William Berry, to drive him to a nearby convenience store so he could purchase some orange juice to counteract the reaction. Berry agreed, but when Graham entered the store, he saw a number of people ahead of him in the check outline. Concerned about the delay, he hurried out of the store and asked Berry to drive him to a friend's house instead.

Respondent Connor, an officer of the Charlotte, North Carolina, Police Department, saw Graham hastily enter and leave the store. The officer became suspicious that something was amiss and followed Berry's car. About one-half mile from the store, he made an investigative stop. Although Berry told Connor that Graham was simply suffering from a "sugar reaction," the officer ordered Berry and Graham to wait while he found out what, if anything, had happened at the convenience store. When Officer Connor returned to his patrol car to call for backup assistance, Graham got out of the car, ran around it twice, and finally sat down on the curb, where he passed out briefly.

In the ensuing confusion, a number of other Charlotte police officers arrived on the scene in response to Officer Connor's request for backup. One of the officers rolled Graham over on the sidewalk and cuffed his hands tightly behind his back, ignoring Berry's pleas to get him some sugar. Another officer said: "I've seen a lot of people with sugar diabetes that never acted like this. Ain't nothing wrong with the M.F. but drunk. Lock the S.B. up." Several officers then lifted Graham up from behind, carried him over to Berry's car, and placed him face down on its hood. Regaining consciousness, Graham asked the officers to check in his wallet for a diabetic decal that he carried. In response, one of the officers told him to "shut up" and shoved his face down against the hood of the car. Four officers grabbed Graham and threw him headfirst into the police car. A friend of Graham's brought some orange juice to the car, but the officers refused to let him have it. Finally, Officer Connor received a report that Graham had done nothing wrong at the convenience store, and the officers drove him home and released him.

At some point during his encounter with the police, Graham sustained a broken foot, cuts on his wrists, a bruised forehead, and an injured shoulder; he also claims to have developed a loud ringing in his right ear that continues to this day. He commenced this action under 42 U.S.C. §1983 against the individual officers involved in the incident, all of whom are respondents here, alleging that they had used excessive force in making the investigatory stop, in violation of "rights secured to him under the Fourteenth Amendment to the United States Constitution and 42 U.S.C. §1983." The case was tried before a jury. At the close of petitioner's evidence, respondents moved for a directed verdict. In ruling on that motion, the District Court considered the following four factors, which it identified as "[t]he factors to be considered in determining when the excessive use of force gives rise to a cause of action under §1983": (1) the need for the application of force; (2) the relationship between that need and the amount of force that was used; (3) the extent of the injury inflicted; and (4) "[w]hether the force was applied in a good faith effort to maintain and restore discipline or maliciously and sadistically for the very purpose of causing harm." Finding that the amount of force used by the officers was "appropriate under the circumstances," that "[t]here was no discernable injury inflicted," and that the force used "was not applied maliciously or sadistically for the very purpose of causing harm," but in "a good faith effort to maintain or restore order in the face of a potentially explosive situation," the District Court granted respondents' motion for a directed verdict. A divided panel of the Court of Appeals for the Fourth Circuit affirmed.

Fifteen years ago, in *Johnson v. Glick*, the Court of Appeals for the Second Circuit addressed a §1983 damages claim filed by a pretrial detainee who claimed that a guard had assaulted him without justification. In evaluating the detainee's claim, Judge Friendly applied neither the Fourth Amendment nor the Eighth, the two most textually obvious sources of constitutional protection against physically abusive governmental conduct. Instead, he looked to "substantive due process," holding that "quite apart from any 'specific' of the Bill of Rights, application of undue force by law enforcement officers deprives a suspect of liberty without due process of law."

We reject this notion that all excessive force claims brought under §1983 are governed by a single generic standard. In addressing an excessive force claim brought under §1983, analysis begins by identifying the specific constitutional right allegedly infringed by the challenged application of force. In most instances, that will be either the Fourth Amendment's prohibition against unreasonable seizures of the person, or the Eighth Amendment's ban on cruel and unusual punishments, which are the two primary sources of constitutional protection against physically abusive governmental conduct. The validity of the claim must then be judged by reference to the specific constitutional standard which governs that right, rather than to some generalized "excessive force" standard.

Where, as here, the excessive force claim arises in the context of an arrest or investigatory stop of a free citizen, it is most properly characterized as one invoking the protections of the Fourth Amendment, which guarantees citizens the right "to be secure in their persons . . . against unreasonable . . . seizures" of the person. This much is clear from our decision in *Tennessee v. Garner*. In *Garner*, we addressed a claim that the use of deadly force to apprehend a fleeing suspect who did not appear to be armed or otherwise dangerous violated the suspect's constitutional rights, notwithstanding the existence of probable cause to arrest. Though the complaint alleged violations of both the Fourth Amendment and the Due Process Clause, we analyzed the constitutionality of the challenged application of force solely by reference to the Fourth Amendment's prohibition against unreasonable seizures of the person, holding that the "reasonableness" of a particular seizure depends not only on *when* it is made, but also on *how* it is carried out. Today we make explicit what was implicit in *Garner*'s analysis, and hold that *all* claims that law enforcement officers have used excessive force— deadly or not—in the course of an arrest, investigatory stop, or other "seizure" of a free citizen should be analyzed under the Fourth Amendment and its "reasonableness" standard, rather than under a "substantive due process" approach. Because the Fourth Amendment provides an explicit textual source of constitutional protection against this sort of physically intrusive governmental conduct, that Amendment, not the more generalized notion of "substantive due process," must be the guide for analyzing these claims.

Determining whether the force used to effect a particular seizure is "reasonable" under the Fourth Amendment requires a careful balancing of "'the nature and quality of the intrusion on the individual's Fourth Amendment interests'" against the countervailing governmental interests at stake. Our Fourth Amendment jurisprudence has long recognized that the right to make an arrest or investigatory stop necessarily carries with it the right to use some degree of physical coercion or threat thereof to effect it. Because "[t]he test of reasonableness under the Fourth Amendment is not capable of precise definition or mechanical application," however, its proper application requires careful attention to the facts and circumstances of each particular case, including the severity of the crime at issue, whether the suspect poses an immediate threat to the safety of the officers or others, and whether he is actively resisting arrest or attempting to evade arrest by flight.

The "reasonableness" of a particular use of force must be judged from the perspective of a reasonable officer on the scene, rather than with the 20/20 vision of hindsight. The Fourth Amendment is not violated by an arrest based on probable cause, even though the wrong person is arrested, nor by the mistaken execution of a valid search warrant on the wrong premises. With respect to a claim of excessive force, the same standard of reasonableness at the moment applies: "Not every push or shove, even if it may later seem unnecessary in the peace of a judge's chambers," violates the Fourth Amendment. The calculus of reasonableness must embody allowance for the fact that police officers are often forced to make split-second judgments—in circumstances that are tense, uncertain, and rapidly evolving—about the amount of force that is necessary in a particular situation.

As in other Fourth Amendment contexts, however, the "reasonableness" inquiry in an excessive force case is an objective one: the question is whether the officers' actions are "objectively reasonable" in light of the facts and circumstances confronting them, without regard to their underlying intent or motivation. An officer's evil intentions will not make a Fourth Amendment violation out of an objectively reasonable use of force; nor will an officer's good intentions make an objectively unreasonable use of force constitutional.

Chapter 3

THE EXCLUSIONARY RULE

D. Who Can Object to the Introduction of Evidence and Raise the Exclusionary Rule? (casebook p. 480)

In *Byrd v. United States*, the Court considered whether an unauthorized driver of a rental car can object to the introduction of evidence and raise the exclusionary rule.

Byrd v. United States
138 S. Ct. 1518 (2018)

Justice KENNEDY delivered the opinion of the Court.

In September 2014, Pennsylvania State Troopers pulled over a car driven by petitioner Terrence Byrd. Byrd was the only person in the car. In the course of the traffic stop the troopers learned that the car was rented and that Byrd was not listed on the rental agreement as an authorized driver. For this reason, the troopers told Byrd they did not need his consent to search the car, including its trunk where he had stored personal effects. A search of the trunk uncovered body armor and 49 bricks of heroin.

The evidence was turned over to federal authorities, who charged Byrd with distribution and possession of heroin with the intent to distribute and possession of body armor by a prohibited person. Byrd moved to suppress the evidence as the fruit of an unlawful search. The United States District Court for the Middle District of Pennsylvania denied the motion, and the Court of Appeals for the Third Circuit affirmed. Both courts concluded that, because Byrd was not listed on the rental agreement, he lacked a reasonable expectation of privacy in the car. Based on this conclusion, it appears that both the District Court and Court of Appeals deemed it unnecessary to consider whether the troopers had probable cause to search the car.

This Court granted certiorari to address the question whether a driver has a reasonable expectation of privacy in a rental car when he or she is not listed as an authorized driver on the rental agreement. The Court now holds that, as a general rule, someone in otherwise lawful possession and control of a rental car has a reasonable expectation of privacy in it even if the rental agreement does not list him or her as an authorized driver.

The Court concludes a remand is necessary to address in the first instance the Government's argument that this general rule is inapplicable because, in the circumstances here, Byrd had no greater expectation of privacy than a car thief. If that is so, our cases make clear he would lack a legitimate expectation of privacy. It is necessary to remand as well to determine whether, even if Byrd had a right to object to the search, probable cause justified it in any event.

I

On September 17, 2014, petitioner Terrence Byrd and Latasha Reed drove in Byrd's Honda Accord to a Budget car-rental facility in Wayne, New Jersey. Byrd stayed in the parking lot in the Honda while Reed went to the Budget desk and rented a Ford Fusion. The agreement Reed signed required her to certify that she had a valid driver's license and had not committed certain vehicle-related offenses within the previous three years. An addendum to the agreement, which Reed initialed, provides the following restriction on who may drive the rental car:

> "I understand that the only ones permitted to drive the vehicle other than the renter are the renter's spouse, the renter's co-employee (with the renter's permission, while on company business), or a person who appears at the time of the rental and signs an Additional Driver Form. These other drivers must also be at least 25 years old and validly licensed.
> "PERMITTING AN UNAUTHORIZED DRIVER TO OPERATE THE VEHICLE IS A VIOLATION OF THE RENTAL AGREEMENT. THIS MAY RESULT IN ANY AND ALL COVERAGE OTHERWISE PROVIDED BY THE RENTAL AGREEMENT BEING VOID AND MY BEING FULLY RESPONSIBLE FOR ALL LOSS OR DAMAGE, INCLUDING LIABILITY TO THIRD PARTIES."

In filling out the paperwork for the rental agreement, Reed did not list an additional driver. With the rental keys in hand, Reed returned to the parking lot and gave them to Byrd. The two then left the facility in separate cars—she in his Honda, he in the rental car. Byrd returned to his home in Patterson, New Jersey, and put his personal belongings in the trunk of the rental car. Later that afternoon, he departed in the car alone and headed toward Pittsburgh, Pennsylvania.

After driving nearly three hours, or roughly half the distance to Pittsburgh, Byrd passed State Trooper David Long, who was parked in the median of Interstate 81 near Harrisburg, Pennsylvania. Long was suspicious of Byrd because he was driving with his hands at the "10 and 2" position on the steering wheel, sitting far back from the steering wheel, and driving a rental car. Long knew the Ford Fusion was a rental car because one of its windows contained a barcode. Based on these observations, he decided to follow Byrd and, a short time later, stopped him for a possible traffic infraction.

When Long approached the passenger window of Byrd's car to explain the basis for the stop and to ask for identification, Byrd was "visibly nervous" and "was shaking and had a hard time obtaining his driver's license." He handed an interim license and the rental agreement to Long, stating that a friend had rented the car.

Long returned to his vehicle to verify Byrd's license and noticed Byrd was not listed as an additional driver on the rental agreement. Around this time another trooper, Travis Martin, arrived at the scene. While Long processed Byrd's license, Martin conversed with Byrd, who again stated that a friend had rented the vehicle. After Martin walked back to Long's patrol car, Long commented to Martin that Byrd was "not on the renter agreement," to which Martin replied, "yeah, he has no expectation of privacy."

A computer search based on Byrd's identification returned two different names. Further inquiry suggested the other name might be an alias and also revealed that Byrd had prior convictions for weapons and drug charges as well as an outstanding warrant in New Jersey for a probation violation. After learning that New Jersey did not want Byrd arrested for extradition, the troopers asked Byrd to step out of the vehicle and patted him down.

Long asked Byrd if he had anything illegal in the car. When Byrd said he did not, the troopers asked for his consent to search the car. At that point Byrd said he had a "blunt" in the car and offered to retrieve it for them. The officers understood "blunt" to mean a marijuana cigarette. They declined to let him retrieve it and continued to seek his consent to search the car, though they stated they did not need consent because he was not listed on the rental agreement. The troopers then opened the passenger and driver doors and began a thorough search of the passenger compartment.

Martin proceeded from there to search the car's trunk, including by opening up and taking things out of a large cardboard box, where he found a laundry bag containing body armor. At this point, the troopers decided to detain Byrd. As Martin walked toward Byrd and said he would be placing him in handcuffs, Byrd began to run away. A third trooper who had arrived on the scene joined Long and Martin in pursuit. When the troopers caught up to Byrd, he surrendered and admitted there was heroin in the car. Back at the car, the troopers resumed their search of the laundry bag and found 49 bricks of heroin.

II

Few protections are as essential to individual liberty as the right to be free from unreasonable searches and seizures. Whether a warrant is required is a separate question from the one the Court addresses here, which is whether the person claiming a constitutional violation "has had his own Fourth Amendment rights infringed by the search and seizure which he seeks to challenge." Answering that question requires examination of whether the person claiming the constitutional violation had a "legitimate expectation of privacy in the premises" searched. "Expectations of privacy protected by the Fourth Amendment, of course, need not be based on a common-law interest in real or personal property, or on the invasion of such an interest." Still, "property concepts" are instructive in "determining the presence or absence of the privacy interests protected by that Amendment."

Indeed, more recent Fourth Amendment cases have clarified that the test most often associated with legitimate expectations of privacy, which was derived from the second Justice Harlan's concurrence in *Katz v. United States* (1967), supplements, rather than displaces, "the traditional property-based understanding of the Fourth Amendment." *Florida v. Jardines* (2013). Reference to property concepts, however, aids the Court in assessing the precise question here: Does a driver of a rental car have a reasonable expectation of privacy in the car when he or she is not listed as an authorized driver on the rental agreement?

III

One who owns and possesses a car, like one who owns and possesses a house, almost always has a reasonable expectation of privacy in it. More difficult to define and delineate are the legitimate expectations of privacy of others.

On the one hand, as noted above, it is by now well established that a person need not always have a recognized common-law property interest in the place searched to be able to claim a reasonable expectation of privacy in it.

On the other hand, it is also clear that legitimate presence on the premises of the place searched, standing alone, is not enough to accord a reasonable expectation of privacy, because it "creates too broad a gauge for measurement of Fourth Amendment rights."

Although the Court has not set forth a single metric or exhaustive list of considerations to resolve the circumstances in which a person can be said to have a reasonable expectation of privacy, it has explained that "[l]egitimation of expectations of privacy by law must have a source outside of the Fourth Amendment, either by reference to concepts of real or personal property law or to understandings that are recognized and permitted by society." The two concepts in cases like this one are often linked. "One of the main rights attaching to property is the right to exclude others," and, in the main, "one who owns or lawfully possesses or controls property will in all likelihood have a legitimate expectation of privacy by virtue of the right to exclude." This general property-based concept guides resolution of this case.

Here, the Government contends that drivers who are not listed on rental agreements always lack an expectation of privacy in the automobile based on the rental company's lack of authorization alone. This *per se* rule rests on too restrictive a view of the Fourth Amendment's protections. Byrd, by contrast, contends that the sole occupant of a rental car always has an expectation of privacy in it based on mere possession and control. There is more to recommend Byrd's proposed rule than the Government's; but, without qualification, it would include within its ambit thieves and others who, not least because of their lack of any property-based justification, would not have a reasonable expectation of privacy.

Stripped to its essentials, the Government's position is that only authorized drivers of rental cars have expectations of privacy in those vehicles. This position is based on the following syllogism: Under *Rakas* [*v. Illinois* (1978)], passengers do not have an expectation of privacy in an automobile glove compartment or like places; an unauthorized driver like Byrd would have been the passenger had the renter been driving; and the unauthorized driver cannot obtain greater protection when he takes the wheel and leaves the renter behind. The flaw in this syllogism is its major premise, for it is a misreading of *Rakas*.

The Court in *Rakas* did not hold that passengers cannot have an expectation of privacy in automobiles. To the contrary, the Court disclaimed any intent to hold "that a passenger lawfully in an automobile may not invoke the exclusionary rule and challenge a search of that vehicle unless he happens to own or have a possessory interest in it." The Court instead rejected the argument that legitimate presence alone was sufficient to assert a Fourth Amendment interest, which was fatal to the petitioners' case there because they had "claimed only that they were 'legitimately on [the] premises' and did not claim that they had any legitimate expectation of privacy in the areas of the car which were searched."

What is more, the Government's syllogism is beside the point, because this case does not involve a passenger at all but instead the driver and sole occupant of a rental car. As Justice Powell observed in his concurring opinion in *Rakas*, a "distinction . . . may be made in some circumstances between the Fourth Amendment rights of passengers and the rights of an individual who has exclusive control of an automobile or of its locked compartments."

The Court sees no reason why the expectation of privacy that comes from lawful possession and control and the attendant right to exclude would differ depending on whether the car in question is rented or privately owned by someone other than the person in current possession of it, much as it did not seem to matter whether the friend of the defendant in *Jones* owned or leased the apartment he permitted the defendant to use in his absence. Both would have the expectation of privacy that comes with the right to exclude. Indeed, the Government conceded at oral argument that an unauthorized driver in sole possession of a rental car would be permitted to exclude third parties from it, such as a carjacker.

The Government further stresses that Byrd's driving the rental car violated the rental agreement that Reed signed, and it contends this violation meant Byrd could not have had any basis for claiming an expectation of privacy in the rental car at the time of the search. As anyone who has rented a car knows, car-rental agreements are filled with long lists of restrictions. Examples include prohibitions on driving the car on unpaved roads or driving while using a handheld cellphone. Few would contend that violating provisions like these has anything to do with a driver's reasonable expectation of privacy in the rental car—as even the Government agrees.

Despite this concession, the Government argues that permitting an unauthorized driver to take the wheel of a rental car is a breach different in kind from these others, so serious that the rental company would consider the agreement "void" the moment an unauthorized driver takes the wheel. To begin with, that is not what the contract says. It states: "Permitting an unauthorized driver to operate the vehicle is a violation of the rental agreement. This may result in any and all coverage otherwise provided by the rental agreement being void and my being fully responsible for all loss or damage, including liability to third parties."

Putting the Government's misreading of the contract aside, there may be countless innocuous reasons why an unauthorized driver might get behind the wheel of a rental car and drive it—perhaps the renter is drowsy or inebriated and the two think it safer for the friend to drive them to their destination. True, this constitutes a breach of the rental agreement, and perhaps a serious one, but the Government fails to explain what bearing this breach of contract, standing alone, has on expectations of privacy in the car. Stated in different terms, for Fourth Amendment purposes there is no meaningful difference between the authorized-driver provision and the other provisions the Government agrees do not eliminate an expectation of privacy, all of which concern risk allocation between private parties—violators might pay additional fees, lose insurance coverage, or assume liability for damage resulting from the breach. But that risk allocation has little to do with whether one would have a reasonable expectation of privacy in the rental car if, for example, he or she otherwise has lawful possession of and control over the car.

The central inquiry at this point turns on the concept of lawful possession, and this is where an important qualification of Byrd's proposed rule comes into play. *Rakas* makes clear that "'wrongful' presence at the scene of a search would not enable a defendant to object to the legality of the search." "A burglar plying his trade in a summer cabin during the off season," for example, "may have a thoroughly justified subjective expectation of privacy, but it is not one which the law recognizes as 'legitimate.'" Likewise, "a person present in a stolen automobile at the time of the search may [not] object to the lawfulness of the search of the automobile." No matter the degree of possession and control, the car thief would not have a reasonable expectation of privacy in a stolen car.

Though new, the fact pattern here continues a well-traveled path in this Court's Fourth Amendment jurisprudence. Those cases support the proposition, and the Court now holds, that the mere fact that a driver in lawful possession or control of a rental car is not listed on the rental agreement will not defeat his or her otherwise reasonable expectation of privacy. The Court leaves for remand two of the Government's arguments: that one who intentionally uses a third party to procure a rental car by a fraudulent scheme for the purpose of committing a crime is no better situated than a car thief; and that probable cause justified the search in any event.

Justice THOMAS, with whom Justice GORSUCH joins, concurring.

Although I have serious doubts about the "reasonable expectation of privacy" test from *Katz v. United States*, (1967) (Harlan, J., concurring), I join the Court's opinion because it correctly navigates our precedents, which no party has asked us to reconsider. As the Court notes, Byrd also argued that he should prevail under the original meaning of the Fourth Amendment because the police interfered with a property interest that he had in the rental car. I agree with the Court's decision not to review this argument in the first instance. In my view, it would be especially "unwise" to reach that issue, because the parties fail to adequately address several threshold questions.

The Fourth Amendment guarantees the people's right to be secure from unreasonable searches of "their persons, houses, papers, and effects." With this language, the Fourth Amendment gives "*each* person . . . the right to be secure against unreasonable searches and seizures in *his own* person, house, papers, and effects." The issue, then, is whether Byrd can prove that the rental car was *his* effect.

That issue seems to turn on at least three threshold questions. First, what kind of property interest do individuals need before something can be considered "their . . . effec[t]" under the original meaning of the Fourth Amendment? Second, what body of law determines whether that property interest is present—modern state law, the common law of 1791, or something else? Third, is the unauthorized use of a rental car illegal or otherwise wrongful under the relevant law, and, if so, does that illegality or wrongfulness affect the Fourth Amendment analysis?

The parties largely gloss over these questions, but the answers seem vitally important to assessing whether Byrd can claim that the rental car is his effect. In an appropriate case, I would welcome briefing and argument on these questions.

E. Civil Remedies Against the Police (new; casebook p. 495)

Other than the exclusionary rule, what remedies are available against police? There might be suits for injunctive relief or for money damages. The following are the leading Supreme Court cases on such civil suits.

1. Suits for Injunctive Relief

In *City of Los Angeles v. Lyons*, the Court limited the ability to sue cities to enjoin police practices. In reading the case, it is important to consider when suits for injunctive relief will be allowed.

City of Los Angeles v. Lyons
461 U.S. 95 (1983)

Justice WHITE delivered the opinion of the Court. . . .

The complaint alleged that on October 6, 1976, at 2 A.M., [Adolph] Lyons was stopped by the defendant officers for a traffic or vehicle code violation and that although Lyons offered no resistance or threat whatsoever, the officers, without provocation or justification, seized Lyons and applied a "chokehold"[1] — either the "bar arm control" hold or the "carotid-artery control" hold or both — rendering him unconscious and causing damage to his larynx.

Counts I through IV of the complaint sought damages against the officers and the City. Count V, with which we are principally concerned here, sought a preliminary and permanent injunction against the City barring the use of the control holds. That count alleged that the city's police officers, "pursuant to the authorization, instruction and encouragement of defendant City of Los Angeles, regularly and routinely apply these choke holds in innumerable situations where they are not threatened by the use of any deadly force whatsoever," that numerous persons have been injured as the result of the application of the chokeholds, that Lyons and others similarly situated are threatened with irreparable injury in the form of bodily injury and loss of life, and that Lyons "justifiably fears that any contact he has with Los Angeles police officers may result in his being choked and strangled to death without provocation, justification or other legal excuse." . . .

The District Court found that Lyons had been stopped for a traffic infringement and that without provocation or legal justification the officers involved had applied a "department-authorized chokehold which resulted in injuries to the plaintiff." The court further found that the department authorizes the use of the holds in situations where no one is threatened by death or grievous bodily harm, that officers are insufficiently trained, that the use of the holds involves a high risk of injury or death as then employed, and that their continued use in situations where neither death nor serious bodily injury is threatened "is unconscionable in a civilized society." The court concluded that such use violated Lyons' substantive due process rights under the Fourteenth Amendment. A preliminary injunction was entered enjoining "the use of both the carotid-artery and bar arm holds under circumstances which do not threaten death or serious bodily injury." An improved training program and regular reporting and record keeping were also ordered. The Court of Appeals affirmed in a brief per curiam opinion . . . .

[Lyons'] first amended complaint alleged that 10 chokehold-related deaths had occurred. By May, 1982, there had been five more such deaths. On May 6, 1982, the Chief of Police in Los Angeles prohibited the use of the bar-arm chokehold in any circumstances. A few days later, on May 12, 1982, the Board of Police Commissioners imposed a six-month moratorium on the use of the carotid-artery chokehold except under circumstances where deadly force is authorized.

---

[1] The police control procedures at issue in this case are referred to as "control holds," "chokeholds," "strangleholds," and "neck restraints." All these terms refer to two basic control procedures: the "carotid" hold and the "bar arm" hold. In the "carotid" hold, an officer positioned behind a subject places one arm around the subject's neck and holds the wrist of that arm with his other hand. The officer, by using his lower forearm and bicep muscle, applies pressure concentrating on the carotid arteries located on the sides of the subject's neck. The "carotid" hold is capable of rendering the subject unconscious by diminishing the flow of oxygenated blood to the brain. The "bar arm" hold, which is administered similarly, applies pressure at the front of the subject's neck. "Bar arm" pressure causes pain, reduces the flow of oxygen to the lungs, and may render the subject unconscious.

3. The Exclusionary Rule

Based on these events . . . Lyons [argues] that in light of changed conditions, an injunctive decree is now unnecessary because he is no longer subject to a threat of injury. He urges that the preliminary injunction should be vacated [because the case is moot]. The City, on the other hand, while acknowledging that subsequent events have significantly changed the posture of this case, again asserts that the case is not moot because the moratorium is not permanent and may be lifted at any time.

We agree with the City that the case is not moot, since the moratorium by its terms is not permanent. . . . We nevertheless hold, for another reason, that the federal courts are without jurisdiction to entertain Lyons' claim for injunctive relief.

It goes without saying that those who seek to invoke the jurisdiction of the federal courts must satisfy the threshhold requirement imposed by Article III of the Constitution by alleging an actual case or controversy. Plaintiffs must demonstrate a "personal stake in the outcome" in order to "assure that concrete adverseness which sharpens the presentation of issues" necessary for the proper resolution of constitutional questions. Abstract injury is not enough. The plaintiff must show that he "has sustained or is immediately in danger of sustaining some direct injury" as the result of the challenged official conduct and the injury or threat of injury must be both "real and immediate," not "conjectural" or "hypothetical."

In *O'Shea v. Littleton*, we dealt with a case brought by a class of plaintiffs claiming that they had been subjected to discriminatory enforcement of the criminal law. Among other things, a county magistrate and judge were accused of discriminatory conduct in various respects, such as sentencing members of plaintiff's class more harshly than other defendants. . . . [We held that the] complaint [failed] to allege a case or controversy. Although it was claimed in that case that particular members of the plaintiff class had actually suffered from the alleged unconstitutional practices, we observed that "[p]ast exposure to illegal conduct does not in itself show a present case or controversy regarding injunctive relief . . . if unaccompanied by any continuing, present adverse effects." Past wrongs were evidence bearing on "whether there is a real and immediate threat of repeated injury." But the prospect of future injury rested "on the likelihood that [plaintiffs] will again be arrested for and charged with violations of the criminal law and will again be subjected to bond proceedings, trial, or sentencing before petitioners." The most that could be said for plaintiffs' standing was "that if [plaintiffs] proceed to violate an unchallenged law and if they are charged, held to answer, and tried in any proceedings before petitioners, they will be subjected to the discriminatory practices that petitioners are alleged to have followed." We could not find a case or controversy in those circumstances: the threat to the plaintiffs was not "sufficiently real and immediate to show an existing controversy simply because they anticipate violating lawful criminal statutes and being tried for their offenses. . . ."

Another relevant decision for present purposes is *Rizzo v. Goode*, a case in which plaintiffs alleged widespread illegal and unconstitutional police conduct aimed at minority citizens and against City residents in general. The Court reiterated the holding in *O'Shea* that past wrongs do not in themselves amount to that real and immediate threat of injury necessary to make out a case or controversy. The claim of injury rested upon "what one or a small, unnamed minority of policemen might do to them in the future because of that unknown policeman's perception" of departmental procedures. This hypothesis was "even more attenuated than those allegations of future injury found insufficient in *O'Shea* to warrant [the] invocation of federal jurisdiction." The Court also held that plaintiffs' showing at trial of a relatively few instances of violations by individual police officers, without any showing of a deliberate policy on behalf of the named defendants, did not provide a basis for equitable relief. . . .

No extension of *O'Shea* and *Rizzo* is necessary to hold that respondent Lyons has failed to demonstrate a case or controversy with the City that would justify the equitable relief sought. Lyons' standing to seek the injunction requested depended on whether he was likely to suffer future injury from the use of the chokeholds by police officers. Count V of the complaint alleged the traffic stop and choking incident five months before. That Lyons may have been illegally choked by the police on October 6, 1976, while presumably affording Lyons standing to claim damages against the individual officers and perhaps against the City, does nothing to establish a real and immediate threat that he would again be stopped for a traffic violation, or for any other offense, by an officer or officers who would illegally choke him into unconsciousness without any provocation or resistance on his part. The additional allegation in the complaint that the police in Los Angeles routinely apply chokeholds in situations where they are not threatened by the use of deadly force falls far short of the allegations that would be necessary to establish a case or controversy between these parties.

In order to establish an actual controversy in this case, Lyons would have had not only to allege that he would have another encounter with the police but also to make the incredible assertion either, (1) that all police officers in Los Angeles always choke any citizen with whom they happen to have an encounter, whether for the purpose of arrest, issuing a citation or for questioning or, (2) that the City ordered or authorized police officers to act in such manner. Although Count V alleged that the City authorized the use of the control holds in situations where deadly force was not threatened, it did not indicate why Lyons might be realistically threatened by police officers who acted within the strictures of the City's policy. If, for example, chokeholds were authorized to be used only to counter resistance to an arrest by a suspect, or to thwart an effort to escape, any future threat to Lyons from the City's policy or from the conduct of police officers would be no more real than the possibility that he would again have an encounter with the police and that either he would illegally resist arrest or detention or the officers would disobey their instructions and again render him unconscious without any provocation.[7]

---

[7] The centerpiece of Justice Marshall's dissent is that Lyons had standing to challenge the City's policy because to recover damages he would have to prove that what allegedly occurred on October 6, 1976, was pursuant to City authorization. We agree completely that for Lyons to succeed in his

3. The Exclusionary Rule

Under *O'Shea* and *Rizzo*, these allegations were an insufficient basis to provide a federal court with jurisdiction to entertain Count V of the complaint.[8] [The court of appeals erred in holding otherwise and distinguishing *O'Shea* and *Rizzo*.] . . .

First, the Court of Appeals thought that Lyons was more immediately threatened than the plaintiffs in those cases since, according to the Court of Appeals, Lyons need only be stopped for a minor traffic violation to be subject to the strangleholds. But even assuming that Lyons would again be stopped for a traffic or other violation in the reasonably near future, it is untenable to assert, and the complaint made no such allegation, that strangleholds are applied by the Los Angeles police to every citizen who is stopped or arrested regardless of the conduct of the person stopped. We cannot agree that the "odds," that Lyons would not only again be stopped for a traffic violation but would also be subjected to a chokehold without any provocation whatsoever are sufficient to make out a federal case for equitable relief. We note that five months elapsed between October 6, 1976, and the filing of the complaint, yet there was no allegation of further unfortunate encounters between Lyons and the police.

Of course, it may be that among the countless encounters between the police and the citizens of a great city such as Los Angeles, there will be certain instances in which strangleholds will be illegally applied and injury and death unconstitutionally inflicted on the victim. As we have said, however, it is no more

---

damages action, it would be necessary to prove that what happened to him—that is, as alleged, he was choked without any provocation or legal excuse whatsoever—was pursuant to a City policy. . . . [H]owever, it does not follow that Lyons had standing to seek the injunction prayed for in Count V. . . .

Lyons alleges . . . official policies of the City . . . authoriz[ed] the use of chokeholds "in situations where [the officers] are threatened by far less than deadly force." This is not equivalent to the unbelievable assertion that the City either orders or authorizes application of the chokeholds where there is no resistance or other provocation. . . .

[E]ven if the complaint must be read as containing an allegation that officers are authorized to apply the chokeholds where there is no resistance or other provocation, it does not follow that Lyons has standing to seek an injunction against the application of the restraint holds in situations that he has not experienced, as for example, where the suspect resists arrest or tries to escape but does not threaten the use of deadly force. Yet that is precisely the scope of the injunction that Lyons prayed for in Count V. . . .

[T]o have a case or controversy with the City that could sustain Count V, Lyons would have to credibly allege that he faced a realistic threat from the future application of the City's policy. Justice Marshall nowhere confronts this requirement—the necessity that Lyons demonstrate that he, himself, will not only again be stopped by the police but will be choked without any provocation or legal excuse. Justice Marshall plainly does not agree with that requirement, and he was in dissent in *O'Shea*. We are at issue in that respect.

[8] As previously indicated, Lyons alleged that he feared he would be choked in any future encounter with the police. The reasonableness of Lyons' fear is dependent upon the likelihood of a recurrence of the allegedly unlawful conduct. It is the reality of the threat of repeated injury that is relevant to the standing inquiry, not the plaintiff's subjective apprehensions. The emotional consequences of a prior act simply are not a sufficient basis for an injunction absent a real and immediate threat of future injury by the defendant. Of course, emotional upset is a relevant consideration in a damages action.

than conjecture to suggest that in every instance of a traffic stop, arrest, or other encounter between the police and a citizen, the police will act unconstitutionally and inflict injury without provocation or legal excuse. And it is surely no more than speculation to assert either that Lyons himself will again be involved in one of those unfortunate instances, or that he will be arrested in the future and provoke the use of a chokehold by resisting arrest, attempting to escape, or threatening deadly force or serious bodily injury.

Second, the Court of Appeals viewed O'Shea and Rizzo as cases in which the plaintiffs sought "massive structural" relief against the local law enforcement systems and therefore that the holdings in those cases were inapposite to cases such as this where the plaintiff, according to the Court of Appeals, seeks to enjoin only an "established," "sanctioned" police practice assertedly violative of constitutional rights. O'Shea and Rizzo, however, cannot be so easily confined . . . . If Lyons has made no showing that he is realistically threatened by a repetition of his experience of October, 1976, then he has not met the requirements for seeking an injunction in a federal court, whether the injunction contemplates intrusive structural relief or the cessation of a discrete practice. . . .

The record and findings made on remand do not improve Lyons' position with respect to standing. . . . There was no finding that Lyons faced a real and immediate threat of again being illegally choked. The City's policy was described as authorizing the use of the strangleholds "under circumstances where no one is threatened with death or grievous bodily harm." That policy was not further described, but the record before the court contained the department's existing policy with respect to the employment of chokeholds. Nothing in that policy, contained in a Police Department manual, suggests that the chokeholds, or other kinds of force for that matter, are authorized absent some resistance or other provocation by the arrestee or other suspect. On the contrary, police officers were instructed to use chokeholds only when lesser degrees of force do not suffice and then only "to gain control of a suspect who is violently resisting the officer or trying to escape." . . .

Contrary to the view of the Court of Appeals, it is not at all "difficult" under our holding "to see how anyone can ever challenge police or similar administrative practices." The legality of the violence to which Lyons claims he was once subjected is at issue in his suit for damages and can be determined there.

Absent a sufficient likelihood that he will again be wronged in a similar way, Lyons is no more entitled to an injunction than any other citizen of Los Angeles; and a federal court may not entertain a claim by any or all citizens who no more than assert that certain practices of law enforcement officers are unconstitutional. . . .

[R]ecognition of the need for a proper balance between state and federal authority counsels restraint in the issuance of injunctions against state officers engaged in the administration of the states' criminal laws in the absence of irreparable injury which is both great and immediate. . . . In exercising their equitable powers federal courts must recognize "[t]he special delicacy of the adjustment to be preserved between federal equitable power and State administration of its own law." ...

Justice MARSHALL, with whom Justice BRENNAN, Justice BLACKMUN and Justice STEVENS join, dissenting.

The District Court found that the City of Los Angeles authorizes its police officers to apply life-threatening chokeholds to citizens who pose no threat of violence, and that respondent, Adolph Lyons, was subjected to such a chokehold. The Court today holds that a federal court is without power to enjoin the enforcement of the City's policy, no matter how flagrantly unconstitutional it may be. Since no one can show that he will be choked in the future, no one—not even a person who, like Lyons, has almost been choked to death—has standing to challenge the continuation of the policy. The City is free to continue the policy indefinitely as long as it is willing to pay damages for the injuries and deaths that result. I dissent from this unprecedented and unwarranted approach to standing. ...

Respondent Adolph Lyons is a 24-year-old Negro male who resides in Los Angeles. According to the uncontradicted evidence in the record, at about 2:30 A.M. on October 6, 1976, Lyons was pulled over to the curb by two officers of the Los Angeles Police Department (LAPD) for a traffic infraction because one of his taillights was burned out. The officers greeted him with drawn revolvers as he exited from his car. Lyons was told to face his car and spread his legs. He did so. He was then ordered to clasp his hands and put them on top of his head. He again complied. After one of the officers completed a pat-down search, Lyons dropped his hands, but was ordered to place them back above his head, and one of the officers grabbed Lyons' hands and slammed them onto his head. Lyons complained about the pain caused by the ring of keys he was holding in his hand. Within five to ten seconds, the officer began to choke Lyons by applying a forearm against his throat. As Lyons struggled for air, the officer handcuffed him, but continued to apply the chokehold until he blacked out. When Lyons regained consciousness, he was lying face down on the ground, choking, gasping for air, and spitting up blood and dirt. He had urinated and defecated. He was issued a traffic citation and released. ...

Although the City instructs its officers that use of a chokehold does not constitute deadly force, since 1975 no less than 16 persons have died following the use of a chokehold by an LAPD police officer. Twelve have been Negro males.[3] The evidence submitted to the District Court established that for many years it has been the official policy of the City to permit police officers to employ chokeholds in a variety of situations where they face no threat of violence. In reported "altercations" between LAPD officers and citizens the chokeholds are used more

---

[3] Thus in a City where Negro males constitute 9% of the population, they have accounted for 75% of the deaths resulting from the use of chokeholds. In addition to his other allegations, Lyons alleged racial discrimination in violation of the Equal Protection Clause of the Fourteenth Amendment. Of the 16 deaths, 10 occurred prior to the District Court's issuance of the preliminary injunction, although at that time the parties and the Court were aware of only nine.

frequently than any other means of physical restraint. Between February 1975 and July 1980, LAPD officers applied chokeholds on at least 975 occasions, which represented more than three-quarters of the reported altercations.

It is undisputed that chokeholds pose a high and unpredictable risk of serious injury or death. Chokeholds are intended to bring a subject under control by causing pain and rendering him unconscious. Depending on the position of the officer's arm and the force applied, the victim's voluntary or involuntary reaction, and his state of health, an officer may inadvertently crush the victim's larynx, trachea, or thyroid. The result may be death caused by either cardiac arrest or asphyxiation. An LAPD officer described the reaction of a person to being choked as "do[ing] the chicken," in reference apparently to the reactions of a chicken when its neck is wrung. The victim experiences extreme pain. His face turns blue as he is deprived of oxygen, he goes into spasmodic convulsions, his eyes roll back, his body wriggles, his feet kick up and down, and his arms move about wildly.

Although there has been no occasion to determine the precise contours of the City's chokehold policy, the evidence submitted to the District Court provides some indications. LAPD training officer Terry Speer testified that an officer is authorized to deploy a chokehold whenever he "feels that there's about to be a bodily attack made on him." A training bulletin states that "[c]ontrol holds . . . allow officers to subdue any resistance by the suspects." . . .

The training given LAPD officers provides additional revealing evidence of the City's chokehold policy. Officer Speer testified that in instructing officers concerning the use of force, the LAPD does not distinguish between felony and misdemeanor suspects. Moreover, the officers are taught to maintain the chokehold until the suspect goes limp, despite substantial evidence that the application of a chokehold invariably induces a "flight or flee" syndrome, producing an involuntary struggle by the victim which can easily be misinterpreted by the officer as willful resistance that must be overcome by prolonging the chokehold and increasing the force applied. In addition, officers are instructed that the chokeholds can be safely deployed for up to three or four minutes. Robert Jarvis, the City's expert who has taught at the Los Angeles Police Academy for the past twelve years, admitted that officers are never told that the bar-arm control can cause death if applied for just two seconds. Of the nine deaths for which evidence was submitted to the District Court, the average duration of the choke where specified was approximately 40 seconds. . . .

It is simply disingenuous for the Court to assert that its decision requires "[n]o extension" of *O'Shea v. Littleton* and *Rizzo v. Goode*. In contrast to this case *O'Shea* and *Rizzo* involved disputes focusing solely on the threat of future injury which the plaintiffs in those cases alleged they faced. In *O'Shea* the plaintiffs did not allege past injury and did not seek compensatory relief. In *Rizzo*, the plaintiffs sought only declaratory and injunctive relief and alleged past instances of police misconduct only in an attempt to establish the substantiality of the threat of future injury. . . .

3. The Exclusionary Rule

By contrast, Lyons' request for prospective relief is coupled with his claim for damages based on past injury. In addition to the risk that he will be subjected to a chokehold in the future, Lyons has suffered past injury. Because he has a live claim for damages, he need not rely solely on the threat of future injury to establish his personal stake in the outcome of the controversy. In the cases relied on by the majority, the Court simply had no occasion to decide whether a plaintiff who has standing to litigate a dispute must clear a separate standing hurdle with respect to each form of relief sought.

The Court's decision likewise finds no support in the fundamental policy underlying the Article III standing requirement—the concern that a federal court not decide a legal issue if the plaintiff lacks a sufficient "personal stake in the outcome of the controversy. . . ."

Because Lyons has a claim for damages against the City, and because he cannot prevail on that claim unless he demonstrates that the City's chokehold policy violates the Constitution, his personal stake in the outcome of the controversy adequately assures an adversary presentation of his challenge to the constitutionality of the policy. Moreover, the resolution of this challenge will be largely dispositive of his requests for declaratory and injunctive relief. No doubt the requests for injunctive relief may raise additional questions. But these questions involve familiar issues relating to the appropriateness of particular forms of relief, and have never been thought to implicate a litigant's standing to sue. The denial of standing separately to seek injunctive relief therefore cannot be justified by the basic concern underlying the Article III standing requirement.

Our cases uniformly state that the touchstone of the Article III standing requirement is the plaintiff's personal stake in the underlying dispute, not in the particular types of relief sought. Once a plaintiff establishes a personal stake in a dispute, he has done all that is necessary to "invok[e] the court's authority . . . to challenge the action sought to be adjudicated." . . .

The federal practice has been to reserve consideration of the appropriate relief until after a determination of the merits, not to foreclose certain forms of relief by a ruling on the pleadings. The prayer for relief is no part of the plaintiff's cause of action. Rather, "[t]he usual rule is that where legal rights have been invaded and a cause of action is available, a federal court may use any available remedy to make good the wrong done." . . .

Apart from the question of standing, the only remaining question presented in the petition for certiorari is whether the preliminary injunction issued by the District Court must be set aside because it "constitute[s] a substantial interference in the operation of a municipal police department." Petition for Certiorari i. In my view it does not. . . .

The principles of federalism simply do not preclude the limited preliminary injunction issued in this case. Unlike the permanent injunction at issue in *Rizzo*, the preliminary injunction involved here entails no federal supervision of the LAPD's activities. The preliminary injunction merely forbids the use of chokeholds absent the threat of deadly force, permitting their continued use where such a threat does exist. This limited ban takes the form of a preventive injunction, which has traditionally been regarded as the least intrusive form of equitable relief. Moreover, the City can remove the ban by obtaining approval of a training plan. Although the preliminary injunction also requires the City to provide records of the uses of chokeholds to respondent and to allow the court access to such records, this requirement is hardly onerous, since the LAPD already maintains records concerning the use of chokeholds. . . .

The Court's decision removes an entire class of constitutional violations from the equitable powers of a federal court. It immunizes from prospective equitable relief any policy that authorizes persistent deprivations of constitutional rights as long as no individual can establish with substantial certainty that he will be injured, or injured again, in the future. THE CHIEF JUSTICE asked in *Bivens* (dissenting opinion), "what would be the judicial response to a police order authorizing 'shoot to kill' with respect to every fugitive?" His answer was that it would be "easy to predict our collective wrath and outrage." We now learn that wrath and outrage cannot be translated into an order to cease the unconstitutional practice, but only an award of damages to those who are victimized by the practice and live to sue and to the survivors of those who are not so fortunate. Under the view expressed by the majority today, if the police adopt a policy of "shoot to kill," or a policy of shooting one out of ten suspects, the federal courts will be powerless to enjoin its continuation. The federal judicial power is now limited to levying a toll for such a systematic constitutional violation.

2. Suits for Money Damages

Local governments might be sued because of police misconduct, but *Monell v. Department of Social Services* holds that they are liable only if their own policy or custom violates the Constitution.

Monell v. Department of Social Services
436 U.S. 658 (1978)

Mr. Justice BRENNAN delivered the opinion of the Court.

Petitioners, a class of female employees of the Department of Social Services and of the Board of Education of the city of New York, commenced this action under 42 U.S.C. §1983 in July 1971. The gravamen of the complaint was that the Board and the Department had as a matter of official policy compelled pregnant employees to take unpaid leaves of absence before such leaves were required for medical reasons.[2] The suit sought injunctive relief and backpay for periods of

---

[2] The plaintiffs alleged that New York had a citywide policy of forcing women to take maternity leave after the fifth month of pregnancy unless a city physician and the head of an employee's

unlawful forced leave. Named as defendants in the action were the Department and its Commissioner, the Board and its Chancellor, and the city of New York and its Mayor. In each case, the individual defendants were sued solely in their official capacities.

[The district court] held moot petitioners' claims for injunctive and declaratory relief since the City of New York and the Board, after the filing of the complaint, had changed their policies . . . No one now challenges this conclusion. . . . [P]laintiffs' prayers for backpay were denied because any such damages would come ultimately from the City of New York and, therefore, to hold otherwise would be to "circumven[t]" the immunity conferred on municipalities by *Monroe v. Pape*. [The court of appeals affirmed.] . . .

In *Monroe*, we held that "Congress did not undertake to bring municipal corporations within the ambit of [§1983]." The sole basis for this conclusion was an inference drawn from Congress' rejection of the "Sherman amendment" to the bill which became the Civil Rights Act of 1871, the precursor of §1983. The Amendment would have held a municipal corporation liable for damage done to the person or property of its inhabitants by private persons "riotously and tumultuously assembled." Although the Sherman amendment did not seek to amend §1 of the Act, which is now §1983, and although the nature of the obligation created by that amendment was vastly different from that created by §1, the Court nonetheless concluded in *Monroe* that Congress must have meant to exclude municipal corporations from the coverage of §1 because " 'the House [in voting against the Sherman amendment] had solemnly decided that in their judgment Congress had no constitutional power to impose any obligation upon county and town organizations, the mere instrumentality for the administration of state law.' " This statement, we thought, showed that Congress doubted its "constitutional power . . . to impose civil liability on municipalities," and that such doubt would have extended to any type of civil liability.

A fresh analysis of the debate on the Civil Rights Act of 1871, and particularly of the case law which each side mustered in its support, shows, however, that *Monroe* incorrectly equated the "obligation" of which Representative Poland spoke with "civil liability." . . .

The main features of the conference committee draft of the Sherman amendment were these: First, a cause of action was given to persons injured by

> "any persons riotously and tumultuously assembled together . . . with intent to deprive any person of any right conferred upon him by the Constitution and laws of the United States, or to deter him or punish him for exercising such right, or by reason of his race, color, or previous condition of servitude . . . ."

Second, the bill provided that the action would be against the county, city, or parish in which the riot had occurred . . . . Third, . . . the conference substitute made

---

agency allowed up to an additional two months of work. The defendants did not deny this, but stated that this policy had been changed after suit was instituted. . . .

the government defendant liable on the judgment if it was not satisfied against individual defendants who had committed the violence. . . .

In the ensuing debate on the first conference report, which was the first debate of any kind on the Sherman amendment, Senator Sherman explained that the purpose of his amendment was to enlist the aid of persons of property in the enforcement of the civil rights laws by making their property "responsible" for Ku Klux Klan damage. . . .

The first conference substitute passed the Senate but was rejected by the House. . . .

House opponents of the Sherman amendment—whose views are particularly important since only the House voted down the amendment—. . . argued that the local units of government upon which the amendment fastened liability were not obligated to keep the peace at state law and further that the Federal Government could not constitutionally require local governments to create police forces, whether this requirement was levied directly, or indirectly by imposing damages for breach of the peace on municipalities. The most complete statement of this position is that of Representative Blair:

> "The proposition known as the Sherman amendment. . . is entirely new. It is alto-gether without a precedent in this country. . . . That amendment claims the power in the General Government to go into the States of this Union and lay such obliga-tions as it may please upon the municipalities, which are the creations of the States alone. . . ."

[Then-recent cases provided] support for Blair's view that the Sherman amendment, by putting municipalities to the Hobson's choice of keeping the peace or paying civil damages, attempted to impose obligations on municipalities by indirection that could not be imposed directly, thereby threatening to "destroy the government of the States."

If municipal liability under §1 of the Civil Rights Act of 1871 created a simi-lar Hobson's choice, we might conclude, as *Monroe* did, that Congress could not have intended municipalities to be among the "persons" to which that section applied. But this is not the case.

First, opponents expressly distinguished between imposing an obligation to keep the peace and merely imposing civil liability for damages on a municipality that was obligated by state law to keep the peace, but which had not in violation of the Fourteenth Amendment. Representative Poland, for example, reasoning from Contract Clause precedents, indicated that Congress could constitutionally confer jurisdiction on the federal courts to entertain suits seeking to hold munici-palities liable for using their authorized powers in violation of the Constitution— which is as far as §1 of the Civil Rights Act went:

> "I presume . . . that where a State had imposed a duty [to keep the peace] upon [a] municipality . . . an action would be allowed to be maintained against them in the courts of the United States under the ordinary restrictions as to jurisdiction. But the

enforcing a liability, existing by their own contract, or by a State law, in the courts, is a very widely different thing from devolving a new duty or liability upon them by the national Government, which has no power either to create or destroy them, and no power or control over them whatever."

Second, . . . [i]t must be remembered that [at the time, the Supreme Court] vigorously enforced the Contract Clause against municipalities—an enforcement effort which included various forms of "positive" relief, such as ordering that taxes be levied and collected to discharge federal-court judgments, once a constitutional infraction was found. Thus, federal judicial enforcement of the Constitution's express limits on state power, since it was done so frequently, must, . . . have been permissible . . . .

From the foregoing discussion, it is readily apparent that nothing said in debate on the Sherman amendment would have prevented holding a municipality liable under §1 of the Civil Rights Act for its own violations of the Fourteenth Amendment. The question remains, however, whether the general language describing those to be liable under §1—"any person"—covers more than natural persons. An examination of the debate on §1 and application of appropriate rules of construction show unequivocally that §1 was intended to cover legal as well as natural persons. . . .

In both Houses, statements of the supporters of §1 corroborated that Congress, in enacting §1, intended to give a broad remedy for violations of federally protected civil rights. Moreover, since municipalities through their official acts could, equally with natural persons, create the harms intended to be remedied by §1, and, further, since Congress intended §1 to be broadly construed, there is no reason to suppose that municipal corporations would have been excluded from the sweep of §1. One need not rely on this inference alone, however, for the debates show that Members of Congress understood "persons" to include municipal corporations.

Representative Bingham, for example, in discussing §1 of the bill, explained that he had drafted §1 of the Fourteenth Amendment with the case of *Barron v. Mayor of Baltimore*, 7 Pet. 243 (1833), especially in mind. "In [that] case the city had taken private property for public use, without COMPENSATION . . . , AND THERE WAS NO REDRESS FOR THE wrong . . . ." Bingham's further remarks clearly indicate his view that such takings by cities, as had occurred in Barron, would be redressable under §1 of the bill. More generally, and as Bingham's remarks confirm, §1 of the bill would logically be the vehicle by which Congress provided redress for takings, since that section provided the only civil remedy for Fourteenth Amendment violations and that Amendment unequivocally prohibited uncompensated takings. Given this purpose, it beggars reason to suppose that Congress would have exempted municipalities from suit, insisting instead that compensation for a taking come from an officer in his individual capacity rather than from the government unit that had the benefit of the property taken.

In addition, by 1871, it was well understood that corporations should be treated as natural persons for virtually all purposes of constitutional and statutory analysis. . . .

That the "usual" meaning of the word "person" would extend to municipal corporations is also evidenced by an Act of Congress which had been passed only months before the Civil Rights Act was passed. This Act provided that

> "in all acts hereafter passed . . . the word 'person' may extend and be applied to bodies politic and corporate . . . unless the context shows that such words were intended to be used in a more limited sense."

Municipal corporations in 1871 were included within the phrase "bodies politic and corporate" and, accordingly, the "plain meaning" of §1 is that local government bodies were to be included within the ambit of the persons who could be sued under §1 of the Civil Rights Act. Indeed, a Circuit Judge, writing in 1873 in what is apparently the first reported case under §1, read the Dictionary Act in precisely this way in a case involving a corporate plaintiff and a municipal defendant.

Our analysis of the legislative history of the Civil Rights Act of 1871 compels the conclusion that Congress did intend municipalities and other local government units to be included among those persons to whom §1983 applies. Local governing bodies,[55] therefore, can be sued directly under §1983 for monetary, declaratory, or injunctive relief where, as here, the action that is alleged to be unconstitutional implements or executes a policy statement, ordinance, regulation, or decision officially adopted and promulgated by that body's officers. Moreover, although the touchstone of the §1983 action against a government body is an allegation that official policy is responsible for a deprivation of rights protected by the Constitution, local governments, like every other §1983 "person," by the very terms of the statute, may be sued for constitutional deprivations visited pursuant to governmental "custom" even though such a custom has not received formal approval through the body's official decisionmaking channels. . . .

On the other hand, the language of §1983, read against the background of the same legislative history, compels the conclusion that Congress did not intend municipalities to be held liable unless action pursuant to official municipal policy of some nature caused a constitutional tort. In particular, we conclude that a municipality cannot be held liable solely because it employs a tortfeasor—or, in other words, a municipality cannot be held liable under §1983 on a respondeat superior theory.

---

[55] Since official-capacity suits generally represent only another way of pleading an action against an entity of which an officer is an agent—at least where Eleventh Amendment considerations do not control analysis—our holding today that local governments can be sued under §1983 necessarily decides that local government officials sued in their official capacities are "persons" under §1983 in those cases in which, as here, a local government would be suable in its own name.

3. The Exclusionary Rule

We begin with the language of §1983 as originally passed:

"*[A]ny person who*, under color of any law, statute, ordinance, regulation, custom, or usage of any State, *shall subject, or cause to be subjected*, any person . . . to the deprivation of any rights, privileges, or immunities secured by the Constitution of the United States, shall, any such law, statute, ordinance, regulation, custom, or usage of the State to the contrary notwithstanding, be liable to the party injured in any action at law, suit in equity, or other proper proceeding for redress . . . ." (emphasis added).

The italicized language plainly imposes liability on a government that, under color of some official policy, "causes" an employee to violate another's constitutional rights. At the same time, that language cannot be easily read to impose liability vicariously on governing bodies solely on the basis of the existence of an employer-employee relationship with a tortfeasor. Indeed, the fact that Congress did specifically provide that A's tort became B's liability if B "caused" A to subject another to a tort suggests that Congress did not intend §1983 liability to attach where such causation was absent.

The primary constitutional justification for the Sherman amendment was that it was a necessary and proper remedy for the failure of localities to protect citizens as the Privileges or Immunities Clause of the Fourteenth Amendment required. And according to Sherman, Shellabarger, and Edmunds, the amendment came into play only when a locality was at fault or had knowingly neglected its duty to provide protection. But other proponents of the amendment apparently viewed it as a form of vicarious liability for the unlawful acts of the citizens of the locality. And whether intended or not, the amendment as drafted did impose a species of vicarious liability on municipalities since it could be construed to impose liability even if a municipality did not know of an impending or ensuing riot or did not have the wherewithal to do anything about it. Indeed, the amendment held a municipality liable even if it had done everything in its power to curb the riot. . . . Strictly speaking, of course, the fact that Congress refused to impose vicarious liability for the wrongs of a few private citizens does not conclusively establish that it would similarly have refused to impose vicarious liability for the torts of a municipality's employees. Nonetheless, when Congress' rejection of the only form of vicarious liability presented to it is combined with the absence of any language in §1983 which can easily be construed to create respondeat superior liability, the inference that Congress did not intend to impose such liability is quite strong.

Equally important, creation of a federal law of respondeat superior would have raised all the constitutional problems associated with the obligation to keep the peace, an obligation Congress chose not to impose . . . . To this day, there is disagreement about the basis for imposing liability on an employer for the torts of an employee when the sole nexus between the employer and the tort is the fact of the employer-employee relationship. Nonetheless, two justifications tend to stand out. First is the common-sense notion that no matter how blameless an employer appears to be in an individual case, accidents might nonetheless be reduced if employers had to bear the cost of accidents. Second is the argument that the cost of accidents should be spread to the community as a whole on an insurance theory.

The first justification is of the same sort that was offered for statutes like the Sherman amendment: "The obligation to make compensation for injury resulting from riot is, by arbitrary enactment of statutes, affirmatory law, and the reason of passing the statute is to secure a more perfect police regulation." This justification was obviously insufficient to sustain the amendment against perceived constitutional difficulties and there is no reason to suppose that a more general liability imposed for a similar reason would have been thought less constitutionally objectionable. The second justification was similarly put forward as a justification for the Sherman amendment: "we do not look upon [the Sherman amendment] as a punishment . . . . It is a mutual insurance." Again, this justification was insufficient to sustain the amendment.

We conclude, therefore, that a local government may not be sued under §1983 for an injury inflicted solely by its employees or agents. Instead, it is when execution of a government's policy or custom, whether made by its lawmakers or by those whose edicts or acts may fairly be said to represent official policy, inflicts the injury that the government as an entity is responsible under §1983. Since this case unquestionably involves official policy as the moving force of the constitutional violation found by the District Court, we must reverse the judgment below. In so doing, we have no occasion to address, and do not address, what the full contours of municipal liability under §1983 may be. We have attempted only to sketch so much of the §1983 cause of action against a local government as is apparent from the history of the 1871 Act and our prior cases, and we expressly leave further development of this action to another day.

Although we have stated that stare decisis has more force in statutory analysis than in constitutional adjudication because, in the former situation, Congress can correct our mistakes through legislation, we have never applied stare decisis mechanically to prohibit overruling our earlier decisions determining the meaning of statutes. Nor is this a case where we should "place on the shoulders of Congress the burden of the Court's own error."

First, *Monroe v. Pape*, insofar as it completely immunizes municipalities from suit under §1983, was a departure from prior practice [including five cases from 1873 to 1955], in each of which municipalities were defendants in §1983 suits. Moreover, the constitutional defect that led to the rejection of the Sherman amendment would not have distinguished between municipalities and school boards, each of which is an instrumentality of state administration. For this reason, our cases—decided both before and after *Monroe*—holding school boards liable in §1983 actions are inconsistent with *Monroe* . . . . And although in many of these cases jurisdiction was not questioned, we ought not "disregard the implications of an exercise of judicial authority assumed to be proper for [100] years." Thus, while we have reaffirmed *Monroe* without further examination on three occasions, it can scarcely be said that *Monroe* is so consistent with the warp and woof of civil rights law as to be beyond question.

Second, the principle of blanket immunity established in *Monroe* cannot be cabined short of school boards. Yet such an extension would itself be inconsistent with recent expressions of congressional intent. In the wake of our decisions, Congress not only has shown no hostility to federal-court decisions against school boards, but it has indeed rejected efforts to strip the federal courts of jurisdiction over school boards. Moreover, recognizing that school boards are often defendants in school desegregation suits, which have almost without exception been §1983 suits, Congress has twice passed legislation authorizing grants to school boards to assist them in complying with federal-court decrees. . . .

Third, municipalities can assert no reliance claim which can support an absolute immunity. As Mr. Justice Frankfurter said in *Monroe*, "[t]his is not an area of commercial law in which, presumably, individuals may have arranged their affairs in reliance on the expected stability of decision." (dissenting in part). Indeed, municipalities simply cannot "arrange their affairs" on an assumption that they can violate constitutional rights indefinitely since injunctive suits against local officials under §1983 would prohibit any such arrangement. And it scarcely need be mentioned that nothing in *Monroe* encourages municipalities to violate constitutional rights or even suggests that such violations are anything other than completely wrong.

Finally, . . . there can be no doubt that §1 of the Civil Rights Act was intended to provide a remedy, to be broadly construed, against all forms of official violation of federally protected rights. Therefore, absent a clear statement in the legislative history supporting the conclusion that §1 was not to apply to the official acts of a municipal corporation—which simply is not present—there is no justification for excluding municipalities from the "persons" covered by §1. . . .

Mr. Justice POWELL, concurring.

I join the opinion of the Court, and express these additional views. . . .

The Court correctly rejects a view of the legislative history that would produce the anomalous result of immunizing local government units from monetary liability for action directly causing a constitutional deprivation, even though such actions may be fully consistent with, and thus not remediable under, state law. No conduct of government comes more clearly within the "under color of" state law language of §1983. It is most unlikely that Congress intended public officials acting under the command or the specific authorization of the government employer to be exclusively liable for resulting constitutional injury. . . .

[*Monroe* and its progeny on municipal liability are] difficult to reconcile on a principled basis with a parallel series of cases in which the Court has assumed sub silentio that some local government entities could be sued under §1983. If now, after full consideration of the question, we continued to adhere to *Monroe*, grave doubt would be cast upon the Court's exercise of §1983 jurisdiction over school boards. Since "the principle of blanket immunity established in *Monroe* cannot be cabined short of school boards," the conflict is squarely presented. Although there was an independent basis of jurisdiction in many of the school board cases because of the inclusion of individual public officials as nominal parties, the opinions of this Court make explicit reference to the school board party, particularly in discussions of the relief to be awarded. And, as the Court points out, Congress has focused specifically on this Court's school board decisions in several statutes. Thus the exercise of §1983 jurisdiction over school boards, while perhaps not premised on considered holdings, has been longstanding. Indeed, it predated *Monroe.* . . .

Mr. Justice STEVENS, concurring in part.

Since [the respondeat superior portions] of the opinion of the Court are merely advisory and are not necessary to explain the Court's decision, I join only [the portions holding that municipalities are "persons" and reversing the judgment.]

Mr. Justice REHNQUIST, with whom THE CHIEF JUSTICE joins, dissenting.

Seventeen years ago, in *Monroe v. Pape,* this Court held that the 42d Congress did not intend to subject a municipal corporation to liability as a "person" within the meaning of 42 U.S.C. §1983. Since then, the Congress has remained silent, but this Court has reaffirmed that holding on at least three separate occasions. Today, the Court abandons this long and consistent line of precedents, offering in justification only an elaborate canvass of the same legislative history which was before the Court in 1961. Because I cannot agree that this Court is "free to disregard these precedents," which have been "considered maturely and recently" by this Court, I am compelled to dissent.

As this Court has repeatedly recognized, considerations of stare decisis are at their strongest when this Court confronts its previous constructions of legislation. In all cases, private parties shape their conduct according to this Court's settled construction of the law, but the Congress is at liberty to correct our mistakes of statutory construction, unlike our constitutional interpretations, whenever it sees fit. . . .

Only the most compelling circumstances can justify this Court's abandonment of such firmly established statutory precedents. . . .

The Court does not demonstrate that any exception to this general rule is properly applicable here. The Court's first assertion, that *Monroe* "was a departure from prior practice," is patently erroneous. [In none of the pre-*Monroe* cases the Court cites] was the question now before us raised by any of the litigants or addressed by this Court. . . .

Nor is there any indication that any later Congress has ever approved suit against any municipal corporation under §1983. Of all its recent enactments, only the Civil Rights Attorney's Fees Awards Act of 1976, explicitly deals with the Civil Rights Act of 1871. . . . There is plainly no language in the 1976 Act which would enlarge the parties suable under those substantive sections; it simply provides that parties who are already suable may be made liable for attorney's fees. . . .

The Court's assertion that municipalities have no right to act "on an assumption that they can violate constitutional rights indefinitely," is simply beside the point. Since *Monroe*, municipalities have had the right to expect that they would not be held liable retroactively for their officers' failure to predict this Court's recognition of new constitutional rights. No doubt innumerable municipal insurance policies and indemnity ordinances have been founded on this assumption, which is wholly justifiable under established principles of stare decisis. To obliterate those legitimate expectations without more compelling justifications than those advanced by the Court is a significant departure from our prior practice. . . .

Thus, our only task is to discern the intent of the 42d Congress. That intent was first expounded in *Monroe*, and it has been followed consistently ever since. . . . *Monroe* may not be overruled unless it has been demonstrated "beyond doubt from the legislative history of the 1871 statute that [*Monroe*] misapprehended the meaning of the controlling provision." *Monroe* (Harlan, J., concurring). The Court must show not only that Congress, in rejecting the Sherman amendment, concluded that municipal liability was not unconstitutional, but also that, in enacting §1, it intended to impose that liability. I am satisfied that no such showing has been made. . . .

The [Dictionary] Act expressly provided that corporations need not be included within the scope of the word "person" where the context suggests a more limited reach. Not a word in the legislative history of the Act gives any indication of the contexts in which Congress felt it appropriate to include a corporation as a person. . . .

At the time §1983 was enacted the only federal case to consider the status of corporations under the Fourteenth Amendment had concluded, with impeccable logic, that a corporation was neither a "citizen" nor a "person." *Insurance Co. v. New Orleans*, 13 Fed. Cas. 67 (CC La.1870).

Furthermore . . . no state court had ever held that municipal corporations were always liable in tort in precisely the same manner as other persons.

The general remarks from the floor on the liberal purposes of §1 offer no explicit guidance as to the parties against whom the remedy could be enforced. As the Court concedes, only Representative Bingham raised a concern which could be satisfied only by relief against governmental bodies. Yet he never directly related this concern to §1 of the Act. . . .

Thus, it ought not lightly to be presumed, as the Court does today, that §1983 "should prima facie be construed to include 'bodies politic' among the entities that could be sued." Neither the Dictionary Act, the ambivalent state of judicial decisions, nor the floor debate on §1 of the Act gives any indication that any Member of Congress had any inkling that §1 could be used to impose liability on municipalities. Although Senator Thurman, as the Court emphasizes, expressed his belief that the terms of §1 "are as comprehensive as can be used," an examination of his lengthy remarks demonstrates that it never occurred to him that §1 did impose or could have imposed any liability upon municipal corporations. . . . Only once was that possibility placed squarely before the Congress—in its consideration of the Sherman amendment—and the Congress squarely rejected it.

The Court is probably correct that the rejection of the Sherman amendment does not lead ineluctably to the conclusion that Congress intended municipalities to be immune from liability under all circumstances. . . . The meaning of §1 of the Act of 1871 has been subjected in this case to a more searching and careful analysis than it was in *Monroe,* and it may well be that on the basis of this closer analysis of the legislative debates a conclusion contrary to the *Monroe* holding could have been reached when that case was decided 17 years ago. But the rejection of the Sherman amendment remains instructive in that here alone did the legislative debates squarely focus on the liability of municipal corporations, and that liability was rejected. Any inference which might be drawn from the Dictionary Act or from general expressions of benevolence in the debate on §1 that the word "person" was intended to include municipal corporations falls far short of showing "beyond doubt" that this Court in *Monroe* "misapprehended the meaning of the controlling provision." . . .

The decision in *Monroe v. Pape* was the fountainhead of the torrent of civil rights litigation of the last 17 years. Using §1983 as a vehicle, the courts have articulated new and previously unforeseeable interpretations of the Fourteenth Amendment. At the same time, the doctrine of municipal immunity enunciated in *Monroe* has protected municipalities and their limited treasuries from the consequences of their officials' failure to predict the course of this Court's constitutional jurisprudence. None of the Members of this Court can foresee the practical consequences of today's removal of that protection. Only the Congress, which has the benefit of the advice of every segment of this diverse Nation, is equipped to consider the results of such a drastic change in the law. It seems all but inevitable that it will find it necessary to do so after today's decision.

Individual police officers also may be sued for money damages. But any officer sued can claim qualified immunity as a defense. That means the officer can be held liable only if the officer violates clearly established law that a reasonable officer should know. The standard was initially articulated in *Harlow v. Fitzgerald.*

Harlow v. Fitzgerald
457 U.S. 800 (1982)

Justice POWELL delivered the opinion of the Court. . . .

In this suit for civil damages petitioners Bryce Harlow and Alexander Butterfield are alleged to have participated in a conspiracy to violate the constitutional and statutory rights of the respondent A. Ernest Fitzgerald. Respondent avers that petitioners entered the conspiracy in their capacities as senior White House aides to former President Richard M. Nixon. . . .

[During the waning months of the Johnson Administration in 1968, respondent Fitzgerald, an Air Force management analyst, testified before a congressional Subcommittee about cost overruns and unexpected technical difficulties concerning the development of a particular airplane. In January 1970, a year after President Nixon assumed office, Fitzgerald was dismissed from his job during a departmental reorganization. After administrative proceedings, Fitzgerald sued various Defense Department officials and White House aides allegedly responsible for his dismissal. After motion practice and extensive pretrial discovery, only three defendants remained: two White House aides (Harlow and Butterfield) and former President Nixon. The Court ruled in a separate decision that Nixon enjoyed absolute presidential immunity.]

Together with their codefendant Richard Nixon, petitioners Harlow and Butterfield moved for summary judgment on February 12, 1980. . . . The court found that genuine issues of disputed fact remained for resolution at trial. . . .

The resolution of immunity questions inherently requires a balance between the evils inevitable in any available alternative. In situations of abuse of office, an action for damages may offer the only realistic avenue for vindication of constitutional guarantees. *See Bivens.* It is this recognition that has required the denial of absolute immunity to most public officers. At the same time, however, it cannot be disputed seriously that claims frequently run against the innocent as well as the guilty—at a cost not only to the defendant officials, but to society as a whole. These social costs include the expenses of litigation, the diversion of official energy from pressing public issues, and the deterrence of able citizens from acceptance of public office. Finally, there is the danger that fear of being sued will "dampen the ardor of all but the most resolute, or the most irresponsible [public officials], in the unflinching discharge of their duties."

In identifying qualified immunity as the best attainable accommodation of competing values [in prior cases] we relied on the assumption that this standard would permit "[i]nsubstantial lawsuits [to] be quickly terminated."[23] Yet petitioners advance persuasive arguments that the dismissal of insubstantial lawsuits without trial—a factor presupposed in the balance of competing interests struck by our prior cases—requires an adjustment of the "good faith" standard established by our decisions.

Qualified or "good faith" immunity is an affirmative defense that must be pleaded by a defendant official. Decisions of this Court have established that the "good faith" defense has both an "objective" and a "subjective" aspect. The objective element involves a presumptive knowledge of and respect for "basic,

---

[23] The importance of this consideration hardly needs emphasis. This Court has noted the risk imposed upon political officials who must defend their actions and motives before a jury. . . . "In times of political passion, dishonest or vindictive motives are readily attributed . . . and as readily believed."

unquestioned constitutional rights." *Wood v. Strickland*. The subjective component refers to "permissible intentions." *Ibid.* Characteristically the Court has defined these elements by identifying the circumstances in which qualified immunity would not be available. Referring both to the objective and subjective elements, we have held that qualified immunity would be defeated if an official "knew or reasonably should have known that the action he took within his sphere of official responsibility would violate the constitutional rights of the [plaintiff], or if he took the action with the malicious intention to cause a deprivation of constitutional rights or other injury. . . ." *Ibid.*

The subjective element of the good-faith defense frequently has proved incompatible with our admonition . . . that insubstantial claims should not proceed to trial. Rule 56 of the Federal Rules of Civil Procedure provides that disputed questions of fact ordinarily may not be decided on motions for summary judgment. And an official's subjective good faith has been considered to be a question of fact that some courts have regarded as inherently requiring resolution by a jury.

In the context of [our] attempted balancing of competing values, it now is clear that substantial costs attend the litigation of the subjective good faith of government officials. Not only are there the general costs of subjecting officials to the risks of trial—distraction of officials from their governmental duties, inhibition of discretionary action, and deterrence of able people from public service. There are special costs to "subjective" inquiries of this kind. Immunity generally is available only to officials performing discretionary functions. In contrast with the thought processes accompanying "ministerial" tasks, the judgments surrounding discretionary action almost inevitably are influenced by the decisionmaker's experiences, values, and emotions. These variables explain in part why questions of subjective intent so rarely can be decided by summary judgment. Yet they also frame a background in which there often is no clear end to the relevant evidence. Judicial inquiry into subjective motivation therefore may entail broad-ranging discovery and the deposing of numerous persons, including an official's professional colleagues. Inquiries of this kind can be peculiarly disruptive of effective government.

Consistently with the balance at which we aimed in [prior cases], we conclude today that bare allegations of malice should not suffice to subject government officials either to the costs of trial or to the burdens of broad-reaching discovery. We therefore hold that government officials performing discretionary functions generally are shielded from liability for civil damages insofar as their conduct does not violate clearly established statutory or constitutional rights of which a reasonable person would have known.

Reliance on the objective reasonableness of an official's conduct, as measured by reference to clearly established law, should avoid excessive disruption of government and permit the resolution of many insubstantial claims on summary judgment. On summary judgment, the judge appropriately may determine, not only the currently applicable law, but whether that law was clearly established at the time an action occurred. If the law at that time was not clearly established, an official could not reasonably be expected to anticipate subsequent legal developments, nor could he fairly be said to "know" that the law forbade conduct not previously identified as unlawful. Until this threshold immunity question is resolved, discovery should not be allowed. If the law was clearly established, the immunity defense ordinarily should fail, since a reasonably competent public official should know the law governing his conduct. . . .

By defining the limits of qualified immunity essentially in objective terms, we provide no license to lawless conduct. The public interest in deterrence of unlawful conduct and in compensation of victims remains protected by a test that focuses on the objective legal reasonableness of an official's acts. Where an official could be expected to know that certain conduct would violate statutory or constitutional rights, he should be made to hesitate; and a person who suffers injury caused by such conduct may have a cause of action. But where an official's duties legitimately require action in which clearly established rights are not implicated, the public interest may be better served by action taken "with independence and without fear of consequences." *Pierson v. Ray*.[34] . . .

Justice BRENNAN, with whom Justice MARSHALL, and Justice BLACKMUN join, concurring.

I agree with the substantive standard announced by the Court today. . . . I write separately only to note that given this standard, it seems inescapable to me that some measure of discovery may sometimes be required to determine exactly what a public-official defendant did "know" at the time of his actions. . . .

In *District of Columbia v. Wesby*, 138 S. Ct. 577 (2018), the Court found that police did not violate the Fourth Amendment when they arrested those who were at a party in an unoccupied house. The Court also concluded that even if there had been a Fourth Amendment violation, the officers were protected by qualified immunity. Justice Thomas, writing for the Court, summarized the current law of qualified immunity:

> Under our precedents, officers are entitled to qualified immunity under §1983 unless (1) they violated a federal statutory or constitutional right, and (2) the unlawfulness of their conduct was "clearly established at the time." "Clearly established" means that, at the time of the officer's conduct, the law was "sufficiently clear" that every "reasonable official would understand that what he is doing" is unlawful. In other words, existing law must have placed the constitutionality of the officer's conduct "beyond debate." This demanding standard protects "all but the plainly

---

[34] We emphasize that our decision applies only to suits for civil damages arising from actions within the scope of an official's duties and in "objective" good faith. We express no view as to the conditions in which injunctive or declaratory relief might be available.

incompetent or those who knowingly violate the law." To be clearly established, a legal principle must have a sufficiently clear foundation in then-existing precedent. The rule must be "settled law," which means it is dictated by "controlling authority" or "a robust consensus of cases of persuasive authority." It is not enough that the rule is suggested by then-existing precedent. The precedent must be clear enough that every reasonable official would interpret it to establish the particular rule the plaintiff seeks to apply. Otherwise, the rule is not one that "every reasonable official" would know. The "clearly established" standard also requires that the legal principle clearly prohibit the officer's conduct in the particular circumstances before him. The rule's contours must be so well defined that it is "clear to a reasonable officer that his conduct was unlawful in the situation he confronted." This requires a high "degree of specificity." We have repeatedly stressed that courts must not "define clearly established law at a high level of generality, since doing so avoids the crucial question whether the official acted reasonably in the particular circumstances that he or she faced." A rule is too general if the unlawfulness of the officer's conduct "does not follow immediately from the conclusion that [the rule] was firmly established."

Chapter 9

PLEA BARGAINING AND GUILTY PLEAS

G.   Impact of Guilty Pleas (casebook p. 949)

Generally, a guilty plea waives a defendant's right to challenge pretrial issues, including search and seizure violations. However, in *Class v. United States* (2018), the Supreme Court held that, in limited circumstances, a guilty plea does not bar a subsequent constitutional challenge to the statute of conviction.

Class v. United States
138 S. Ct. 798 (2018)

Justice BREYER delivered the opinion of the Court.

Does a guilty plea bar a criminal defendant from later appealing his conviction on the ground that the statute of conviction violates the Constitution? In our view, a guilty plea by itself does not bar that appeal.

I

In September 2013, a federal grand jury indicted petitioner, Rodney Class, for possessing firearms in his locked jeep, which was parked in a lot on the grounds of the United States Capitol in Washington, D.C. Class alleged that the statute, §5104(e), violates the Second Amendment. He also raised a due process claim, arguing that he was denied fair notice that weapons were banned in the parking lot. Following a hearing, the District Court denied both claims.

Several months later, Class pleaded guilty to "Possession of a Firearm on U.S. Capitol Grounds, in violation of 40 U.S.C. §5104(e)." The Government agreed to drop related charges.

A written plea agreement set forth the terms of Class' guilty plea, including several categories of rights that he expressly agreed to waive. At the same time, the plea agreement expressly enumerated categories of claims that Class could raise on appeal. The agreement said nothing about the right to raise on direct appeal a claim that the statute of conviction was unconstitutional.

Class appealed his conviction. He repeated his constitutional claims, namely, that the statute violates the Second Amendment and the Due Process Clause because it fails to give fair notice of which areas fall within the Capitol Grounds where firearms are banned. The Court of Appeals held that Class could not raise his constitutional claims because, by pleading guilty, he had waived them.

II

The question is whether a guilty plea by itself bars a federal criminal defendant from challenging the constitutionality of the statute of conviction on direct appeal. We hold that it does not. Class did not relinquish his right to appeal the District Court's constitutional determinations simply by pleading guilty.

Fifty years ago this Court directly addressed a similar claim (a claim that the statute of conviction was unconstitutional). And the Court stated that a defendant's "plea of guilty did not . . . waive his previous [constitutional] claim." *Haynes v. United States* (1968). Though Justice Harlan's opinion for the Court in *Haynes* offered little explanation for this statement, subsequent decisions offered a rationale that applies here.

In *Blackledge v. Perry* (1974), North Carolina indicted and convicted Jimmy Seth Perry on a misdemeanor assault charge. When Perry exercised his right under a North Carolina statute to a *de novo* trial in a higher court, the State reindicted him, but this time the State charged a felony, which carried a heavier penalty, for the same conduct. Perry pleaded guilty. He then sought habeas relief on the grounds that the reindictment amounted to an unconstitutional vindictive prosecution. The State argued that Perry's guilty plea barred him from raising his constitutional challenge. But this Court held that it did not.

A year and a half later, in *Menna v. New York* (1975), this Court repeated what it had said and held in *Blackledge*. The Court held that "a plea of guilty to a charge does not waive a claim that—judged on its face—the charge is one which the State may not constitutionally prosecute."

These holdings reflect an understanding of the nature of guilty pleas which, in broad outline, stretches back nearly 150 years:

> "The plea of guilty is, of course, a confession of all the facts charged in the indictment, and also of the evil intent imputed to the defendant. It is a waiver also of all merely technical and formal objections of which the defendant could have availed himself by any other plea or motion. But if the facts alleged and admitted do not constitute a crime against the laws of the Commonwealth, the defendant is entitled to be discharged."

Decisions of federal and state courts throughout the 19th and 20th centuries reflect a similar view of the nature of a guilty plea.

[T]he claims at issue here do not fall within any of the categories of claims that Class' plea agreement forbids him to raise on direct appeal. They challenge the Government's power to criminalize Class' (admitted) conduct. They thereby call into question the Government's power to "constitutionally prosecute" him. . . . A guilty plea does not bar a direct appeal in these circumstances.

Justice ALITO, with whom Justice KENNEDY and Justice THOMAS join, dissenting.

9. Plea Bargaining and Guilty Pleas

Roughly 95% of felony cases in the federal and state courts are resolved by guilty pleas. Therefore it is critically important that defendants, prosecutors, and judges understand the consequences of these pleas. In this case, the parties have asked us to identify the claims that a defendant can raise on appeal after entering an unconditional guilty plea. Regrettably, the Court provides no clear answer.

Blackledge and *Menna* represented marked departures from our prior decisions. Before they were handed down, our precedents were clear: When a defendant pleaded guilty to a crime, he relinquished his right to litigate all nonjurisdictional challenges to his conviction (except for the claim that his plea was not voluntary and intelligent), and the prosecution could assert this forfeiture to defeat a subsequent appeal.

On the strength of that rule, we held that defendants who pleaded guilty forfeited a variety of important constitutional claims. For instance, a defendant who pleaded guilty could not attack his conviction on the ground that the prosecution violated the Equal Protection Clause by systematically excluding African–Americans from grand juries in the county where he was indicted. Nor could he argue that the prosecution unlawfully coerced his confession—even if the confession was the only evidence supporting the conviction. Nor could he assert that his statute of conviction employed an unconstitutional penalty provision; his consent to be punished under the statute precluded this defense.

Blackledge and *Menna* diverged from these prior precedents, but neither case provided a clear or coherent explanation for the departure.

* * *

[T]he governing law in the present case is Rule 11 of the Federal Rules of Criminal Procedure. Under that rule, an unconditional guilty plea waives all nonjurisdictional claims with the possible exception of the "*Menna-Blackledge* doctrine" created years ago by this Court. That doctrine is vacuous, has no sound foundation and produces nothing but confusion. At a minimum, I would limit the doctrine to the particular types of claims involved in those cases. I certainly would not expand its reach.

I fear that today's decision will bedevil the lower courts. I respectfully dissent.

Chapter 11

RIGHT TO COUNSEL

D. Standard for "Effective Assistance" of Counsel (casebook p. 1002, after *Strickland v. Washington*)

While great deference is given to defense counsel's strategy, the Supreme Court overturned a death penalty sentence in *Andrus v. Texas* because of defense counsel's failure to provide adequate representation.

Andrus v. Texas
__ S. Ct. __ (2020)

PER CURIAM

Death-sentenced petitioner Terence Andrus was six years old when his mother began selling drugs out of the apartment where Andrus and his four siblings lived. To fund a spiraling drug addiction, Andrus' mother also turned to prostitution. By the time Andrus was 12, his mother regularly spent entire weekends, at times weeks, away from her five children to binge on drugs. When she did spend time around her children, she often was high and brought with her a revolving door of drug-addicted, sometimes physically violent, boyfriends. Before he reached adolescence, Andrus took on the role of caretaker for his four siblings.

When Andrus was 16, he allegedly served as a lookout while his friends robbed a woman. He was sent to a juvenile detention facility where, for 18 months, he was steeped in gang culture, dosed on high quantities of psychotropic drugs, and frequently relegated to extended stints of solitary confinement. The ordeal left an already traumatized Andrus all but suicidal. Those suicidal urges resurfaced later in Andrus' adult life.

During Andrus' capital trial, however, nearly none of this mitigating evidence reached the jury. That is because Andrus' defense counsel not only neglected to present it; he failed even to look for it. Indeed, counsel performed virtually no investigation of the relevant evidence. Those failures also fettered the defense's capacity to contextualize or counter the State's evidence of Andrus' alleged incidences of past violence.

Only years later, during an 8-day evidentiary hearing in Andrus' state habeas proceeding, did the grim facts of Andrus' life history come to light. And when pressed at the hearing to provide his reasons for failing to investigate Andrus' history, Andrus' counsel offered none.

We conclude that the record makes clear that Andrus has demonstrated counsel's deficient performance under *Strickland*.

I

A

In 2008, 20-year-old Terence Andrus unsuccessfully attempted a carjacking in a grocery-store parking lot while under the influence of PCP-laced marijuana. During the bungled attempt, Andrus fired multiple shots, killing car owner Avelino Diaz and bystander Kim-Phuong Vu Bui. The State charged Andrus with capital murder.

At the guilt phase of trial, Andrus' defense counsel declined to present an opening statement. After the State rested its case, the defense immediately rested as well. In his closing argument, defense counsel conceded Andrus' guilt and informed the jury that the trial would "boil down to the punishment phase," emphasizing that "that's where we are going to be fighting." The jury found Andrus guilty of capital murder.

Trial then turned to the punishment phase. Once again, Andrus' counsel presented no opening statement. In its 3-day case in aggravation, the State put forth evidence that Andrus had displayed aggressive and hostile behavior while confined in a juvenile detention center; that Andrus had tattoos indicating gang affiliations; and that Andrus had hit, kicked, and thrown excrement at prison officials while awaiting trial. The State also presented evidence tying Andrus to an aggravated robbery of a dry-cleaning business. Counsel raised no material objections to the State's evidence and cross-examined the State's witnesses only briefly.

When it came to the defense's case in mitigation, counsel first called Andrus' mother to testify. The direct examination focused on Andrus' basic biographical information and did not reveal any difficult circumstances in Andrus' childhood. Andrus' mother testified that Andrus had an "excellent" relationship with his siblings and grandparents. She also insisted that Andrus "didn't have access to" "drugs or pills in [her] household," and that she would have "counsel[ed] him" had she found out that he was using drugs.

The second witness was Andrus' biological father, Michael Davis, with whom Andrus had lived for about a year when Andrus was around 15 years old. Davis had been in and out of prison for much of Andrus' life and, before he appeared to testify, had not seen Andrus in more than six years. The bulk of Davis' direct examination explored such topics as Davis' criminal history and his relationship with Andrus' mother. Toward the end of the direct examination, counsel elicited testimony that Andrus had been "good around [Davis]" during the 1-year period he had lived with Davis.

Once Davis stepped down, Andrus' counsel informed the court that the defense rested its case and did not intend to call any more witnesses. After the court questioned counsel about this choice during a sidebar discussion, however, counsel changed his mind and decided to call additional witnesses.

11.   Right to Counsel

Following a court recess, Andrus' counsel called Dr. John Roache as the defense's only expert witness. Counsel's terse direct examination focused on the general effects of drug use on developing adolescent brains. On cross-examination, the State quizzed Dr. Roache about the relevance and purpose of his testimony, probing pointedly whether Dr. Roache "drove three hours from San Antonio to tell the jury . . . that people change their behavior when they use drugs."

Counsel next called James Martins, a prison counselor who had worked with Andrus. Martins testified that Andrus "started having remorse" in the past two months and was "making progress." *Id.*, at 35. On cross-examination, the State emphasized that Andrus' feelings of remorse had manifested only recently, around the time trial began.

Finally, Andrus himself testified. Contrary to his mother's depiction of his upbringing, he stated that his mother had started selling drugs when he was around six years old, and that he and his siblings were often home alone when they were growing up. He also explained that he first started using drugs regularly around the time he was 15. All told, counsel's questioning about Andrus' childhood comprised four pages of the trial transcript. The State on cross declared, "I have not heard one mitigating circumstance in your life." *Id.*, at 60.

The jury sentenced Andrus to death.

B

After an unsuccessful direct appeal, Andrus filed a state habeas application, principally alleging that his trial counsel was ineffective for failing to investigate or present available mitigation evidence. During an 8-day evidentiary hearing, Andrus presented what the Texas trial court characterized as a "tidal wave of information . . . with regard to mitigation."

The evidence revealed a childhood marked by extreme neglect and privation, a family environment filled with violence and abuse. Andrus was born into a neighborhood of Houston, Texas, known for its frequent shootings, gang fights, and drug overdoses. Andrus' mother had Andrus, her second of five children, when she was 17. The children's fathers never stayed as part of the family. One of them raped Andrus' younger half sister when she was a child. The others—some physically abusive toward Andrus' mother, all addicted to drugs and carrying criminal histories—constantly flitted in and out of the picture.

Starting when Andrus was young, his mother sold drugs and engaged in prostitution. She often made her drug sales at home, in view of Andrus and his siblings. She also habitually used drugs in front of them, and was high more often than not. In her frequently disoriented state, she would leave her children to fend for themselves. Many times, there was not enough food to eat.

After her boyfriend was killed in a shooting, Andrus' mother became increasingly dependent on drugs and neglectful of her children. As a close family friend attested, Andrus' mother "would occasionally just take a week or a weekend and binge [on drugs]. She would get a room somewhere and just go at it."

With the children often left on their own, Andrus assumed responsibility as the head of the household for his four siblings, including his older brother with special needs. Andrus was around 12 years old at the time. He cleaned for his siblings, put them to bed, cooked breakfast for them, made sure they got ready for school, helped them with their homework, and made them dinner. According to his siblings, Andrus was "a protective older brother" who "kept on to [them] to stay out of trouble." Andrus, by their account, was "very caring and very loving," "liked to make people laugh," and "never liked to see people cry." While attempting to care for his siblings, Andrus struggled with mental-health issues: When he was only 10 or 11, he was diagnosed with affective psychosis.

At age 16, Andrus was sentenced to a juvenile detention center run by the Texas Youth Commission (TYC), for allegedly "serv[ing] as the 'lookout'" while he and his friends robbed a woman of her purse. While in TYC custody, Andrus was prescribed high doses of psychotropic drugs carrying serious adverse side effects. He also spent extended periods in isolation, often for purported infractions like reporting that he had heard voices telling him to do bad things. TYC records on Andrus noted multiple instances of self-harm and threats of suicide. After 18 months in TYC custody, Andrus was transferred to an adult prison facility.

Not long after Andrus' release from prison at age 18, Andrus attempted the fatal carjacking that resulted in his capital convictions. While incarcerated awaiting trial, Andrus tried to commit suicide. He slashed his wrist with a razor blade and used his blood to smear messages on the walls, beseeching the world to "[j]ust let [him] die."

II

To prevail on a Sixth Amendment claim alleging ineffective assistance of counsel, a defendant must show that his counsel's performance was deficient and that his counsel's deficient performance prejudiced him. To show deficiency, a defendant must show that "counsel's representation fell below an objective standard of reasonableness." And to establish prejudice, a defendant must show "that there is a reasonable probability that, but for counsel's unprofessional errors, the result of the proceeding would have been different."

To assess whether counsel exercised objectively reasonable judgment under prevailing professional standards, we first ask "whether the investigation supporting counsel's decision not to introduce mitigating evidence of [Andrus'] background was itself reasonable. Here, plainly not. Although counsel nominally put on a case in mitigation in that counsel in fact called witnesses to the stand after the prosecution rested, the record leaves no doubt that counsel's investigation to support that case was an empty exercise.

To start, counsel was, by his own admissions at the habeas hearing, barely acquainted with the witnesses who testified during the case in mitigation. Counsel acknowledged that the first time he met Andrus' mother was when she was subpoenaed to testify, and the first time he met Andrus' biological father was when he showed up at the courthouse to take the stand. Counsel also admitted that he did not get in touch with the third witness (Dr. Roache) until just before *voir dire*, and became aware of the final witness (Martins) only partway through trial.

Over and over during the habeas hearing, counsel acknowledged that he did not look into or present the myriad tragic circumstances that marked Andrus' life. [C]ounsel performed virtually no investigation, either of the few witnesses he called during the case in mitigation, or of the many circumstances in Andrus' life that could have served as powerful mitigating evidence. The untapped body of mitigating evidence was, as the habeas hearing revealed, simply vast.

No doubt due to counsel's failure to investigate the case in mitigation, much of the so-called mitigating evidence he offered unwittingly aided the State's case in aggravation. Counsel's introduction of seemingly *aggravating* evidence confirms the gaping distance between his performance at trial and objectively reasonable professional judgment.

The testimony elicited from Andrus' mother best illustrates this deficiency. First to testify during the case in mitigation, Andrus' mother sketched a portrait of a tranquil upbringing, during which Andrus got himself into trouble despite his family's best efforts. On her account, Andrus fell into drugs entirely on his own: Drugs were not available at home, Andrus did not use them at home, and she would have intervened had she known about Andrus' drug habits. Andrus, his mother related to the jury, "[k]ind of "just decided he didn't want to do what [she] told him to do."

Even though counsel called Andrus' mother as a defense witness, he was ill-prepared for her testimony. [C]ounsel's uninformed decision to call Andrus' mother ultimately undermined Andrus' own testimony.

Counsel also failed to conduct any independent investigation of the State's case in aggravation, despite ample opportunity to do so. During the case in aggravation, the State's task was to prove to the jury that Andrus presented a future danger to society. To that end, the State emphasized that Andrus had acted aggressively in TYC facilities and in prison while awaiting trial. This evidence principally comprised verbal threats, but also included instances of Andrus' kicking, hitting, and throwing excrement at prison officials when they tried to control him. Had counsel genuinely investigated Andrus' experiences in TYC custody, counsel would have learned that Andrus' behavioral problems there were notably mild, and the harms he sustained severe. Or, with sufficient understanding of the violent environments Andrus inhabited his entire life, counsel could have provided a counternarrative of Andrus' later episodes in prison. But instead, counsel left all of that aggravating evidence untouched at trial—even going so far as to inform the jury that the evidence made it "probabl[e]" that Andrus was "a violent kind of guy."

The State's case in aggravation also highlighted Andrus' alleged commission of a knifepoint robbery at a dry-cleaning business. At the time of the offense, "all [that] the crime victim . . . told the police . . . was that he had been the victim of an assault by a black man." Although Andrus stressed to counsel his innocence of the offense, and although the State had not proceeded with charges, Andrus' counsel did not attempt to exclude or rebut the State's evidence.

That is hardly the work of reasonable counsel.

Having found deficient performance, the question remains whether counsel's deficient performance prejudiced Andrus. According to Andrus, effective counsel would have painted a vividly different tableau of aggravating and mitigating evidence than that presented at trial. . . . We conclude that Andrus has shown deficient performance under the first prong of *Strickland*.

Justice ALITO, with whom Justice THOMAS and Justice GORSUCH join, dissenting.

The Court clears this case off the docket, but it does so on a ground that is hard to take seriously. According to the Court, "[i]t is unclear whether the Court of Criminal Appeals considered *Strickland* prejudice at all." But that reading is squarely contradicted by the opinion of the Court of Criminal Appeals (CCA).

Here is what the record shows. According to Andrus's confession, he left his apartment one evening, "'amped up' on embalming fluid [PCP] mixed with marijuana, cocaine, and beer," and looked for a car to "go joy-riding." In the parking lot of a supermarket, he saw Avelino Diaz drop off his wife, Patty, in front of the store. By his own admission, Andrus approached Diaz's car with a gun drawn, but he abandoned the carjacking attempt when he saw that the car had a stick shift, which he could not drive. Alerted by a store employee, Patty Diaz ran out of the store and found her husband lying by the side of the car with a bullet wound in the back of his head. He was subsequently pronounced dead.

After killing Avelino Diaz, Andrus approached a car with two occupants, whom Andrus described as an "old man and old wom[a]n." Andrus fired three shots into the car. The first went through the open driver's side window and hit the passenger, Kim-Phuong Vu Bui, in the head. As the car sped away, Andrus fired a second shot, which entered the back driver's side window, and a third shot, which "entered at an angle indicating that the shot originated from a farther distance." One of these bullets hit the driver, Steve Bui, in the back. Seeing that blood was coming out of his wife's mouth, Steve drove her to a hospital and carried her inside, where she died.

These senseless murders in October 2008 were not Andrus's first crimes. In 2004, he was placed on probation for a drug offense, but just two weeks later, he committed an armed robbery. Andrus and two others followed a woman to her parents' home, where they held her at gunpoint and took her purse and gym bag. The woman identified Andrus as the perpetrator who held the gun.

For this offense, Andrus was sent to a juvenile facility where he showed such "'significant assaultive behavior' toward other youths and staff "that he was eventually transferred to an adult facility. Shortly after his release, he again violated his supervisory conditions and was returned to the adult facility.

When he was released again, he committed an armed robbery of a dry-cleaning establishment. Around 7 A.M. one morning, he entered the business and chased the owner, Tuan Tran, to the back. He beat Tran and threatened him with a knife until Tran gave him money. Less than two months after this crime, Andrus murdered Avelino Diaz and Kim-Phuong Vu Bui.

While awaiting trial for those murders, Andrus carried out a reign of terror in jail. He assaulted another detainee, attacked and injured corrections officers, threw urine in an officer's face, repeatedly made explicit threats to kill officers and staff, flooded his cell and threw excrement on the walls, and engaged in other disruptive acts. Also while awaiting trial for murder, he had the words "murder weapon" tattooed on his hands and a smoking gun tattooed on his forearm.

The CCA has already held once that Andrus failed to establish prejudice. I see no good reason why it should be required to revisit the issue.

3.   Strategic Decisions by Defense Counsel (casebook p. 1009)

In *McCoy v. Louisiana* (2018), the Supreme Court held that where a defendant actually objects to having his attorney concede the defendant's guilt, the *Strickland* standard does not apply. Rather, the attorney's actions violate the defendant's autonomy and, thus, constitute a structural error requiring reversal without a showing of prejudice.

McCoy v. Louisiana
138 S. Ct. 1500 (2018)

Justice GINSBURG delivered the opinion of the Court.

In *Florida v. Nixon* (2004), this Court considered whether the Constitution bars defense counsel from conceding a capital defendant's guilt at trial "when [the] defendant, informed by counsel, neither consents nor objects." In that case, defense counsel had several times explained to the defendant a proposed guilt-phase concession strategy, but the defendant was unresponsive. We held that when counsel confers with the defendant and the defendant remains silent, neither approving nor protesting counsel's proposed concession strategy, "[no] blanket rule demand[s] the defendant's explicit consent" to implementation of that strategy.

In the case now before us, in contrast to *Nixon*, the defendant vociferously insisted that he did not engage in the charged acts and adamantly objected to any admission of guilt. Yet the trial court permitted counsel, at the guilt phase of a capital trial, to tell the jury the defendant "committed three murders. . . . [H]e's guilty." We hold that a defendant has the right to insist that counsel refrain from admitting guilt, even when counsel's experienced-based view is that confessing guilt offers the defendant the best chance to avoid the death penalty. Guaranteeing a defendant the right "to have the *Assistance* of Counsel for *his* defence," the Sixth Amendment so demands. With individual liberty—and, in capital cases, life—at stake, it is the defendant's prerogative, not counsel's, to decide on the objective of his defense: to admit guilt in the hope of gaining mercy at the sentencing stage, or to maintain his innocence, leaving it to the State to prove his guilt beyond a reasonable doubt.

I

On May 5, 2008, Christine and Willie Young and Gregory Colston were shot and killed in the Youngs' home in Bossier City, Louisiana. The three victims were the mother, stepfather, and son of Robert McCoy's estranged wife, Yolanda. Several days later, police arrested McCoy in Idaho. Extradited to Louisiana, McCoy was appointed counsel from the public defender's office. A Bossier Parish grand jury indicted McCoy on three counts of first-degree murder, and the prosecutor gave notice of intent to seek the death penalty. McCoy pleaded not guilty. Throughout the proceedings, he insistently maintained he was out of State at the time of the killings and that corrupt police killed the victims when a drug deal went wrong. At defense counsel's request, a court-appointed sanity commission examined McCoy and found him competent to stand trial.

In December 2009 and January 2010, McCoy told the court his relationship with assigned counsel had broken down irretrievably. He sought and gained leave to represent himself until his parents engaged new counsel for him. In March 2010, Larry English, engaged by McCoy's parents, enrolled as McCoy's counsel. English eventually concluded that the evidence against McCoy was overwhelming and that, absent a concession at the guilt stage that McCoy was the killer, a death sentence would be impossible to avoid at the penalty phase. McCoy, English reported, was "furious" when told, two weeks before trial was scheduled to begin, that English would concede McCoy's commission of the triple murders. McCoy told English "not to make that concession," and English knew of McCoy's "complet[e] oppos[ition] to [English] telling the jury that [McCoy] was guilty of killing the three victims"; instead of any concession, McCoy pressed English to pursue acquittal.

At a July 26, 2011 hearing, McCoy sought to terminate English's representation and English asked to be relieved if McCoy secured other counsel. With trial set to start two days later, the court refused to relieve English and directed that he remain as counsel of record. "[Y]ou are the attorney," the court told English when he expressed disagreement with McCoy's wish to put on a defense case, and "you have to make the trial decision of what you're going to proceed with."

At the beginning of his opening statement at the guilt phase of the trial, English told the jury there was "no way reasonably possible" that they could hear the prosecution's evidence and reach "any other conclusion than Robert McCoy was the cause of these individuals' death." McCoy protested; out of earshot of the jury, McCoy told the court that English was "selling [him] out" by maintaining that McCoy "murdered [his] family." The trial court reiterated that English was "representing" McCoy and told McCoy that the court would not permit "any other outbursts." Continuing his opening statement, English told the jury the evidence is "unambiguous," "my client committed three murders." McCoy testified in his own defense, maintaining his innocence and pressing an alibi difficult to fathom. In his closing argument, English reiterated that McCoy was the killer. On that issue, English told the jury that he "took [the] burden off of [the prosecutor]." The jury then returned a unanimous verdict of guilty of first-degree murder on all three counts. At the penalty phase, English again conceded "Robert McCoy committed these crimes," but urged mercy in view of McCoy's "serious mental and emotional issues." The jury returned three death verdicts.

Represented by new counsel, McCoy unsuccessfully moved for a new trial, arguing that the trial court violated his constitutional rights by allowing English to concede McCoy "committed three murders" over McCoy's objection. We granted certiorari . . . on the question whether it is unconstitutional to allow defense counsel to concede guilt over the defendant's intransigent and unambiguous objection.

II

A

The Sixth Amendment guarantees to each criminal defendant "the Assistance of Counsel for his defence." At common law, self-representation was the norm. As the laws of England and the American Colonies developed, providing for a right to counsel in criminal cases, self-representation remained common and the right to proceed without counsel was recognized. Even now, when most defendants choose to be represented by counsel (0.2% of federal felony defendants proceeded *pro se*), an accused may insist upon representing herself—however counterproductive that course may be. As this Court explained, "[t]he right to defend is personal," and a defendant's choice in exercising that right "must be honored out of 'that respect for the individual which is the lifeblood of the law.'" *Faretta* (1975).

The choice is not all or nothing: To gain assistance, a defendant need not surrender control entirely to counsel. For the Sixth Amendment, in "grant[ing] to the accused personally the right to make his defense," "speaks of the 'assistance' of counsel, and an assistant, however expert, is still an assistant." Trial management is the lawyer's province: Counsel provides his or her assistance by making decisions such as "what arguments to pursue, what evidentiary objections to raise, and what agreements to conclude regarding the admission of evidence." Some decisions, however, are reserved for the client—notably, whether to plead guilty, waive the right to a jury trial, testify in one's own behalf, and forgo an appeal.

Autonomy to decide that the objective of the defense is to assert innocence belongs in this latter category. Just as a defendant may steadfastly refuse to plead guilty in the face of overwhelming evidence against her, or reject the assistance of legal counsel despite the defendant's own inexperience and lack of professional qualifications, so may she insist on maintaining her innocence at the guilt phase of a capital trial. These are not strategic choices about how best to *achieve* a client's objectives; they are choices about what the client's objectives in fact *are*."

Counsel may reasonably assess a concession of guilt as best suited to avoiding the death penalty, as English did in this case. But the client may not share that objective. He may wish to avoid, above all else, the opprobrium that comes with admitting he killed family members. Or he may hold life in prison not worth living and prefer to risk death for any hope, however small, of exoneration. When a client expressly asserts that the objective of "*his* defence" is to maintain innocence of the charged criminal acts, his lawyer must abide by that objective and may not override it by conceding guilt. See ABA Model Rule of Professional Conduct 1.2(a) (2016) (a "lawyer shall abide by a client's decisions concerning the objectives of the representation").

Preserving for the defendant the ability to decide whether to maintain his innocence should not displace counsel's, or the court's, respective trial management roles. If, after consultations with English concerning the management of the defense, McCoy disagreed with English's proposal to concede McCoy committed three murders, it was not open to English to override McCoy's objection.

B

Florida v. Nixon is not to the contrary. Nixon's attorney did not negate Nixon's autonomy by overriding Nixon's desired defense objective, for Nixon never asserted any such objective. Nixon "was generally unresponsive" during discussions of trial strategy, and "never verbally approved or protested" counsel's proposed approach. Nixon complained about the admission of his guilt only after trial. McCoy, in contrast, opposed English's assertion of his guilt at every opportunity, before and during trial, both in conference with his lawyer and in open court. If a client declines to participate in his defense, then an attorney may permissibly guide the defense pursuant to the strategy she believes to be in the defendant's best interest. Presented with express statements of the client's will to maintain innocence, however, counsel may not steer the ship the other way.

III

Because a client's autonomy, not counsel's competence, is in issue, we do not apply our ineffective-assistance-of-counsel jurisprudence, *Strickland v. Washington* (1984), to McCoy's claim. To gain redress for attorney error, a defendant ordinarily must show prejudice. Here, however, the violation of McCoy's protected autonomy right was complete when the court allowed counsel to usurp control of an issue within McCoy's sole prerogative.

Such an admission blocks the defendant's right to make the fundamental choices about his own defense. And the effects of the admission would be immeasurable, because a jury would almost certainly be swayed by a lawyer's concession of his client's guilt. McCoy must therefore be accorded a new trial without any need first to show prejudice.

11. Right to Counsel

Larry English was placed in a difficult position; he had an unruly client and faced a strong government case. He reasonably thought the objective of his representation should be avoidance of the death penalty. But McCoy insistently maintained: "I did not murder my family." Once he communicated that to court and counsel, strenuously objecting to English's proposed strategy, a concession of guilt should have been off the table. The trial court's allowance of English's admission of McCoy's guilt despite McCoy's insistent objections was incompatible with the Sixth Amendment. Because the error was structural, a new trial is the required corrective.

Justice ALITO, with whom Justice THOMAS and Justice GORSUCH join, dissenting.

The Constitution gives us the authority to decide real cases and controversies; we do not have the right to simplify or otherwise change the facts of a case in order to make our work easier or to achieve a desired result. But that is exactly what the Court does in this case.

Retained by petitioner's family, English found himself in a predicament as the trial date approached. . . . Among other things, the evidence showed the following. Before the killings took place, petitioner had abused and threatened to kill his wife, and she was therefore under police protection. On the night of the killings, petitioner's mother-in-law made a 911 call and was heard screaming petitioner's first name. She yelled: "'She ain't here, Robert . . . I don't know where she is. The detectives have her. Talk to the detectives. She ain't in there, Robert.'" Moments later, a gunshot was heard, and the 911 call was disconnected.

Officers were dispatched to the scene, and on arrival, they found three dead or dying victims—petitioner's mother-in-law, her husband, and the teenage son of petitioner's wife. The officers saw a man who fit petitioner's description fleeing in petitioner's car. They chased the suspect, but he abandoned the car along with critical evidence linking him to the crime: the cordless phone petitioner's mother-in-law had used to call 911 and a receipt for the type of ammunition used to kill the victims. Petitioner was eventually arrested while hitchhiking in Idaho, and a loaded gun found in his possession was identified as the one used to shoot the victims. In addition to all this, a witness testified that petitioner had asked to borrow money to purchase bullets shortly before the shootings, and surveillance footage showed petitioner purchasing the ammunition on the day of the killings. And two of petitioner's friends testified that he confessed to killing at least one person.

Despite all this evidence, petitioner, who had been found competent to stand trial and had refused to plead guilty by reason of insanity, insisted that he did not kill the victims. He claimed that the victims were killed by the local police and that he had been framed by a farflung conspiracy of state and federal officials, reaching from Louisiana to Idaho. Petitioner believed that even his attorney and the trial judge had joined the plot.

Unwilling to go along with this incredible and uncorroborated defense, English told petitioner "some eight months" before trial that the only viable strategy was to admit the killings and to concentrate on attempting to avoid a sentence of death. At that point—aware of English's strong views—petitioner could have discharged English and sought new counsel willing to pursue his conspiracy defense; under the Sixth Amendment, that was his right. But petitioner stated "several different times" that he was "confident with Mr. English."

The weekend before trial, however, petitioner changed his mind. He asked the trial court to replace English, and English asked for permission to withdraw. Petitioner stated that he had secured substitute counsel, but he was unable to provide the name of this new counsel, and no new attorney ever appeared. The court refused these requests and also denied petitioner's last-minute request to represent himself. (Petitioner does not challenge these decisions here.) So petitioner and English were stuck with each other, and petitioner availed himself of his right to take the stand to tell his wild story. Under those circumstances, what was English supposed to do?

The Court ignores the question actually presented by the case before us and instead decides this case on the basis of a newly discovered constitutional right that is not implicated by what really occurred at petitioner's trial. I would base our decision on what really took place, and under the highly unusual facts of this case, I would affirm the judgment below.

I therefore respectfully dissent.

Chapter 12

TRIAL BY JURY

A. Trial by Jury

3. Composition of the Jury

b. *Unanimity* (casebook p. 1038)

In 1972, the Supreme Court issued a plurality decision in *Apodaca v. Oregon*, 406 U.S. 404 (1972), holding that the Sixth Amendment does not require a unanimous verdict to convict a defendant. However, in 2020, the Court revisited that issue. In *Ramos v. Louisiana* (2020), the Court overturned *Apodaca* and held that there is a right under the Sixth Amendment to a unanimous verdict.

Ramos v. Louisiana
140 S. Ct. 1390 (2020)

Justice GORSUCH announced the judgment of the Court and delivered the opinion of the Court with respect to Parts I, II-A, III, and IV-B-1, an opinion with respect to Parts II-B, IV-B-2, and V, in which Justice GINSBURG, Justice BREYER, and Justice SOTOMAYOR join, and an opinion with respect to Part IV-A, in which Justice GINSBURG and Justice BREYER join.

Accused of a serious crime, Evangelisto Ramos insisted on his innocence and invoked his right to a jury trial. Eventually, 10 jurors found the evidence against him persuasive. But a pair of jurors believed that the State of Louisiana had failed to prove Mr. Ramos's guilt beyond reasonable doubt; they voted to acquit.

In 48 States and federal court, a single juror's vote to acquit is enough to prevent a conviction. But not in Louisiana. Along with Oregon, Louisiana has long punished people based on 10-to-2 verdicts like the one here. So instead of the mistrial he would have received almost anywhere else, Mr. Ramos was sentenced to life in prison without the possibility of parole.

Why do Louisiana and Oregon allow nonunanimous convictions? Though it's hard to say why these laws persist, their origins are clear. Louisiana first endorsed nonunanimous verdicts for serious crimes at a constitutional convention in 1898. According to one committee chairman, the avowed purpose of that convention was to "establish the supremacy of the white race," and the resulting document included many of the trappings of the Jim Crow era.

Nor was it only the prospect of African-Americans voting that concerned the delegates. Just a week before the convention, the U.S. Senate passed a resolution calling for an investigation into whether Louisiana was systemically excluding African-Americans from juries. Seeking to avoid unwanted national attention, the delegates sought to undermine African-American participation on juries in another way. With a careful eye on racial demographics, the convention delegates sculpted a "facially race-neutral" rule permitting 10-to-2 verdicts in order "to ensure that African-American juror service would be meaningless."

Adopted in the 1930s, Oregon's rule permitting nonunanimous verdicts can be similarly traced to the rise of the Ku Klux Klan and efforts to dilute "the influence of racial, ethnic, and religious minorities on Oregon juries." In fact, no one before us contests any of this; courts in both Louisiana and Oregon have frankly acknowledged that race was a motivating factor in the adoption of their States' respective nonunanimity rules.

We took this case to decide whether the Sixth Amendment right to a jury trial—as incorporated against the States by way of the Fourteenth Amendment—requires a unanimous verdict to convict a defendant of a serious offense.

I

The Sixth Amendment promises that "[i]n all criminal prosecutions, the accused shall enjoy the right to a speedy and public trial, by an impartial jury of the State and district wherein the crime shall have been committed, which district shall have been previously ascertained by law." The Amendment goes on to preserve other rights for criminal defendants but says nothing else about what a "trial by an impartial jury" entails.

The text and structure of the Constitution clearly suggest that the term "trial by an impartial jury" carried with it some meaning about the content and requirements of a jury trial.

One of these requirements was unanimity. Wherever we might look to determine what the term "trial by an impartial jury trial" meant at the time of the Sixth Amendment's adoption—whether it's the common law, state practices in the founding era, or opinions and treatises written soon afterward—the answer is unmistakable. A jury must reach a unanimous verdict in order to convict.

The requirement of juror unanimity emerged in 14th century England and was soon accepted as a vital right protected by the common law. As Blackstone explained, "'[a] verdict, taken from eleven, was no verdict'" at all.

This same rule applied in the young American States. Six State Constitutions explicitly required unanimity. Another four preserved the right to a jury trial in more general terms.

It was against this backdrop that James Madison drafted and the States ratified the Sixth Amendment in 1791. By that time, unanimous verdicts had been required for about 400 years.

II

A

How, despite these seemingly straightforward principles, have Louisiana's and Oregon's laws managed to hang on for so long? It turns out that the Sixth Amendment's otherwise simple story took a strange turn in 1972. That year, the Court confronted these States' unconventional schemes for the first time—in *Apodaca v. Oregon* and a companion case, *Johnson v. Louisiana*. Ultimately, the Court could do no more than issue a badly fractured set of opinions. Four dissenting Justices would not have hesitated to strike down the States' laws, recognizing that the Sixth Amendment requires unanimity. . . . But a four-Justice plurality took a very different view of the Sixth Amendment. These Justices declared that the real question before them was whether unanimity serves an important "function" in "contemporary society." Then, having reframed the question, the plurality wasted few words before concluding that unanimity's costs outweigh its benefits in the modern era, so the Sixth Amendment should not stand in the way of Louisiana or Oregon.

B

In the years following *Apodaca*, both Louisiana and Oregon chose to continue allowing nonunanimous verdicts. But their practices have always stood on shaky ground.

III

[W]ho can say whether any particular hung jury is a waste, rather than an example of a jury doing exactly what the plurality said it should—deliberating carefully and safeguarding against overzealous prosecutions? And what about the fact, too, that some studies suggest that the elimination of unanimity has only a small effect on the rate of hung juries? Or the fact that others profess to have found that requiring unanimity may provide other possible benefits, including more open-minded and more thorough deliberations?

IV

A

If Louisiana's path to an affirmance is a difficult one, the dissent's is trickier still. The dissent doesn't dispute that the Sixth Amendment protects the right to a unanimous jury verdict, or that the Fourteenth Amendment extends this right to state-court trials. But, it insists, we must affirm Mr. Ramos's conviction anyway. Why? Because the doctrine of stare decisis supposedly commands it. There are two independent reasons why that answer falls short.

In the first place and as we've seen, not even Louisiana tries to suggest that *Apodaca* supplies a governing precedent. Remember, Justice Powell agreed that the Sixth Amendment requires a unanimous verdict to convict, so he would have no objection to that aspect of our holding today. Justice Powell reached a different result only by relying on a dual-track theory of incorporation that a majority of the Court had already rejected (and continues to reject). And to accept that reasoning as precedential, we would have to embrace a new and dubious proposition: that a single Justice writing only for himself has the authority to bind this Court to propositions it has already rejected.

B

1

There's another obstacle the dissent must overcome. Even if we accepted the premise that *Apodaca* established a precedent, no one on the Court today is prepared to say it was rightly decided, and stare decisis isn't supposed to be the art of methodically ignoring what everyone knows to be true. Of course, the precedents of this Court warrant our deep respect as embodying the considered views of those who have come before. But stare decisis has never been treated as "an inexorable command." And the doctrine is "at its weakest when we interpret the Constitution" because a mistaken judicial interpretation of that supreme law is often "practically impossible" to correct through other means.

Start with the quality of the reasoning. Whether we look to the plurality opinion or Justice Powell's separate concurrence, *Apodaca* was gravely mistaken. . . .

Apodaca sits uneasily with 120 years of preceding case law. Given how unmoored it was from the start, it might seem unlikely that later developments could have done more to undermine the decision. Yet they have. While Justice Powell's dual-track theory of incorporation was already foreclosed in 1972. . . .

When it comes to reliance interests, it's notable that neither Louisiana nor Oregon claims anything like the prospective economic, regulatory, or social disruption litigants seeking to preserve precedent usually invoke. No one, it seems, has signed a contract, entered a marriage, purchased a home, or opened a business based on the expectation that, should a crime occur, at least the accused may be sent away by a 10-to-2 verdict. Nor does anyone suggest that nonunanimous verdicts have "become part of our national culture." It would be quite surprising if they had, given that nonunanimous verdicts are insufficient to convict in 48 States and federal court.

2

The second and related reliance interest the dissent seizes upon involves the interest Louisiana and Oregon have in the security of their final criminal judgments. In light of our decision today, the dissent worries that defendants whose appeals are already complete might seek to challenge their nonunanimous convictions through collateral (i.e., habeas) review.

But again the worries outstrip the facts. Under *Teague v. Lane*, newly recognized rules of criminal procedure do not normally apply in collateral review.

In the final accounting, the dissent's stare decisis arguments round to zero. We have an admittedly mistaken decision, on a constitutional issue, an outlier on the day it was decided, one that's become lonelier with time.

V

On what ground would anyone have us leave Mr. Ramos in prison for the rest of his life? Not a single Member of this Court is prepared to say Louisiana secured his conviction constitutionally under the Sixth Amendment. No one before us suggests that the error was harmless. Louisiana does not claim precedent commands an affirmance. In the end, the best anyone can seem to muster against Mr. Ramos is that, if we dared to admit in his case what we all know to be true about the Sixth Amendment, we might have to say the same in some others. But where is the justice in that?

Reversed.

Justice SOTOMAYOR, concurring as to all but Part IV-A.

I agree with most of the Court's rationale, and so I join all but Part IV-A of its opinion. I write separately, however, to underscore three points. First, overruling precedent here is not only warranted, but compelled. Second, the interests at stake point far more clearly to that outcome than those in other recent cases. And finally, the racially biased origins of the Louisiana and Oregon laws uniquely matter here.

Justice KAVANAUGH, concurring in part.

In *Apodaca v. Oregon*, this Court held that state juries need not be unanimous in order to convict a criminal defendant. Two States, Louisiana and Oregon, have continued to use non-unanimous juries in criminal cases. Today, the Court overrules *Apodaca* and holds that state juries must be unanimous in order to convict a criminal defendant.

I agree with the Court that the time has come to overrule *Apodaca*. I write separately to explain my view of how stare decisis applies to this case.

The stare decisis factors identified by the Court in its past cases include:

> the quality of the precedent's reasoning;
> the precedent's consistency and coherence with previous or subsequent decisions;
> changed law since the prior decision;
> changed facts since the prior decision;
> the workability of the precedent;
> the reliance interests of those who have relied on the precedent; and
> the age of the precedent.

Applying the three broad stare decisis considerations to this case, I agree with the Court's decision to overrule *Apodaca*.

First, *Apodaca* is egregiously wrong.

Second, *Apodaca* causes significant negative consequences. It is true that *Apodaca* is workable. But *Apodaca* sanctions the conviction at trial or by guilty plea of some defendants who might not be convicted under the proper constitutional rule (although exactly how many is of course unknowable).

In light of the racist origins of the non-unanimous jury, it is no surprise that non-unanimous juries can make a difference in practice, especially in cases involving black defendants, victims, or jurors.

Third, overruling *Apodaca* would not unduly upset reliance interests. Only Louisiana and Oregon employ non-unanimous juries in criminal cases.

In sum, *Apodaca* is egregiously wrong, it has significant negative consequences, and overruling it would not unduly upset reliance interests. I therefore agree with the Court's decision to overrule *Apodaca*.

Justice THOMAS, concurring in the judgment.

I agree with the Court that petitioner Evangelisto Ramos' felony conviction by a nonunanimous jury was unconstitutional. I write separately because I would resolve this case based on the Court's longstanding view that the Sixth Amendment includes a protection against nonunanimous felony guilty verdicts, without undertaking a fresh analysis of the meaning of "trial . . . by an impartial jury."

Justice ALITO, with whom THE CHIEF JUSTICE joins, and with whom Justice KAGAN joins as to all but Part III-D, dissenting.

The doctrine of stare decisis gets rough treatment in today's decision. Lowering the bar for overruling our precedents, a badly fractured majority casts aside an important and long-established decision with little regard for the enormous reliance the decision has engendered. If the majority's approach is not just a way to dispose of this one case, the decision marks an important turn.

Nearly a half century ago in *Apodaca v. Oregon* (1972), the Court held that the Sixth Amendment permits non-unanimous verdicts in state criminal trials, and in all the years since then, no Justice has even hinted that *Apodaca* should be reconsidered. Understandably thinking that *Apodaca* was good law, the state courts in Louisiana and Oregon have tried thousands of cases under rules that permit such verdicts. But today, the Court does away with *Apodaca* and, in so doing, imposes a potentially crushing burden on the courts and criminal justice systems of those States.

To add insult to injury, the Court tars Louisiana and Oregon with the charge of racism for permitting nonunanimous verdicts—even though this Court found such verdicts to be constitutional and even though there are entirely legitimate arguments for allowing them.

I would not overrule *Apodaca*. Whatever one may think about the correctness of the decision, it has elicited enormous and entirely reasonable reliance. And before this Court decided to intervene, the decision appeared to have little practical importance going forward. Louisiana has now abolished non-unanimous verdicts, and Oregon seemed on the verge of doing the same until the Court intervened.

Too much public discourse today is sullied by ad hominem rhetoric, that is, attempts to discredit an argument not by proving that it is unsound but by attacking the character or motives of the argument's proponents. The majority regrettably succumbs to this trend. At the start of its opinion, the majority asks this rhetorical question: "Why do Louisiana and Oregon allow nonunanimous convictions?" And the answer it suggests? Racism, white supremacy, the Ku Klux Klan.

If Louisiana and Oregon originally adopted their laws allowing non-unanimous verdicts for these reasons, that is deplorable, but what does that have to do with the broad constitutional question before us? The answer is: nothing.

That history would be relevant if there were no legitimate reasons why anyone might think that allowing non-unanimous verdicts is good policy. But that is undeniably false.

Some years ago the British Parliament enacted a law allowing non-unanimous verdicts. Was Parliament under the sway of the Klan? The Constitution of Puerto Rico permits non-unanimous verdicts. Non-unanimous verdicts were once advocated by the American Law Institute and the American Bar Association. Was their aim to promote white supremacy? And how about the prominent scholars who have taken the same position? Racists all? Of course not. We should set an example of rational and civil discourse instead of contributing to the worst current trends.

Now to what matters.

I begin with the question whether *Apodaca* was a precedent at all. It is remarkable that it is even necessary to address this question, but in Part IV-A of the principal opinion, three Justices take the position that *Apodaca* was never a precedent. The only truly fitting response to this argument is: "Really?"

Consider what it would mean if *Apodaca* was never a precedent. It would mean that the entire legal profession was fooled for the past 48 years. Believing that *Apodaca* was a precedent, the courts of Louisiana and Oregon tried thousands of cases under rules allowing conviction by a vote of 11 to 1 or 10 to 2, and appellate courts in those States upheld these convictions based on *Apodaca*. But according to three Justices in the majority, these courts were deluded.

[Additionally], Stare decisis has been a fundamental part of our jurisprudence since the founding, and it is an important doctrine. But, as we have said many times, it is not an "inexorable command."

What is the majority's justification for overruling *Apodaca*? With no apparent appreciation of the irony, today's majority, which is divided into four separate camps, criticizes the *Apodaca* majority as "badly fractured." But many important decisions currently regarded as precedents were decided without an opinion of the Court. Does the majority mean to suggest that all such precedents are fair game?

Even now, our cases do not hold that every provision of the Bill of Rights applies in the same way to the Federal Government and the States. A notable exception is the Grand Jury Clause of the Fifth Amendment, a provision that, like the Sixth Amendment jury-trial right, reflects the importance that the founding generation attached to juries as safeguards against oppression. In *Hurtado v. California* (1884), the Court held that the Grand Jury Clause does not bind the States and that they may substitute preliminary hearings at which the decision to allow a prosecution to go forward is made by a judge rather than a defendant's peers.

While the majority worries that *Apodaca* is inconsistent with our cases on incorporation, the majority ignores something far more important: the way in which *Apodaca* is intertwined with the body of our Sixth Amendment case law. As I have explained, the *Apodaca* plurality's reasoning was based on the same fundamental mode of analysis as that in *Williams v. Florida* (1970), which had held just two years earlier that the Sixth Amendment did not constitutionalize the common law's requirement that a jury have 12 members. Although only one State, Oregon, now permits non-unanimous verdicts, many more allow sixperson juries. Repudiating the reasoning of *Apodaca* will almost certainly prompt calls to overrule *Williams*.

Up to this point, I have discussed the majority's reasons for overruling *Apodaca*, but that is only half the picture. What convinces me that *Apodaca* should be retained are the enormous reliance interests of Louisiana and Oregon. For 48 years, Louisiana and Oregon, trusting that *Apodaca* is good law, have conducted thousands and thousands of trials under rules allowing non-unanimous verdicts. Now, those States face a potential tsunami of litigation on the jury unanimity issue.

The majority cannot have it both ways. As long as retroactive application on collateral review remains a real possibility, the crushing burden that this would entail cannot be ignored. And while it is true that this Court has been chary in recognizing new watershed rules, it is by no means clear that *Teague* will preclude the application of today's decision on collateral review.

Under the approach to stare decisis that we have taken in recent years, Apodaca should not be overruled. I would therefore affirm the judgment below, and I respectfully dissent.

B. Jury Composition and Selection

2. Selecting the Petit Jury (casebook p. 1059)

Recently, the Supreme Court applied *Batson* to overturn a death penalty conviction in *Flowers v. Mississippi* (2019). Flowers was tried six times. Over the course of his six trials, the prosecutor used his peremptory challenges to strike 41 of 42 prospective black jurors. The Court found that the facts of the case showed ample evidence of a pattern to discriminate against jurors on the basis of their race.

Flowers v. Mississippi
139 S. Ct. 2228 (2019)

Justice KAVANAUGH delivered the opinion of the Court.

In *Batson v. Kentucky* (1986), this Court ruled that a State may not discriminate on the basis of race when exercising peremptory challenges against prospective jurors in a criminal trial.

In 1996, Curtis Flowers allegedly murdered four people in Winona, Mississippi. Flowers is black. He has been tried six separate times before a jury for murder. The same lead prosecutor represented the State in all six trials. In the initial three trials, Flowers was convicted, but the Mississippi Supreme Court reversed each conviction. In the first trial, Flowers was convicted, but the Mississippi Supreme Court reversed the conviction due to "numerous instances of prosecutorial misconduct." In the second trial, the trial court found that the prosecutor discriminated on the basis of race in the peremptory challenge of a black juror. The trial court seated the black juror. Flowers was then convicted, but the Mississippi Supreme Court again reversed the conviction because of prosecutorial misconduct at trial. In the third trial, Flowers was convicted, but the Mississippi Supreme Court yet again reversed the conviction, this time because the court concluded that the prosecutor had again discriminated against black prospective jurors in the jury selection process. The fourth and fifth trials of Flowers ended in mistrials due to hung juries. In his sixth trial, which is the one at issue here, Flowers was convicted. The State struck five of the six black prospective jurors. On appeal, Flowers argued that the State again violated Batson in exercising peremptory strikes against black prospective jurors.

Four critical facts, taken together, require reversal. First, in the six trials combined, the State employed its peremptory challenges to strike 41 of the 42 black prospective jurors that it could have struck. Second, in the most recent trial, the sixth trial, the State exercised peremptory strikes against five of the six black prospective jurors. Third, at the sixth trial, in an apparent effort to find pretextual reasons to strike black prospective jurors, the State engaged in dramatically disparate questioning of black and white prospective jurors. Fourth, the State then struck at least one black prospective juror, Carolyn Wright, who was similarly situated to white prospective jurors who were not struck by the State.

We need not and do not decide that any one of those four facts alone would require reversal. All that we need to decide, and all that we do decide, is that all of the relevant facts and circumstances taken together establish that the trial court committed clear error in concluding that the State's peremptory strike of black prospective juror Carolyn Wright was not "motivated in substantial part by discriminatory intent."

I

The underlying events that gave rise to this case took place in Winona, Mississippi. Winona is a small town in northern Mississippi. The total population of Winona is about 5,000. The town is about 53 percent black and about 46 percent white. In 1996, Bertha Tardy, Robert Golden, Derrick Stewart, and Carmen Rigby were murdered at the Tardy Furniture store in Winona. All four victims worked at the Tardy Furniture store. Three of the four victims were white; one was black. In 1997, the State charged Curtis Flowers with murder. Flowers is black. Since then, Flowers has been tried six separate times for the murders. In each of the first two trials, Flowers was tried for one individual murder. In each subsequent trial, Flowers was tried for all four of the murders together. The same state prosecutor tried Flowers each time. The prosecutor is white.

At Flowers' first trial, 36 prospective jurors—5 black and 31 white—were presented to potentially serve on the jury. The State exercised a total of 12 peremptory strikes, and it used 5 of them to strike the five qualified black prospective jurors. Flowers objected, arguing under *Batson* that the State had exercised its peremptory strikes in a racially discriminatory manner. At the second trial, 30 prospective jurors—5 black and 25 white—were presented to potentially serve on the jury. As in Flowers' first trial, the State again used its strikes against all five black prospective jurors. But this time, the trial court determined that the State's asserted reason for one of the strikes was a pretext for discrimination. Specifically, the trial court determined that one of the State's proffered reasons—that the juror had been inattentive and was nodding off during jury selection—for striking that juror was false, and the trial court therefore sustained Flowers' *Batson* challenge. The jury at Flowers' second trial consisted of 11 white jurors and 1 black juror. The jury convicted Flowers and sentenced him to death.

At Flowers' third trial, 45 prospective jurors—17 black and 28 white—were presented to potentially serve on the jury. One of the black prospective jurors was struck for cause, leaving 16. The State exercised a total of 15 peremptory strikes, and it used all 15 against black prospective jurors. Flowers again argued that the State had used its peremptory strikes in a racially discriminatory manner.

On appeal, the Mississippi Supreme Court yet again reversed. The court's lead opinion stated: "The instant case presents us with as strong a prima facie case of racial discrimination as we have ever seen in the context of a *Batson* challenge."

At Flowers' fourth trial, 36 prospective jurors—16 black and 20 white—were presented to potentially serve on the jury. The State exercised a total of 11 peremptory strikes, and it used all 11 against black prospective jurors.

At the sixth trial, which we consider here, 26 prospective jurors—6 black and 20 white—were presented to potentially serve on the jury. The State exercised a total of six peremptory strikes, and it used five of the six against black prospective jurors, leaving one black juror to sit on the jury.

II

A

Other than voting, serving on a jury is the most substantial opportunity that most citizens have to participate in the democratic process.

Under *Batson*, once a prima facie case of discrimination has been shown by a defendant, the State must provide race-neutral reasons for its peremptory strikes. The trial judge must determine whether the prosecutor's stated reasons were the actual reasons or instead were a pretext for discrimination. Four parts of *Batson* warrant particular emphasis here.

First, the *Batson* Court rejected Swain's insistence that a defendant demonstrate a history of racially discriminatory strikes in order to make out a claim of race discrimination. In the eyes of the Constitution, one racially discriminatory peremptory strike is one too many. For those reasons, the *Batson* Court held that a criminal defendant could show "purposeful discrimination in selection of the petit jury solely on evidence concerning the prosecutor's exercise of peremptory challenges at the defendant's trial."

Second, the *Batson* Court rejected Swain's statement that a prosecutor could strike a black juror based on an assumption or belief that the black juror would favor a black defendant. In some of the most critical sentences in the Batson opinion, the Court emphasized that a prosecutor may not rebut a claim of discrimination "by stating merely that he challenged jurors of the defendant's race on the assumption—or his intuitive judgment—that they would be partial to the defendant because of their shared race."

Third, the *Batson* Court did not accept the argument that race-based peremptories should be permissible because black, white, Asian, and Hispanic defendants and jurors were all "equally" subject to race-based discrimination.

Fourth, the *Batson* Court did not accept the argument that race-based peremptories are permissible because both the prosecution and defense could employ them in any individual case and in essence balance things out.

B

Equal justice under law requires a criminal trial free of racial discrimination in the jury selection process. Enforcing that constitutional principle, *Batson* ended the widespread practice in which prosecutors could (and often would) routinely strike all black prospective jurors in cases involving black defendants. By taking steps to eradicate racial discrimination from the jury selection process, *Batson* sought to protect the rights of defendants and jurors, and to enhance public confidence in the fairness of the criminal justice system. *Batson* immediately revolutionized the jury selection process that takes place every day in federal and state criminal courtrooms throughout the United States.

In the decades since *Batson*, this Court's cases have vigorously enforced and reinforced the decision, and guarded against any backsliding. Our precedents allow criminal defendants raising Batson challenges to present a variety of evidence to support a claim that a prosecutor's peremptory strikes were made on the basis of race. For example, defendants may present:

- statistical evidence about the prosecutor's use of peremptory strikes against black prospective jurors as compared to white prospective jurors in the case;
- evidence of a prosecutor's disparate questioning and investigation of black and white prospective jurors in the case;
- side-by-side comparisons of black prospective jurors who were struck and white prospective jurors who were not struck in the case;
- a prosecutor's misrepresentations of the record when defending the strikes during the Batson hearing;
- relevant history of the State's peremptory strikes in past cases; or
- other relevant circumstances that bear upon the issue of racial discrimination.

As the *Batson* Court explained and as the Court later reiterated, once a prima facie case of racial discrimination has been established, the prosecutor must provide race-neutral reasons for the strikes. The trial court must consider the prosecutor's race-neutral explanations in light of all of the relevant facts and circumstances, and in light of the arguments of the parties.

An appeals court looks at the same factors as the trial judge, but is necessarily doing so on a paper record. "Since the trial judge's findings in the context under consideration here largely will turn on evaluation of credibility, a reviewing court ordinarily should give those findings great deference."

III

In accord with the principles set forth in *Batson*, we now address Flowers' case.

The Constitution forbids striking even a single prospective juror for a discriminatory purpose. The question for this Court is whether the Mississippi trial court clearly erred in concluding that the State was not "motivated in substantial part by discriminatory intent" when exercising peremptory strikes at Flowers' sixth trial.

First, we consider the relevant history of the case. Here, our review of the history of the prosecutor's peremptory strikes in Flowers' first four trials strongly supports the conclusion that his use of peremptory strikes in Flowers' sixth trial was motivated in substantial part by discriminatory intent. (Recall that there is no record evidence from the fifth trial regarding the race of the prospective jurors.)

The numbers speak loudly. Over the course of the first four trials, there were 36 black prospective jurors against whom the State could have exercised a peremptory strike. The State tried to strike all 36. Not only did the State's use of peremptory strikes in Flowers' first four trials reveal a blatant pattern of striking black prospective jurors, the Mississippi courts themselves concluded on two separate occasions that the State violated *Batson*. Stretching across Flowers' first four trials, the State employed its peremptory strikes to remove as many black prospective jurors as possible.

We turn now to the State's strikes of five of the six black prospective jurors at Flowers' sixth trial, the trial at issue here. The State's use of peremptory strikes in Flowers' sixth trial followed the same pattern as the first four trials, with one modest exception: It is true that the State accepted one black juror for Flowers' sixth trial. But especially given the history of the case, that fact alone cannot insulate the State from a *Batson* challenge. In *Miller-El II*, this Court skeptically viewed the State's decision to accept one black juror, explaining that a prosecutor might do so in an attempt "to obscure the otherwise consistent pattern of opposition to" seating black jurors. The overall record of this case suggests that the same tactic may have been employed here.

We next consider the State's dramatically disparate questioning of black and white prospective jurors in the jury selection process for Flowers' sixth trial. One can slice and dice the statistics and come up with all sorts of ways to compare the State's questioning of excluded black jurors with the State's questioning of the accepted white jurors. But any meaningful comparison yields the same basic assessment: The State spent far more time questioning the black prospective jurors than the accepted white jurors.

Why did the State ask so many more questions—and conduct more vigorous inquiry—of black prospective jurors than it did of white prospective jurors? No one can know for certain. But this Court's cases explain that disparate questioning and investigation of prospective jurors on the basis of race can arm a prosecutor with seemingly race-neutral reasons to strike the prospective jurors of a particular race. *See Miller-El I*. In other words, by asking a lot of questions of the black prospective jurors or conducting additional inquiry into their backgrounds, a prosecutor can try to find some pretextual reason—any reason—that the prosecutor can later articulate to justify what is in reality a racially motivated strike. And by not doing the same for white prospective jurors, by not asking white prospective jurors those same questions, the prosecutor can try to distort the record so as to thereby avoid being accused of treating black and white jurors differently.

A court confronting that kind of pattern cannot ignore it. The lopsidedness of the prosecutor's questioning and inquiry can itself be evidence of the prosecutor's objective as much as it is of the actual qualifications of the black and white prospective jurors who are struck or seated. The prosecutor's dramatically disparate questioning of black and white prospective jurors—at least if it rises to a certain level of disparity—can supply a clue that the prosecutor may have been seeking to paper the record and disguise a discriminatory intent.

To be clear, disparate questioning or investigation alone does not constitute a *Batson* violation. The disparate questioning or investigation of black and white prospective jurors may reflect ordinary race-neutral considerations. But the disparate questioning or investigation can also, along with other evidence, inform the trial court's evaluation of whether discrimination occurred.

Finally, in combination with the other facts and circumstances in this case, the record of jury selection at the sixth trial shows that the peremptory strike of at least one of the black prospective jurors (Carolyn Wright) was motivated in substantial part by discriminatory intent. In this case, Carolyn Wright was a black prospective juror who said she was strongly in favor of the death penalty as a general matter. And she had a family member who was a prison security guard. Yet the State exercised a peremptory strike against Wright. The State said it struck Wright in part because she knew several defense witnesses and had worked at Wal-Mart where Flowers' father also worked.

Winona is a small town. Wright had some sort of connection to 34 people involved in Flowers' case, both on the prosecution witness side and the defense witness side. But three white prospective jurors—Pamela Chesteen, Harold Waller, and Bobby Lester—also knew many individuals involved in the case. Yet as we explained above, the State did not ask Chesteen, Waller, and Lester individual follow-up questions about their connections to witnesses.

To be sure, the back and forth of a Batson hearing can be hurried, and prosecutors can make mistakes when providing explanations. That is entirely understandable, and mistaken explanations should not be confused with racial discrimination. But when considered with other evidence of discrimination, a series of factually inaccurate explanations for striking black prospective jurors can be telling. So it is here. To reiterate, we need not and do not decide that any one of those four facts alone would require reversal. All that we need to decide, and all that we do decide, is that all of the relevant facts and circumstances taken together establish that the trial court at Flowers' sixth trial committed clear error in concluding that the State's peremptory strike of black prospective juror Carolyn Wright was not motivated in substantial part by discriminatory intent. In reaching that conclusion, we break no new legal ground. We simply enforce and reinforce Batson by applying it to the extraordinary facts of this case.

Justice ALITO, concurring.

As the Court takes pains to note, this is a highly unusual case. In light of all that had gone before, it was risky for the case to be tried once again by the same prosecutor in Montgomery County. Were it not for the unique combinations of circumstances present here, I would have no trouble affirming the decision of the Supreme Court of Mississippi, which conscientiously applied the legal standards applicable in less unusual cases. But viewing the totality of the circumstances present here, I agree with the Court that petitioner's capital conviction cannot stand.

12. Trial by Jury

Justice THOMAS, with whom Justice GORSUCH joins as to Parts I, II, and III, dissenting.[1]

The Court today does not dispute that the evidence was sufficient to convict Flowers or that he was tried by an impartial jury. Instead, the Court vacates Flowers' convictions on the ground that the state courts clearly erred in finding that the State did not discriminate based on race when it struck Carolyn Wright from the jury.

The only clear errors in this case are committed by today's majority. Today's decision distorts the record of this case, eviscerates our standard of review, and vacates four murder convictions because the State struck a juror who would have been stricken by any competent attorney. I dissent.

If this case required us to decide whether the state courts were correct that no Batson violation occurred here, I would find the case easy enough. As I have demonstrated, the evidence overwhelmingly supports the conclusion that the State did not engage in purposeful race discrimination. Any competent prosecutor would have struck the jurors struck below. Indeed, some of the jurors' conflicts might even have justified for-cause strikes. But this case is easier yet. The question before us is not whether we "'would have decided the case differently,'" but instead whether the state courts were clearly wrong. And the answer to that question is obviously no.

Much of the Court's opinion is a paean to *Batson v. Kentucky*, which requires that a duly convicted criminal go free because a juror was arguably deprived of his right to serve on the jury. That rule was suspect when it was announced, and I am even less confident of it today.

Flowers should not have standing to assert the excluded juror's claim. He does not dispute that the jury that convicted him was impartial, and as the Court has said many times. He therefore suffered no legally cognizable injury.

Today, the Court holds that Carolyn Wright was denied equal protection by being excluded from jury service. But she is not the person challenging Flowers' convictions (she would lack standing to do so), and I do not understand how Flowers can have standing to assert her claim. The "entire line of cases following *Batson*" is "a misguided effort to remedy a general societal wrong by using the Constitution to regulate the traditionally discretionary exercise of peremptory challenges."

---

[1] Editor's Note: In Part IV of his dissent, Justice Thomas challenges the ongoing validity of *Batson v. Kentucky*.

Chapter 13

SENTENCING

D. The Death Penalty

3. Recent Limits on the Scope of the Death Penalty (casebook p. 1230)

In 2019, the Supreme Court held in *Madison v. Alabama* (2019) that the Eighth Amendment may permit executing a prisoner even if the prisoner cannot remember committing the crime, but it may prohibit executing a prisoner who suffers from dementia or another disorder rather than psychotic delusions.

Madison v. Alabama
139 S. Ct. 718 (2019)

Justice KAGAN delivered the opinion of the Court.

The Eighth Amendment, this Court has held, prohibits the execution of a prisoner whose mental illness prevents him from "rational[ly] understanding" why the State seeks to impose that punishment. In this case, Vernon Madison argued that his memory loss and dementia entitled him to a stay of execution, but an Alabama court denied the relief. We now address two questions relating to the Eighth Amendment's bar, disputed below but not in this Court. First, does the Eighth Amendment forbid execution whenever a prisoner shows that a mental disorder has left him without any memory of committing his crime? We (and, now, the parties) think not, because a person lacking such a memory may still be able to form a rational understanding of the reasons for his death sentence. Second, does the Eighth Amendment apply similarly to a prisoner suffering from dementia as to one experiencing psychotic delusions? We (and, now, the parties) think so, because either condition may—or, then again, may not—impede the requisite comprehension of his punishment. The only issue left, on which the parties still disagree, is what those rulings mean for Madison's own execution. We direct that issue to the state court for further consideration in light of this opinion.

I

A

This Court decided in *Ford v. Wainwright* (1986), that the Eighth Amendment's ban on cruel and unusual punishments precludes executing a prisoner who has "lost his sanity" after sentencing. While on death row, Alvin Ford was beset by "pervasive delusion[s]" associated with "[p]aranoid [s]chizophrenia." Surveying both the common law and state statutes, the Court found a uniform practice against taking the life of such a prisoner. Among the reasons for that time-honored bar, the Court explained, was a moral "intuition" that "killing one who has no capacity" to understand his crime or punishment "simply offends humanity." Another rationale rested on the lack of "retributive value" in executing a person who has no comprehension of the meaning of the community's judgment.

The Court clarified the scope of that category in *Panetti v. Quarterman* by focusing on whether a prisoner can "reach a rational understanding of the reason for [his] execution." The critical question is whether a "prisoner's mental state is so distorted by a mental illness" that he lacks a "rational understanding" of "the State's rationale for [his] execution."

B

Vernon Madison killed a police officer in 1985 during a domestic dispute. An Alabama jury found him guilty of capital murder, and the trial court sentenced him to death. He has spent most of the ensuing decades on the State's death row.

In recent years, Madison's mental condition has sharply deteriorated. Madison suffered a series of strokes, including major ones in 2015 and 2016. He was diagnosed as having vascular dementia, with attendant disorientation and confusion, cognitive impairment, and memory loss. In particular, Madison claims that he can no longer recollect committing the crime for which he has been sentenced to die.

After his 2016 stroke, Madison petitioned the trial court for a stay of execution on the ground that he had become mentally incompetent. Citing *Ford* and *Panetti*, he argued that "he no longer understands" the "status of his case" or the "nature of his conviction and sentence." And in a later filing, Madison emphasized that he could not "independently recall the facts of the offense he is convicted of."

Expert reports from two psychologists largely aligned with the parties' contending positions. Dr. John Goff, Madison's expert, found that although Madison "underst[ood] the nature of execution" in the abstract, he did not comprehend the "reasoning behind" Alabama's effort to execute him. At a competency hearing, Alabama similarly stressed Madison's absence of psychotic episodes or delusions.

II

Two issues relating to *Panetti*'s application are before us. The first question presented is whether *Panetti* prohibits executing Madison merely because he cannot remember committing his crime. The second question raised is whether *Panetti* permits executing Madison merely because he suffers from dementia, rather than psychotic delusions. As the parties now recognize, the standard set out in *Panetti* supplies the answers to both questions. First, a person lacking memory of his crime may yet rationally understand why the State seeks to execute him; if so, the Eighth Amendment poses no bar to his execution. Second, a person suffering from dementia may be unable to rationally understand the reasons for his sentence; if so, the Eighth Amendment does not allow his execution. What matters is whether a person has the "rational understanding" *Panetti* requires—not whether he has any particular memory or any particular mental illness.

In evaluating competency to be executed, a judge must therefore look beyond any given diagnosis to a downstream consequence. As *Ford* and *Panetti* recognized, a delusional disorder can be of such severity—can "so impair the prisoner's concept of reality"—that someone in its thrall will be unable "to come to grips with" the punishment's meaning. But delusions come in many shapes and sizes, and not all will interfere with the understanding that the Eighth Amendment requires. And much the same is true of dementia. That mental condition can cause such disorientation and cognitive decline as to prevent a person from sustaining a rational understanding of why the State wants to execute him. But dementia also has milder forms, which allow a person to preserve that understanding. Hence the need—for dementia as for delusions as for any other mental disorder—to attend to the particular circumstances of a case and make the precise judgment *Panetti* requires.

III

The only question left—and the only one on which the parties now disagree—is whether Madison's execution may go forward based on the state court's decision below.

[W]e must return this case to the state court for renewed consideration of Madison's competency (assuming Alabama sets a new execution date). In that proceeding, two matters disputed below should now be clear. First, under *Ford* and *Panetti*, the Eighth Amendment may permit executing Madison even if he cannot remember committing his crime. Second, under those same decisions, the Eighth Amendment may prohibit executing Madison even though he suffers from dementia, rather than delusions. The sole question on which Madison's competency depends is whether he can reach a "rational understanding" of why the State wants to execute him.

d. *Method of Execution* (casebook p. 1266)

In Glossip v. Gross, 135 S. Ct. 2726 (2015), the Supreme Court clarified that the plurality opinion in Baze v. Rees, 553 U.S. 35 (2008), was controlling. Under *Baze v. Rees* and *Glossip v. Gross*, an inmate challenging a method of execution must demonstrate that there is an alternative form of execution that would not cause the severe pain in the challenged execution method. In *Bucklew v. Precythe* (2019), the condemned inmate failed to make that necessary showing.

Bucklew v. Precythe
139 S. Ct. 1112 (2019)

Justice GORSUCH delivered the opinion of the Court.

Russell Bucklew concedes that the State of Missouri lawfully convicted him of murder and a variety of other crimes. He acknowledges that the U.S. Constitution permits a sentence of execution for his crimes. He accepts, too, that the State's lethal injection protocol is constitutional in most applications. But because of his unusual medical condition, he contends the protocol is unconstitutional as applied to him.

I

A

In 1996, when Stephanie Ray announced that she wanted to end their relationship, Mr. Bucklew grew violent. He cut her jaw, punched her in the face, and threatened her with a knife. Frightened to remain in the home they had shared, Ms. Ray sought refuge with her children in Michael Sanders' nearby residence. But then one night Mr. Bucklew invaded that home. Bearing a pistol in each hand, he shot Mr. Sanders in the chest; fired at Mr. Sanders' 6-year-old son (thankfully, he missed); and pistol-whipped Ms. Ray, this time breaking her jaw. Then Mr. Bucklew handcuffed Ms. Ray, drove her to a secluded spot, and raped her at gunpoint. After a trooper spotted Mr. Bucklew, a shootout followed and he was finally arrested. While all this played out, Mr. Sanders bled to death. As a coda, Mr. Bucklew escaped from jail while awaiting trial and attacked Ms. Ray's mother with a hammer before he could be recaptured.

A jury had convicted him of murder and other crimes and recommended a death sentence, which the court had imposed.

Mr. Bucklew's case soon became caught up in a wave of litigation over lethal injection procedures. Like many States, Missouri has periodically sought to improve its administration of the death penalty. Early in the 20th century, the State replaced hanging with the gas chamber. Later in the century, it authorized the use of lethal injection as an alternative to lethal gas. By the time Mr. Bucklew's post-conviction proceedings ended, Missouri's protocol called for lethal injections to be carried out using three drugs: sodium thiopental, pancuronium bromide, and potassium chloride. And by that time, too, various inmates were in the process of challenging the constitutionality of the State's protocol and others like it around the country.

While all this played out, pressure from anti-death-penalty advocates induced the company that manufactured sodium thiopental to stop supplying it for use in executions. As a result, the State was unable to proceed with executions until it could change its lethal injection protocol again. This it did in 2012, prescribing the use of a single drug, the sedative propofol. Soon after that, Mr. Bucklew and other inmates sued to invalidate this new protocol as well, alleging that it would produce excruciating pain and violate the Eighth Amendment on its face. After the State revised the protocol in 2013 to use the sedative pentobarbital instead of propofol, the inmates amended their complaint to allege that pentobarbital would likewise violate the Constitution.

Things came to a head in 2014. With its new protocol in place and the necessary drugs now available, the State scheduled Mr. Bucklew's execution for May 21. But 12 days before the execution Mr. Bucklew filed yet another lawsuit, the one now before us. In this case, he presented an as-applied Eighth Amendment challenge to the State's new protocol. Whether or not it would cause excruciating pain for all prisoners, as his previous lawsuit alleged, Mr. Bucklew now contended that the State's protocol would cause him severe pain because of his particular medical condition. Mr. Bucklew suffers from a disease called cavernous hemangioma, which causes vascular tumors—clumps of blood vessels—to grow in his head, neck, and throat. His complaint alleged that this condition could prevent the pentobarbital from circulating properly in his body; that the use of a chemical dye to flush the intravenous line could cause his blood pressure to spike and his tumors to rupture; and that pentobarbital could interact adversely with his other medications.

[In] *Glossip v. Gross* (2015), this Court reject[ed] a challenge to Oklahoma's lethal injection protocol. There, the Court clarified that . . . an inmate cannot successfully challenge a method of execution under the Eighth Amendment unless he identifies "an alternative that is 'feasible, readily implemented, and in fact significantly reduces a substantial risk of severe pain.'" Justice Thomas, joined by Justice Scalia, reiterated his view that the Eighth Amendment "prohibits only those methods of execution that are deliberately designed to inflict pain," but he joined the Court's opinion because it correctly explained why petitioners' claim failed even under the controlling opinion in *Baze*.

Despite . . . express instructions, when Mr. Bucklew returned to the district court in 2015 he still refused to identify an alternative procedure that would significantly reduce his alleged risk of pain. Mr. Bucklew's contentions about the pain he might suffer had evolved considerably. He no longer complained about circulation of the drug, the use of dye, or adverse drug interactions. Instead, his main claim now was that he would experience pain during the period after the pentobarbital started to take effect but before it rendered him fully unconscious. According to his expert, Dr. Joel Zivot, while in this semiconscious "twilight stage" Mr. Bucklew would be unable to prevent his tumors from obstructing his breathing, which would make him feel like he was suffocating.

II

We begin with Mr. Bucklew's suggestion that the test for lethal injection protocol challenges announced in *Baze* and *Glossip* should govern only facial challenges, not as-applied challenges like his.

The Constitution allows capital punishment. In fact, death was "the standard penalty for all serious crimes" at the time of the founding. Of course, that doesn't mean the American people must continue to use the death penalty. The same Constitution that permits States to authorize capital punishment also allows them to outlaw it. But it does mean that the judiciary bears no license to end a debate reserved for the people and their representatives.

While the Eighth Amendment doesn't forbid capital punishment, it does speak to how States may carry out that punishment, prohibiting methods that are "cruel and unusual." What does this term mean? At the time of the framing, English law still formally tolerated certain punishments even though they had largely fallen into disuse—punishments in which "terror, pain, or disgrace [were] superadded" to the penalty of death. These included such "[d]isgusting" practices as dragging the prisoner to the place of execution, disemboweling, quartering, public dissection, and burning alive, all of which Blackstone observed "savor[ed] of torture or cruelty."

Methods of execution like these readily qualified as "cruel and unusual," as a reader at the time of the Eighth Amendment's adoption would have understood those words. They were undoubtedly "cruel," a term often defined to mean "[p]leased with hurting others; inhuman; hard-hearted; void of pity; wanting compassion; savage; barbarous; unrelenting,"

Consistent with the Constitution's original understanding, this Court in *Wilkerson v. Utah* (1879), permitted an execution by firing squad while observing that the Eighth Amendment forbade the gruesome methods of execution described by Blackstone "and all others in the same line of unnecessary cruelty." A few years later, the Court upheld a sentence of death by electrocution while observing that, though electrocution was a new mode of punishment and therefore perhaps could be considered "unusual," it was not "cruel" in the constitutional sense.

At the time of the [Eighth] Amendment's adoption, the predominant method of execution in this country was hanging. While hanging was considered more humane than some of the punishments of the Old World, it was no guarantee of a quick and painless death.

What does all this tell us about how the Eighth Amendment applies to methods of execution? For one thing, it tells us that the Eighth Amendment does not guarantee a prisoner a painless death—something that, of course, isn't guaranteed to many people, including most victims of capital crimes. Instead, what unites the punishments the Eighth Amendment was understood to forbid, and distinguishes them from those it was understood to allow, is that the former were long disused (unusual) forms of punishment that intensified the sentence of death with a (cruel) "'superadd[ition]'" of "'terror, pain, or disgrace.'"

This Court has yet to hold that a State's method of execution qualifies as cruel and unusual, and perhaps understandably so. Far from seeking to superadd terror, pain, or disgrace to their executions, the States have often sought more nearly the opposite. Notably, all of these innovations occurred not through this Court's intervention, but through the initiative of the people and their representatives.

III

Having (re)confirmed that anyone bringing a method of execution claim alleging the infliction of unconstitutionally cruel pain must meet the *Baze-Glossip* test, we can now turn to the question whether Mr. Bucklew is able to satisfy that test. Has he identified a feasible and readily implemented alternative method of execution the State refused to adopt without a legitimate reason, even though it would significantly reduce a substantial risk of severe pain? Because the case comes to us after the entry of summary judgment, this appeal turns on whether Mr. Bucklew has shown a genuine issue of material fact warranting a trial.

We begin with the question of a proposed alternative method. Through much of this case and despite many opportunities, Mr. Bucklew refused to identify any alternative method of execution, choosing instead to stand on his argument that *Baze* and *Glossip*'s legal standard doesn't govern as-applied challenges like his (even after the Eighth Circuit rejected that argument). Only when the district court warned that his continued refusal to abide this Court's precedents would result in immediate dismissal did Mr. Bucklew finally point to nitrogen hypoxia. The district court then afforded Mr. Bucklew "extensive discovery" to explore the viability of that alternative. But even after all that, we conclude Mr. Bucklew has failed for two independent reasons to present a triable question on the viability of nitrogen hypoxia as an alternative to the State's lethal injection protocol.

First, an inmate must show that his proposed alternative method is not just theoretically "'feasible'" but also "'readily implemented.'" This means the inmate's proposal must be sufficiently detailed to permit a finding that the State could carry it out "relatively easily and reasonably quickly." Mr. Bucklew's bare-bones proposal falls well short of that standard. He has presented no evidence on essential questions like how nitrogen gas should be administered (using a gas chamber, a tent, a hood, a mask, or some other delivery device); in what concentration (pure nitrogen or some mixture of gases); how quickly and for how long it should be introduced; or how the State might ensure the safety of the execution team, including protecting them against the risk of gas leaks.

Second, and relatedly, the State had a "legitimate" reason for declining to switch from its current method of execution as a matter of law. Rather than point to a proven alternative method, Mr. Bucklew sought the adoption of an entirely new method—one that had "never been used to carry out an execution" and had "no track record of successful use."

Even if a prisoner can carry his burden of showing a readily available alternative, he must still show that it would significantly reduce a substantial risk of severe pain. A minor reduction in risk is insufficient; the difference must be clear and considerable. Over the course of this litigation, Mr. Bucklew's explanation why nitrogen hypoxia meets this standard has evolved significantly. But neither of the two theories he has advanced in this Court turns out to be supported by record evidence.

First, Mr. Bucklew points to several risks that he alleges could result from use of the State's lethal injection protocol that would not be present if the State used nitrogen gas. For example, he says the execution team might try to insert an IV into one of his peripheral veins, which could cause the vein to rupture; or the team might instead use an allegedly painful "cut-down" procedure to access his femoral vein. He also says that he might be forced to lie flat on his back during the execution, which could impair his breathing even before the pentobarbital is administered. And he says the stress from all this could cause his tumors to bleed, further impairing his breathing. These risks, we may assume, would not exist if Mr. Bucklew were executed by his preferred method of nitrogen hypoxia.

The problem with all of these contentions is that they rest on speculation unsupported, if not affirmatively contradicted, by the evidence in this case. . . . In sum, even if execution by nitrogen hypoxia were a feasible and readily implemented alternative to the State's chosen method, Mr. Bucklew has still failed to present any evidence suggesting that it would significantly reduce his risk of pain. For that reason as well, the State was entitled to summary judgment on Mr. Bucklew's Eighth Amendment claim.

IV

"Both the State and the victims of crime have an important interest in the timely enforcement of a sentence." Those interests have been frustrated in this case. Mr. Bucklew committed his crimes more than two decades ago. He exhausted his appeal and separate state and federal habeas challenges more than a decade ago. Yet since then he has managed to secure delay through lawsuit after lawsuit.

The people of Missouri, the surviving victims of Mr. Bucklew's crimes, and others like them deserve better. Last-minute stays should be the extreme exception.

The judgment of the court of appeals is affirmed.

Justice THOMAS, concurring.
I adhere to my view that "a method of execution violates the Eighth Amendment only if it is deliberately designed to inflict pain."

Justice KAVANAUGH, concurring.
When an inmate raises an as-applied constitutional challenge to a particular method of execution—that is, a challenge to a method of execution that is constitutional in general but that the inmate says is very likely to cause him severe pain—one question is whether the inmate must identify an available alternative method of execution that would significantly reduce the risk of severe pain. Applying our recent decisions in *Glossip v. Gross* and *Baze v. Rees*, the Court's answer to that question is yes. Under those precedents, I agree with the Court's holding and join the Court's opinion.

13. Sentencing

Justice BREYER with whom Justice GINSBURG, Justice SOTOMAYOR, and Justice KAGAN join as to all but Part III, dissenting.

Bucklew has easily established a genuine issue of material fact regarding whether an execution by lethal injection would subject him to impermissible suffering. The record indicates that Bucklew suffers from a congenital condition known as cavernous hemangioma that causes tumors filled with blood vessels to grow throughout his body, including in his head, face, neck, and oral cavity. The condition is rare. One study estimates that hemangiomas in the oral cavity occur in less than one percent of the population, and that hemangiomas like Bucklew's have been identified in five cases.

Tumors grow out of Bucklew's lip and over his mouth, as well as on his hard and soft palates. One tumor also grows directly on Bucklew's uvula, which has become "grossly enlarged" as a result. Bucklew's tumors obstruct his airway and make it difficult for him to breathe. His difficulty breathing is chronic, but is particularly acute when he lies flat and gravity pulls his engorged uvula into his airway. He often has to adjust the positioning of his head to prevent his uvula from obstructing his breathing. He sleeps at a 45-degree angle to facilitate breathing, and he often wakes up in the middle of the night gasping for air.

Due to the sensitivity of his tumors, even minimal contact may cause them to hemorrhage. He has described past hemorrhages as "'squirting'" or "leaking" blood, and he states that the first thing he does each morning is to wipe the blood off his face that leaked from his nose and mouth as he slept. Bucklew's condition is progressive and, due to the risk of significant blood loss caused by the sensitivity of his tumors, cannot be treated by surgery.

Bucklew maintains that, as a result of this medical condition, executing him by lethal injection would prove excruciatingly painful. In support of this claim, Bucklew submitted sworn declarations and deposition testimony from an expert witness, Dr. Joel Zivot, an anesthesiologist. The State asked the District Court to grant summary judgment in its favor on the theory that Bucklew failed to identify a genuine factual issue regarding whether an execution by lethal injection would be impermissibly painful. The District Court refused.

The District Court was right. The evidence, taken in the light most favorable to Bucklew, creates a genuine factual issue as to whether Missouri's lethal injection protocol would subject him to several minutes of "severe pain and suffering,"

I accept the *Glossip* majority opinion as governing. I nonetheless do not believe its "alternative method" requirement applies in this case. [W]hile I acknowledge that the Court in *Glossip* spoke in unqualified terms, the circumstances in *Glossip* were indeed "different" in relevant respects from the circumstances presented here.

The *Glossip* Court, in adopting the "alternative method" requirement, relied on the Chief Justice's plurality opinion in *Baze*, which discussed the need to avoid "intrud[ing] on the role of state legislatures in implementing their execution procedures." But no such intrusion problem exists in a case like this one.

When adopting a method of execution, a state legislature will rarely consider the method's application to an individual who, like Bucklew, suffers from a rare disease. It is impossible to believe that Missouri's legislature, when adopting lethal injection, considered the possibility that it would cause prisoners to choke on their own blood for up to several minutes before they die. Exempting a prisoner from the State's chosen method of execution in these circumstances does not interfere with any legislative judgment.

Even assuming for argument's sake that Bucklew must bear the burden of showing the existence of a "known and available" alternative method of execution that "significantly reduces a substantial risk of severe pain," Bucklew has satisfied that burden. Bucklew identified as an alternative method of execution the use of nitrogen hypoxia, which is a form of execution by lethal gas. Missouri law permits the use of this method of execution. Three other States—Alabama, Mississippi, and Oklahoma—have specifically authorized nitrogen hypoxia as a method of execution. Presented with evidence such as Bucklew's, I believe a State should take at least minimal steps to determine the feasibility of the proposed alternative.

Justice Thomas concurs in the majority's imposition of an "alternative method" requirement, but would also permit Bucklew's execution on the theory that a method of execution violates the Eighth Amendment "'only if it is deliberately designed to inflict pain.'" But that is not the proper standard.

Today's majority appears to believe that because "[t]he Constitution allows capital punishment," the Constitution must allow capital punishment to occur quickly. It may be that there is no way to execute a prisoner quickly while affording him the protections that our Constitution guarantees to those who have been singled out for our law's most severe sanction. And it may be that, as our Nation comes to place ever greater importance upon ensuring that we accurately identify, through procedurally fair methods, those who may lawfully be put to death, there simply is no constitutional way to implement the death penalty.

Justice SOTOMAYOR, dissenting.

As I have maintained ever since the Court started down this wayward path in *Glossip v. Gross*, there is no sound basis in the Constitution for requiring condemned inmates to identify an available means for their own executions. I am [also] especially troubled by the majority's statement that "[l]ast-minute stays should be the extreme exception," which could be read to intimate that late-occurring stay requests from capital prisoners should be reviewed with an especially jaundiced eye.

There are higher values than ensuring that executions run on time. If a death sentence or the manner in which it is carried out violates the Constitution, that stain can never come out. Our jurisprudence must remain one of vigilance and care, not one of dismissiveness.

Chapter 14

DOUBLE JEOPARDY

D. Exceptions to the Double Jeopardy Rule

2. Dual Sovereignty (casebook p. 1295)

In *Gamble v. United States* (2019), the Supreme Court reaffirmed the separate sovereign exception to the double jeopardy rule.

Gamble v. United States
138 S. Ct. 2707 (2019)

Justice ALITO delivered the opinion of the Court.

We consider in this case whether to overrule a longstanding interpretation of the *Double Jeopardy Clause of the Fifth Amendment*. That Clause provides that no person may be "twice put in jeopardy" "for the same offence." Our double jeopardy case law is complex, but at its core, the Clause means that those acquitted or convicted of a particular "offence" cannot be tried a second time for the same "offence." But what does the Clause mean by an "offence"?

We have long held that a crime under one sovereign's laws is not "the same offence" as a crime under the laws of another sovereign. Under this "dual-sovereignty" doctrine, a State may prosecute a defendant under state law even if the Federal Government has prosecuted him for the same conduct under a federal statute.

Or the reverse may happen, as it did here. Terance Gamble, convicted by Alabama for possessing a firearm as a felon, now faces prosecution by the United States under its own felon-in-possession law. Attacking this second prosecution on double jeopardy grounds, Gamble asks us to overrule the dual-sovereignty doctrine. He contends that it departs from the founding-era understanding of the right enshrined by the Double Jeopardy Clause. But the historical evidence assembled by Gamble is feeble; pointing the other way are the Clause's text, other historical evidence, and 170 years of precedent. Today we affirm that precedent, and with it the decision below.

I

In November 2015, a local police officer in Mobile, Alabama, pulled Gamble over for a damaged headlight. Smelling marijuana, the officer searched

Gamble's car, where he found a loaded 9-mm handgun. Since Gamble had been convicted of second-degree robbery, his possession of the handgun violated an Alabama law providing that no one convicted of "a crime of violence" "shall own a firearm or have one in his or her possession."

Gamble moved to dismiss on one ground: The federal indictment was for "the same offence" as the one at issue in his state conviction and thus exposed him to double jeopardy. But because this Court has long held that two offenses "are not the 'same offence'" for double jeopardy purposes if "prosecuted by different sovereigns." The District Court denied Gamble's motion to dismiss.

II

Gamble contends that the Double Jeopardy Clause must forbid successive prosecutions by different sovereigns because that is what the founding-era common law did. But before turning to that historical claim, see Part III infra, we review the Clause's text and some of the cases Gamble asks us to overturn.

A

We start with the text of the Fifth Amendment. Although the dual-sovereignty rule is often dubbed an "exception" to the double jeopardy right, it is not an exception at all. On the contrary, it follows from the text that defines that right in the first place. "[T]he language of the Clause . . . protects individuals from being twice put in jeopardy 'for the same offence,' not for the same conduct or actions."

Faced with this reading, Gamble falls back on an episode from the Double Jeopardy Clause's drafting history. The first Congress, working on an earlier draft that would have banned "'more than one trial or one punishment for the same offence,'" voted down a proposal to add "'by any law of the United States.'" In rejecting this addition, Gamble surmises, Congress must have intended to bar successive prosecutions regardless of the sovereign bringing the charge.

Even if that inference were justified—something that the Government disputes—it would count for little. The private intent behind a drafter's rejection of one version of a text is shoddy evidence of the public meaning of an altogether different text.

Besides, if we allowed conjectures about purpose to inform our reading of the text, the Government's conjecture would prevail. The Government notes that the Declaration of Independence denounced King George III for "protecting [British troops] by a mock Trial, from punishment for any Murders which they should commit on the Inhabitants of these States." The Declaration was alluding to "the so-called Murderers' Act, passed by Parliament after the Boston Massacre," a law that allowed British officials indicted for murder in America to be "'tried in England, beyond the control of local juries.'" Yet on Gamble's reading, the same Founders who quite literally revolted against the use of acquittals abroad to bar criminal prosecutions here would soon give us an Amendment allowing foreign acquittals to spare domestic criminals. We doubt it.

B

Our cases reflect the same reading. A close look at them reveals how fidelity to the Double Jeopardy Clause's text does more than honor the formal difference between two distinct criminal codes. It honors the substantive differences between the interests that two sovereigns can have in punishing the same act.

The question of successive federal and state prosecutions arose in three antebellum cases implying and then spelling out the dual-sovereignty doctrine. The first involved an Ohio prosecution for the passing of counterfeit coins. The defendant argued that since Congress can punish counterfeiting, the States must be barred from doing so, or else a person could face two trials for the same offense, contrary to the Fifth Amendment. We rejected the defendant's premise that under the Double Jeopardy Clause "offences falling within the competency of different authorities to restrain or punish them would not properly be subjected to the consequences which those authorities might ordain and affix to their perpetration." Indeed, we observed, the nature of the crime or its effects on "public safety" might well "deman[d]" separate prosecutions.

This principle comes into still sharper relief when we consider a prosecution in this country for crimes committed abroad. If, as Gamble suggests, only one sovereign may prosecute for a single act, no American court—state or federal—could prosecute conduct already tried in a foreign court. Imagine, for example, that a U.S. national has been murdered in another country. That country could rightfully seek to punish the killer for committing an act of violence within its territory. The foreign country's interest lies in protecting the peace in that territory rather than protecting the American specifically. But the United States looks at the same conduct and sees an act of violence against one of its nationals, a person under the particular protection of its laws. The murder of a U.S. national is an offense to the United States as much as it is to the country where the murder occurred and to which the victim is a stranger. That is why the killing of an American abroad is a federal offense that can be prosecuted in our courts, and why customary international law allows this exercise of jurisdiction.

C

We briefly address two objections to this analysis.

First, the dissents contend that our dual-sovereignty rule errs in treating the Federal and State Governments as two separate sovereigns when in fact sovereignty belongs to the people. . . . The United States is a federal republic; it is not, contrary to Justice Gorsuch's suggestion, unitary state like the United Kingdom.

Gamble and the dissents lodge a second objection to this line of reasoning. They suggest that because the division of federal and state power was meant to promote liberty, it cannot support a rule that exposes Gamble to a second sentence. This argument fundamentally misunderstands the governmental structure established by our Constitution. Our federal system advances individual liberty in many ways. Among other things, it limits the powers of the Federal Government and protects certain basic liberties from infringement. But because the powers of the Federal Government and the States often overlap, allowing both to regulate often results in two layers of regulation. Taxation is an example that comes immediately to mind.

III

Gamble claims that our precedent contradicts the common-law rights that the Double Jeopardy Clause was originally understood to engraft onto the Constitution. The English cases are a muddle. Treatises offer spotty support. And early state and federal cases are by turns equivocal and downright harmful to Gamble's position. All told, this evidence does not establish that those who ratified the Fifth Amendment took it to bar successive prosecutions under different sovereigns' laws—much less do so with enough force to break a chain of precedent linking dozens of cases over 170 years.

Justice GINSBURG, dissenting

Terance Martez Gamble pleaded guilty in Alabama state court to both possession of a firearm by a person convicted of "a crime of violence" and drug possession, and was sentenced to ten years' imprisonment, all but one year suspended. Apparently regarding Alabama's sentence as too lenient, federal prosecutors pursued a parallel charge, possession of a firearm by a convicted felon, in violation of federal law. Gamble again pleaded guilty and received nearly three more years in prison.

Had either the Federal Government or Alabama brought the successive prosecutions, the second would have violated Gamble's right not to be "twice put in jeopardy . . . for the same offence."

I dissent from the Court's adherence to that misguided doctrine. Instead of "fritter[ing] away [Gamble's] libert[y] upon a metaphysical subtlety, two sovereignties," I would hold that the Double Jeopardy Clause bars "successive prosecutions [for the same offense] by parts of the whole USA."

In our "compound republic," the division of authority between the United States and the States was meant to operate as "a double security [for] the rights of the people." The separate-sovereigns doctrine, however, scarcely shores up people's rights. Instead, it invokes federalism to withhold liberty.

The separate-sovereigns doctrine, especially since *Bartkus* and *Abbate,* has been subject to relentless criticism by members of the bench, bar, and academy. Nevertheless, the Court reaffirms the doctrine, thereby diminishing the individual rights shielded by the Double Jeopardy Clause. Different parts of the "WHOLE" United States should not be positioned to prosecute a defendant a second time for the same offense. I would reverse Gamble's federal conviction.

Justice GORSUCH, dissenting.

A free society does not allow its government to try the same individual for the same crime until it's happy with the result. When governments may unleash all their might in multiple prosecutions against an individual, exhausting themselves only when those who hold the reins of power are content with the result, it is "the poor and the weak," and the unpopular and controversial, who suffer first — and there is nothing to stop them from being the last. The separate sovereigns exception was wrong when it was invented, and it remains wrong today.

F.   Collateral Estoppel (casebook p. 1302)

In *Currier v. Virginia*, the Court held that a defendant who agrees to sever charges cannot claim that Double Jeopardy bars a second trial even if the first trial resulted in acquittal and the jury appeared to decide in defendant's favor key issues that would arise in defendant's second trial.

Currier v. Virginia
138 S. Ct. 2144 (2018)

Justice GORSUCH announced the judgment of the Court and delivered the opinion of the Court with respect to Parts I and II, and an opinion with respect to Part III, in which THE CHIEF JUSTICE, Justice THOMAS, and Justice ALITO join.

About to face trial, Michael Currier worried the prosecution would introduce prejudicial but probative evidence against him on one count that could infect the jury's deliberations on others. To address the problem, he agreed to sever the charges and hold two trials instead of one. But after the first trial finished, Mr. Currier turned around and argued that proceeding with the second would violate his right against double jeopardy. All of which raises the question: can a defendant who agrees to have the charges against him considered in two trials later successfully argue that the second trial offends the Fifth Amendment's Double Jeopardy Clause?

I

This case began when police dredged up a safe full of guns from a Virginia river. Paul Garrison, the safe's owner, had reported it stolen from his home. Before the theft, Mr. Garrison said, it contained not just the guns but also $71,000 in cash. Now, most of the money was missing. As the investigation unfolded, the police eventually found their way to Mr. Garrison's nephew. Once confronted, the nephew quickly confessed. Along the way, he pointed to Michael Currier as his accomplice. A neighbor also reported that she saw Mr. Currier leave the Garrison home around the time of the crime. On the strength of this evidence, a grand jury indicted Mr. Currier for burglary, grand larceny, and unlawful possession of a firearm by a convicted felon. The last charge followed in light of Mr. Currier's previous convictions for (as it happens) burglary and larceny.

Because the prosecution could introduce evidence of his prior convictions to prove the felon-in-possession charge, and worried that the evidence might prejudice the jury's consideration of the other charges, Mr. Currier and the government agreed to a severance. They asked the court to try the burglary and larceny charges first. Then, they said, the felon-in-possession charge could follow in a second trial. Some jurisdictions routinely refuse requests like this. Instead, they seek to address the risk of prejudice with an instruction directing the jury to consider the defendant's prior convictions only when assessing the felon-in-possession charge. Other jurisdictions allow parties to stipulate to the defendant's past convictions so the particulars of those crimes don't reach the jury's ears. Others take a more protective approach yet and view severance requests with favor. Because Virginia falls into this last group, the trial court granted the parties' joint request in this case.

The promised two trials followed. At the first, the prosecution produced the nephew and the neighbor who testified to Mr. Currier's involvement in the burglary and larceny. But Mr. Currier argued that the nephew lied and the neighbor was unreliable and, in the end, the jury acquitted. Then, before the second trial on the firearm charge could follow, Mr. Currier sought to stop it. Now, he argued, holding a second trial would amount to double jeopardy. Alternatively and at the least, he asked the court to forbid the government from relitigating in the second trial any issue resolved in his favor at the first. So, for example, he said the court should exclude from the new proceeding any evidence about the burglary and larceny. The court replied that it could find nothing in the Double Jeopardy Clause requiring either result so it allowed the second trial to proceed unfettered. In the end, the jury convicted Mr. Currier on the felon-in-possession charge.

II

The Double Jeopardy Clause, applied to the States through the Fourteenth Amendment, provides that no person may be tried more than once "for the same offence." This guarantee recognizes the vast power of the sovereign, the ordeal of a criminal trial, and the injustice our criminal justice system would invite if prosecutors could treat trials as dress rehearsals until they secure the convictions they seek. At the same time, this Court has said, the Clause was not written or originally understood to pose "an insuperable obstacle to the administration of justice" in cases where "there is no semblance of [these] type[s] of oppressive practices." *Wade v. Hunter* (1949).

On which side of the line does our case fall? Mr. Currier suggests this Court's decision in *Ashe v. Swenson*, 397 U. S. 436 (1970), requires a ruling for him. There, the government accused a defendant of robbing six poker players in a game at a private home. At the first trial, the jury acquitted the defendant of robbing one victim. Then the State sought to try the defendant for robbing a second victim. This Court held the second prosecution violated the Double Jeopardy Clause. To be sure, the Clause speaks of barring successive trials for the same offense. And, to be sure, the State sought to try the defendant for a *different* robbery. But, the Court reasoned, because the first jury necessarily found that the defendant "was not one of the robbers," a second jury could not "rationally" convict the defendant of robbing the second victim without calling into question the earlier acquittal.

Ashe's suggestion that the relitigation of an issue can sometimes amount to the impermissible relitigation of an offense represented a significant innovation in our jurisprudence. To say that the second trial is tantamount to a trial of the same offense as the first and thus forbidden by the Double Jeopardy Clause, we must be able to say that "it would have been *irrational* for the jury" in the first trial to acquit without finding in the defendant's favor on a fact essential to a conviction in the second.

[In this case], a critical difference immediately emerges between our case and *Ashe*. Even assuming without deciding that Mr. Currier's second trial qualified as the retrial of the same offense under *Ashe*, he consented to it. Nor does anyone doubt that trying all three charges in one trial would have prevented any possible *Ashe* complaint Mr. Currier might have had.

How do these features affect the double jeopardy calculus? A precedent points the way. In *Jeffers v. United States* (1977), the defendant sought separate trials on each of the counts against him to reduce the possibility of prejudice. The court granted his request. After the jury convicted the defendant in the first trial of a lesser-included offense, he argued that the prosecution could not later try him for a greater offense. In any other circumstance the defendant likely would have had a good argument. Historically, courts have treated greater and lesser-included offenses as the same offense for double jeopardy purposes, so a conviction on one normally precludes a later trial on the other. But, *Jeffers* concluded, it's different when the defendant consents to two trials where one could have done.

What was true in *Jeffers*, we hold, can be no less true here. If a defendant's consent to two trials can overcome concerns lying at the historic core of the Double Jeopardy Clause, so too we think it must overcome a double jeopardy complaint under *Ashe*. While we acknowledge that *Ashe*'s protections apply only to trials following acquittals, as a general rule, the Double Jeopardy Clause "'protects against a second prosecution for the same offense after conviction'" as well as "'against a second prosecution for the same offense after acquittal.'" Because the Clause applies equally in both situations, consent to a second trial should in general have equal effect in both situations.

Mr. Currier replies that he had no real choice but to seek two trials. Without a second trial, he says, evidence of his prior convictions would have tainted the jury's consideration of the burglary and larceny charges . . . . But litigants every day face difficult decisions. This Court has held repeatedly that difficult strategic choices like these are "not the same as no choice," and the Constitution "does not . . . forbid requiring" a litigant to make them.

III

Even if he voluntarily consented to holding the second trial, Mr. Currier argues, that consent did not extend to the relitigation of any issues the first jury resolved in his favor. So, Mr. Currier says, the court should have excluded evidence suggesting he possessed the guns in Mr. Garrison's home, leaving the prosecution to prove that he possessed them only later, maybe down by the river. To support this argument, Mr. Currier points to issue preclusion principles in civil cases and invites us to import them for the first time into the criminal law through the Double Jeopardy Clause.

We cannot.

Mr. Currier's problems begin with the text of the Double Jeopardy Clause. As we've seen, the Clause speaks not about prohibiting the relitigation of issues or evidence but offenses.

The Double Jeopardy Clause took its cue from English common law pleas that prevented courts from retrying a criminal defendant previously acquitted or convicted of the crime in question. But those pleas barred only repeated "prosecution for the same identical act *and* crime," not the retrial of particular issues or evidence.

Both English and early American cases illustrate the point. In *Turner's Case* (K. B. 1663), for example, a jury acquitted the defendant of breaking into a home and stealing money from the owner. Even so, the court held that the defendant could be tried later for the theft of money "stolen at the same time" from the owner's servant.

On its own terms, too, any effort to transplant civil preclusion principles into the Double Jeopardy Clause would quickly meet trouble. While the Clause embodies a kind of "claim preclusion" rule, even this rule bears little in common with its civil counterpart. In civil cases, a claim generally may not be tried if it arises out of the same transaction or common nucleus of operative facts as another already tried. But in a criminal case, *Blockburger* precludes a trial on an offense only if a court has previously heard the same offense as measured by its statutory elements.

It isn't even clear that civil preclusion principles would help defendants like Mr. Currier. Issue preclusion addresses the effect in a current case of a prior adjudication in *another case*. So it doesn't often have much to say about the preclusive effects of rulings "within the framework of a continuing action."

The fact is, civil preclusion principles and double jeopardy are different doctrines, with different histories, serving different purposes. Historically, both claim and issue preclusion have sought to "promot[e] judicial economy by preventing needless litigation." That interest may make special sense in civil cases where often only money is at stake. But the Double Jeopardy Clause and the common law principles it built upon govern *criminal* cases and concern more than efficiency. They aim instead, as we've seen, to balance vital interests against abusive prosecutorial practices with consideration to the public's safety. The Clause's terms and history simply do not contain the rights Mr. Currier seeks.

Affirmed.

Justice KENNEDY, concurring in part.

I join Parts I and II of the Court's opinion, which, in my view, suffice to resolve this case in a full and proper way.

The Double Jeopardy Clause reflects the principle that "the State with all its resources and power should not be allowed to make repeated attempts to convict an individual for an alleged offense, thereby subjecting him to embarrassment, expense and ordeal and compelling him to live in a continuing state of anxiety and insecurity, as well as enhancing the possibility that even though innocent he may be found guilty." But this "is not a principle which can be expanded to include situations in which the defendant is responsible for the second prosecution."

Justice GINSBURG, with whom Justice BREYER, Justice SOTOMAYOR, and Justice KAGAN join, dissenting.

This Court's decisions "have recognized that the [Double Jeopardy] Clause embodies two vitally important interests." "The first is the 'deeply ingrained' principle that 'the State with all its resources and power should not be allowed to make repeated attempts to convict an individual for an alleged offense, thereby subjecting him to embarrassment, expense and ordeal and compelling him to live in a continuing state of anxiety and insecurity, as well as enhancing the possibility that even though innocent he may be found guilty.'" The second interest the Clause serves is preservation of the "finality of judgments."

The Clause effectuates its overall guarantee through multiple protections. Historically, among those protections, the Court has safeguarded the right not to be subject to multiple trials for the "same offense."

Also shielded by the Double Jeopardy Clause is the issue-preclusive effect of an acquittal. First articulated in *Ashe v. Swenson* (1970), the issue-preclusive aspect of the Double Jeopardy Clause prohibits the government from relitigating issues necessarily resolved in a defendant's favor at an earlier trial presenting factually related offenses. *Ashe* involved the robbery of six poker players by a group of masked men. Missouri tried Ashe first for the robbery of Donald Knight. At trial, proof that Knight was the victim of a robbery was "unassailable"; the sole issue in dispute was whether Ashe was one of the robbers. A jury found Ashe not guilty. Missouri then tried Ashe for robbing a different poker player at the same table. The witnesses at the second trial "were for the most part the same," although their testimony for the prosecution was "substantially stronger" than it was at the first trial. The State also "refined its case" by declining to call a witness whose identification testimony at the first trial had been "conspicuously negative." The second time around, the State secured a conviction.

Although the second prosecution involved a different victim and thus a different "offense," this Court held that the second prosecution violated the Double

Jeopardy Clause. A component of that Clause, the Court explained, rests on the principle that "when an issue of ultimate fact has once been determined by a valid and final judgment, that issue cannot again be litigated between the same parties in any future lawsuit."

Toward the end of the 19th century, courts increasingly concluded that greater protections than those traditionally afforded under the Double Jeopardy Clause were needed to spare defendants from prosecutorial excesses. Federal courts, cognizant of the increased potential for exposing defendants to multiple charges based on the same criminal episode, borrowed issue-preclusion principles from the civil context to bar relitigation of issues necessarily resolved against the government in a criminal trial.

Since *Ashe*, this Court has reaffirmed that issue preclusion ranks with claim preclusion as a Double Jeopardy Clause component.

The sole issue in dispute at the first trial, Currier maintains, was whether he participated in the break-in and theft. The case was submitted to the jury, which acquitted Currier of both offenses.

Despite the jury's acquittal verdicts, the prosecution proceeded against Currier on the felon-in-possession charge. At the second trial, the prosecution shored up its attempt to prove Currier's participation in the break-in and theft. The witnesses refined their testimony. Remedying its earlier procedural lapse by timely notifying Currier, the prosecution introduced the cigarette butt evidence. And, of course, to show Currier was a felon, the prosecution introduced his prior burglary and larceny convictions. The jury found Currier guilty of the felon-in-possession offense.

III

The Court holds that even if Currier could have asserted a double jeopardy issue-preclusion defense in opposition to the second trial, he relinquished that right by acquiescing in severance of the felon-in-possession charge. This holding is not sustainable. A defendant's consent to severance does not waive his right to rely on the issue-preclusive effect of an acquittal.

FEDERAL RULES OF CRIMINAL PROCEDURE

Rule 4. Arrest Warrant or Summons on a Complaint

(a) Issuance.

If the complaint or one or more affidavits filed with the complaint establish probable cause to believe that an offense has been committed and that the defendant committed it, the judge must issue an arrest warrant to an officer authorized to execute it. At the request of an attorney for the government, the judge must issue a summons, instead of a warrant, to a person authorized to serve it. A judge may issue more than one warrant or summons on the same complaint. If a defendant fails to appear in response to a summons, a judge may, and upon request of an attorney for the government must, issue a warrant. If an organizational defendant fails to appear in response to a summons, a judge may take any action authorized by United States law.

(b) Form.

(1) Warrant.

A warrant must:

(A) contain the defendant's name or, if it is unknown, a name or description by which the defendant can be identified with reasonable certainty;

(B) describe the offense charged in the complaint;

(C) command that the defendant be arrested and brought without unnecessary delay before a magistrate judge or, if none is reasonably available, before a state or local judicial officer; and

(D) be signed by a judge.

(2) Summons.

A summons must be in the same form as a warrant except that it must require the defendant to appear before a magistrate judge at a stated time and place.

(c)   Execution or Service, and Return.

(1)   By Whom.

Only a marshal or other authorized officer may execute a warrant. Any person authorized to serve a summons in a federal civil action may serve a summons.

(2)   Location.

A warrant may be executed, or a summons served, within the jurisdiction of the United States or anywhere else a federal statute authorizes an arrest. A summons to an organization under Rule 4(c)(3)(D) may also be served at a place not within a judicial district of the United States.

(3)   Manner.

(A) A warrant is executed by arresting the defendant. Upon arrest, an officer possessing the original or a duplicate original warrant must show it to the defendant. If the officer does not possess the warrant, the officer must inform the defendant of the warrant's existence and of the offense charged and, at the defendant's request, must show the original or a duplicate original warrant to the defendant as soon as possible.

(B) A summons is served on an individual defendant:

(i) by delivering a copy to the defendant personally; or

(ii) by leaving a copy at the defendant's residence or usual place of abode with a person of suitable age and discretion residing at that location and by mailing a copy to the defendant's last known address.

(C) A summons is served on an organization by delivering a copy to an officer, to a managing or general agent, or to another agent appointed or legally authorized to receive service of process. If the agent is one authorized by statute and the statute so requires, a copy must also be mailed to the organization.

* * *

(4)   Return.

(A) After executing a warrant, the officer must return it to the judge before whom the defendant is brought in accordance with Rule 5. The officer may do so by reliable electronic means. At the request of an attorney for the government, an unexecuted warrant must be brought back to and canceled by a magistrate judge or, if none is reasonably available, by a state or local judicial officer.

(B) The person to whom a summons was delivered for service must return it on or before the return day.

(C) At the request of an attorney for the government, a judge may deliver an unexecuted warrant, an unserved summons, or a copy of the warrant or summons to the marshal or other authorized person for execution or service.

(d)   Warrant by Telephone or Other Reliable Electronic Means.

In accordance with Rule 4.1, a magistrate judge may issue a warrant or summons based on information communicated by telephone or other reliable electronic means.

Rule 4.1.   Complaint, Warrant, or Summons by Telephone or Other Reliable Electronic Means

(a)   In General.

A magistrate judge may consider information communicated by telephone or other reliable electronic means when reviewing a complaint or deciding whether to issue a warrant or summons.

(b)   Procedures.

If a magistrate judge decides to proceed under this rule, the following procedures apply:

(1)   Taking Testimony Under Oath.

The judge must place under oath — and may examine — the applicant and any person on whose testimony the application is based.

(2)   Creating a Record of the Testimony and Exhibits.

(A) Testimony Limited to Attestation. If the applicant does no more than attest to the contents of a written affidavit submitted by reliable electronic means, the judge must acknowledge the attestation in writing on the affidavit.

(B) Additional Testimony or Exhibits. If the judge considers additional testimony or exhibits, the judge must:

(i) have the testimony recorded verbatim by an electronic recording device, by a court reporter, or in writing;

(ii) have any recording or reporter's notes transcribed, have the transcription certified as accurate, and file it;

(iii) sign any other written record, certify its accuracy, and file it; and

(iv) make sure that the exhibits are filed.

(3)   Preparing a Proposed Duplicate Original of a Complaint, Warrant, or Summons.

The applicant must prepare a proposed duplicate original of a complaint, warrant, or summons, and must read or otherwise transmit its contents verbatim to the judge.

(4)   Preparing an Original Complaint, Warrant, or Summons.

If the applicant reads the contents of the proposed duplicate original, the judge must enter those contents into an original complaint, warrant, or summons. If the applicant transmits the contents by reliable electronic means, the transmission received by the judge may serve as the original.

(5)   Modification.

The judge may modify the complaint, warrant, or summons. The judge must then:

(A) transmit the modified version to the applicant by reliable electronic means; or

(B) file the modified original and direct the applicant to modify the proposed duplicate original accordingly.

(6)   Issuance.

To issue the warrant or summons, the judge must:

(A) sign the original documents;

(B) enter the date and time of issuance on the warrant or summons; and

(C) transmit the warrant or summons by reliable electronic means to the applicant or direct the applicant to sign the judge's name and enter the date and time on the duplicate original.

(c) ***Suppression Limited.***

Absent a finding of bad faith, evidence obtained from a warrant issued under this rule is not subject to suppression on the ground that issuing the warrant in this manner was unreasonable under the circumstances.

Rule 5. Initial Appearance

(a) ***In General.***

(1) Appearance Upon an Arrest.

(A) A person making an arrest within the United States must take the defendant without unnecessary delay before a magistrate judge, or before a state or local judicial officer as Rule 5(c) provides, unless a statute provides otherwise.

(B) A person making an arrest outside the United States must take the defendant without unnecessary delay before a magistrate judge, unless a statute provides otherwise.

(2) Exceptions.

(A) An officer making an arrest under a warrant issued upon a complaint charging solely a violation of 18 U.S.C. §1073 need not comply with this rule if:

(i) the person arrested is transferred without unnecessary delay to the custody of appropriate state or local authorities in the district of arrest; and

(ii) an attorney for the government moves promptly, in the district where the warrant was issued, to dismiss the complaint.

(B) If a defendant is arrested for violating probation or supervised release, Rule 32.1 applies.

(C) If a defendant is arrested for failing to appear in another district, Rule 40 applies.

(3) Appearance Upon a Summons.

When a defendant appears in response to a summons under Rule 4, a magistrate judge must proceed under Rule 5(d) or (e), as applicable.

(b)   Arrest Without a Warrant.

If a defendant is arrested without a warrant, a complaint meeting Rule 4(a)'s requirement of probable cause must be promptly filed in the district where the offense was allegedly committed.

(c)   Place of Initial Appearance; Transfer to Another District.

(1)   Arrest in the District Where the Offense Was Allegedly Committed.

If the defendant is arrested in the district where the offense was allegedly committed:

(A) the initial appearance must be in that district; and

(B) if a magistrate judge is not reasonably available, the initial appearance may be before a state or local judicial officer.

(2)   Arrest in a District Other Than Where the Offense Was Allegedly Committed.

If the defendant was arrested in a district other than where the offense was allegedly committed, the initial appearance must be:

(A) in the district of arrest; or

(B) in an adjacent district if:

(i) the appearance can occur more promptly there; or

(ii) the offense was allegedly committed there and the initial appearance will occur on the day of arrest.

* * *

(d)   Procedure in a Felony Case.

(1)   Advice.

If the defendant is charged with a felony, the judge must inform the defendant of the following:

(A) the complaint against the defendant, and any affidavit filed with it;

(B) the defendant's right to retain counsel or to request that counsel be appointed if the defendant cannot obtain counsel;

(C) the circumstances, if any, under which the defendant may secure pre-trial release;

(D) any right to a preliminary hearing; and

(E) the defendant's right not to make a statement, and that any statement made may be used against the defendant.

(F) that a defendant who is not a United States citizen may request that an attorney for the government or a federal law enforcement official notify a consular officer from the defendant's country of nationality that the defendant has been arrested – but that even without defendant's request, a treat or other international agreement may require consular notification.

(2)   Consulting with Counsel.

The judge must allow the defendant reasonable opportunity to consult with counsel.

(3)   Detention or Release.

The judge must detain or release the defendant as provided by statute or these rules.

(4)   Plea.

A defendant may be asked to plead only under Rule 10.

(e)   Procedure in a Misdemeanor Case.

If the defendant is charged with a misdemeanor only, the judge must inform the defendant in accordance with Rule 58(b)(2).

(f)   Video Teleconferencing.

Video teleconferencing may be used to conduct an appearance under this rule if the defendant consents.

Rule 5.1.   Preliminary Hearing

(a)   *In General.*

If a defendant is charged with an offense other than a petty offense, a magistrate judge must conduct a preliminary hearing unless:

(1)   the defendant waives the hearing;

(2)   the defendant is indicted;

(3)   the government files an information under Rule 7(b) charging the defendant with a felony;

(4)   the government files an information charging the defendant with a misdemeanor; or

(5)   the defendant is charged with a misdemeanor and consents to trial before a magistrate judge.

(b)   *Selecting a District.*

A defendant arrested in a district other than where the offense was allegedly committed may elect to have the preliminary hearing conducted in the district where the prosecution is pending.

(c)   *Scheduling.*

The magistrate judge must hold the preliminary hearing within a reasonable time, but no later than 14 days after the initial appearance if the defendant is in custody and no later than 21 days if not in custody.

(d)   *Extending the Time.*

With the defendant's consent and upon a showing of good cause—taking into account the public interest in the prompt disposition of criminal cases— a magistrate judge may extend the time limits in Rule 5.1(c) one or more times. If the defendant does not consent, the magistrate judge may extend the time limits only on a showing that extraordinary circumstances exist and justice requires the delay.

(e) Hearing and Finding.

At the preliminary hearing, the defendant may cross-examine adverse witnesses and may introduce evidence but may not object to evidence on the ground that it was unlawfully acquired. If the magistrate judge finds probable cause to believe an offense has been committed and the defendant committed it, the magistrate judge must promptly require the defendant to appear for further proceedings.

(f) Discharging the Defendant.

If the magistrate judge finds no probable cause to believe an offense has been committed or the defendant committed it, the magistrate judge must dismiss the complaint and discharge the defendant. A discharge does not preclude the government from later prosecuting the defendant for the same offense.

(g) Recording the Proceedings.

The preliminary hearing must be recorded by a court reporter or by a suitable recording device. A recording of the proceeding may be made available to any party upon request. A copy of the recording and a transcript may be provided to any party upon request and upon any payment required by applicable Judicial Conference regulations.

(h) Producing a Statement.

(1) In General.

Rule 26.2(a)-(d) and (f) applies at any hearing under this rule, unless the magistrate judge for good cause rules otherwise in a particular case.

(2) Sanctions for Not Producing a Statement.

If a party disobeys a Rule 26.2 order to deliver a statement to the moving party, the magistrate judge must not consider the testimony of a witness whose statement is withheld.

Rule 6.   The Grand Jury

(a)   Summoning a Grand Jury.

(1)   In General.

When the public interest so requires, the court must order that one or more grand juries be summoned. A grand jury must have 16 to 23 members, and the court must order that enough legally qualified persons be summoned to meet this requirement.

(2)   Alternate Jurors.

When a grand jury is selected, the court may also select alternate jurors. Alternate jurors must have the same qualifications and be selected in the same manner as any other juror. Alternate jurors replace jurors in the same sequence in which the alternates were selected. An alternate juror who replaces a juror is subject to the same challenges, takes the same oath, and has the same authority as the other jurors.

(b)   Objection to the Grand Jury or to a Grand Juror.

(1)   Challenges.

Either the government or a defendant may challenge the grand jury on the ground that it was not lawfully drawn, summoned, or selected, and may challenge an individual juror on the ground that the juror is not legally qualified.

(2)   Motion to Dismiss an Indictment.

A party may move to dismiss the indictment based on an objection to the grand jury or on an individual juror's lack of legal qualification, unless the court has previously ruled on the same objection under Rule 6(b)(1). The motion to dismiss is governed by 28 U.S.C. §1867(e). The court must not dismiss the indictment on the ground that a grand juror was not legally qualified if the record shows that at least 12 qualified jurors concurred in the indictment.

(c)   Foreperson and Deputy Foreperson.

The court will appoint one juror as the foreperson and another as the deputy foreperson. In the foreperson's absence, the deputy foreperson will act as the foreperson. The foreperson may administer oaths and affirmations and will sign all indictments. The foreperson—or another juror designated by the foreperson—will record the number of jurors concurring in every indictment and will file the record with the clerk, but the record may not be made public unless the court so orders.

(d) Who May Be Present.

(1) While the Grand Jury Is in Session.

The following persons may be present while the grand jury is in session: attorneys for the government, the witness being questioned, interpreters when needed, and a court reporter or an operator of a recording device.

(2) During Deliberations and Voting.

No person other than the jurors, and any interpreter needed to assist a hearing-impaired or speech-impaired juror, may be present while the grand jury is deliberating or voting.

(e) Recording and Disclosing the Proceedings.

(1) Recording the Proceedings.

Except while the grand jury is deliberating or voting, all proceedings must be recorded by a court reporter or by a suitable recording device. But the validity of a prosecution is not affected by the unintentional failure to make a recording. Unless the court orders otherwise, an attorney for the government will retain control of the recording, the reporter's notes, and any transcript prepared from those notes.

(2) Secrecy.

(A) No obligation of secrecy may be imposed on any person except in accordance with Rule 6(e)(2)(B).

(B) Unless these rules provide otherwise, the following persons must not disclose a matter occurring before the grand jury:

(i) a grand juror;

(ii) an interpreter;

(iii) a court reporter;

(iv) an operator of a recording device;

(v) a person who transcribes recorded testimony;

(vi) an attorney for the government; or

(vii) a person to whom disclosure is made under Rule 6(e)(3)(A)(ii) or (iii).

(3)   Exceptions.

(A) Disclosure of a grand-jury matter—other than the grand jury's deliberations or any grand juror's vote—may be made to:

(i) an attorney for the government for use in performing that attorney's duty;

(ii) any government personnel—including those of a state, state subdivision, Indian tribe, or foreign government—that an attorney for the government considers necessary to assist in performing that attorney's duty to enforce federal criminal law; or

(iii) a person authorized by 18 U.S.C. §3322.

(B) A person to whom information is disclosed under Rule 6(e)(3)(A)(ii) may use that information only to assist an attorney for the government in performing that attorney's duty to enforce federal criminal law. An attorney for the government must promptly provide the court that impaneled the grand jury with the names of all persons to whom a disclosure has been made, and must certify that the attorney has advised those persons of their obligation of secrecy under this rule.

(C) An attorney for the government may disclose any grand-jury matter to another federal grand jury.

(D) An attorney for the government may disclose any grand-jury matter involving foreign intelligence, counterintelligence (as defined in 50 U.S.C. §3003), or foreign intelligence information (as defined in Rule 6(e)(3)(D)(iii)) to any federal law enforcement, intelligence, protective, immigration, national defense, or national security official to assist the official receiving the information in the performance of that official's duties. An attorney for the government may also disclose any grand-jury matter involving, within the United States or elsewhere, a threat of attack or other grave hostile acts of a foreign power or its agent, a threat of domestic or international sabotage or terrorism, or clandestine intelligence gathering activities by an intelligence service or network of a foreign power or by its agent, to any appropriate federal, state, state subdivision, Indian tribal, or foreign government official, for the purpose of preventing or responding to such threat or activities.

(i) Any official who receives information under Rule 6(e)(3)(D) may use the information only as necessary in the conduct of that person's official duties subject to any limitations on the unauthorized disclosure of such information. Any state, state subdivision, Indian tribal, or foreign government official who receives information under Rule 6(e)(3)(D) may use the information only in a manner consistent with any guidelines issued by the Attorney General and the Director of National Intelligence.

(ii) Within a reasonable time after disclosure is made under Rule 6(e)(3)(D), an attorney for the government must file, under seal, a notice with the court in the district where the grand jury convened stating that such information was disclosed and the departments, agencies, or entities to which the disclosure was made.

(iii) As used in Rule 6(e)(3)(D), the term "foreign intelligence information" means:

(a) information, whether or not it concerns a United States person, that relates to the ability of the United States to protect against—

- actual or potential attack or other grave hostile acts of a foreign power or its agent;
- sabotage or international terrorism by a foreign power or its agent; or
- clandestine intelligence activities by an intelligence service or network of a foreign power or by its agent; or

(b) information, whether or not it concerns a United States person, with respect to a foreign power or foreign territory that relates to—

- the national defense or the security of the United States; or
- the conduct of the foreign affairs of the United States.

(E) The court may authorize disclosure—at a time, in a manner, and subject to any other conditions that it directs—of a grand-jury matter:

(i) preliminarily to or in connection with a judicial proceeding;

(ii) at the request of a defendant who shows that a ground may exist to dismiss the indictment because of a matter that occurred before the grand jury;

(iii) at the request of the government, when sought by a foreign court or prosecutor for use in an official criminal investigation;

(iv) at the request of the government if it shows that the matter may disclose a violation of State, Indian tribal, or foreign criminal law, as long as the disclosure is to an appropriate state, state-subdivision, Indian tribal, or foreign government official for the purpose of enforcing that law; or

(v) at the request of the government if it shows that the matter may disclose a violation of military criminal law under the Uniform Code of Military Justice, as long as the disclosure is to an appropriate military official for the purpose of enforcing that law.

(F) A petition to disclose a grand-jury matter under Rule 6(e)(3)(E)(i) must be filed in the district where the grand jury convened. Unless the hearing is ex parte—as it may be when the government is the petitioner—the petitioner must serve the petition on, and the court must afford a reasonable opportunity to appear and be heard to:

(i) an attorney for the government;

(ii) the parties to the judicial proceeding; and

(iii) any other person whom the court may designate.

(G) If the petition to disclose arises out of a judicial proceeding in another district, the petitioned court must transfer the petition to the other court unless the petitioned court can reasonably determine whether disclosure is proper. If the petitioned court decides to transfer, it must send to the transferee court the material sought to be disclosed, if feasible, and a written evaluation of the need for continued grand-jury secrecy. The transferee court must afford those persons identified in Rule 6(e)(3)(F) a reasonable opportunity to appear and be heard.

(4)   Sealed Indictment.

The magistrate judge to whom an indictment is returned may direct that the indictment be kept secret until the defendant is in custody or has been released pending trial. The clerk must then seal the indictment, and no person may disclose the indictment's existence except as necessary to issue or execute a warrant or summons.

(5)   Closed Hearing.

Subject to any right to an open hearing in a contempt proceeding, the court must close any hearing to the extent necessary to prevent disclosure of a matter occurring before a grand jury.

(6)   Sealed Records.

Records, orders, and subpoenas relating to grand-jury proceedings must be kept under seal to the extent and as long as necessary to prevent the unauthorized disclosure of a matter occurring before a grand jury.

(7)   Contempt.

A knowing violation of Rule 6, or of any guidelines jointly issued by the Attorney General and the Director of National Intelligence under Rule 6, may be punished as a contempt of court.

(f)   Indictment and Return.

A grand jury may indict only if at least 12 jurors concur. The grand jury—or its foreperson or deputy foreperson—must return the indictment to a magistrate judge in open court. To avoid unnecessary cost or delay, the magistrate may take the return by video conference from the court where the grand jury sits. If a complaint or information is pending against the defendant and 12 jurors do not concur in the indictment, the foreperson must promptly and in writing report the lack of concurrence to the magistrate judge.

(g)   Discharging the Grand Jury.

A grand jury must serve until the court discharges it, but it may serve more than 18 months only if the court, having determined that an extension is in the public interest, extends the grand jury's service. An extension may be granted for no more than 6 months, except as otherwise provided by statute.

(h)   Excusing a Juror.

At any time, for good cause, the court may excuse a juror either temporarily or permanently, and if permanently, the court may impanel an alternate juror in place of the excused juror.

(i)   "Indian Tribe" Defined.

"Indian tribe" means an Indian tribe recognized by the Secretary of the Interior on a list published in the Federal Register under 25 U.S.C. §479a-1.

Rule 7.   The Indictment and the Information

(a)   When Used.

(1)   Felony.

An offense (other than criminal contempt) must be prosecuted by an indictment if it is punishable:

(A) by death; or

(B) by imprisonment for more than one year.

(2)   Misdemeanor.

An offense punishable by imprisonment for one year or less may be prosecuted in accordance with Rule 58(b)(1).

(b)   Waiving Indictment.

An offense punishable by imprisonment for more than one year may be prosecuted by information if the defendant—in open court and after being advised of the nature of the charge and of the defendant's rights—waives prosecution by indictment.

(c)   Nature and Contents.

(1)   In General.

The indictment or information must be a plain, concise, and definite written statement of the essential facts constituting the offense charged and must be signed by an attorney for the government. It need not contain a formal introduction or conclusion. A count may incorporate by reference an allegation made in another count. A count may allege that the means by which the defendant committed the offense are unknown or that the defendant committed it by one or more specified means. For each count, the indictment or information must give the official or customary citation of the statute, rule, regulation, or other provision of law that the defendant is alleged to have violated. For purposes of an indictment referred to in section 3282 of title 18, United States Code, for which the identity of the defendant is unknown, it shall be sufficient for the indictment to describe the defendant as an individual whose name is unknown, but who has a particular DNA profile, as that term is defined in that section 3282.

    (2)   Citation Error.

Unless the defendant was misled and thereby prejudiced, neither an error in a citation nor a citation's omission is a ground to dismiss the indictment or information or to reverse a conviction.

(d) Surplusage.

Upon the defendant's motion, the court may strike surplusage from the indictment or information.

(e) Amending an Information.

Unless an additional or different offense is charged or a substantial right of the defendant is prejudiced, the court may permit an information to be amended at any time before the verdict or finding.

(f) Bill of Particulars.

The court may direct the government to file a bill of particulars. The defendant may move for a bill of particulars before or within 14 days after arraignment or at a later time if the court permits. The government may amend a bill of particulars subject to such conditions as justice requires.

Rule 8.   Joinder of Offenses or Defendants

(a) Joinder of Offenses.

The indictment or information may charge a defendant in separate counts with 2 or more offenses if the offenses charged—whether felonies or misdemeanors or both—are of the same or similar character, or are based on the same act or transaction, or are connected with or constitute parts of a common scheme or plan.

(b) Joinder of Defendants.

The indictment or information may charge 2 or more defendants if they are alleged to have participated in the same act or transaction, or in the same series of acts or transactions, constituting an offense or offenses. The defendants may be charged in one or more counts together or separately. All defendants need not be charged in each count.

Rule 11.   Pleas

(a)   Entering a Plea.

(1)   In General.

A defendant may plead not guilty, guilty, or (with the court's consent) nolo contendere.

(2)   Conditional Plea.

With the consent of the court and the government, a defendant may enter a conditional plea of guilty or nolo contendere, reserving in writing the right to have an appellate court review an adverse determination of a specified pretrial motion. A defendant who prevails on appeal may then withdraw the plea.

(3)   Nolo Contendere Plea.

Before accepting a plea of nolo contendere, the court must consider the parties' views and the public interest in the effective administration of justice.

(4)   Failure to Enter a Plea.

If a defendant refuses to enter a plea or if a defendant organization fails to appear, the court must enter a plea of not guilty.

(b)   Considering and Accepting a Guilty or Nolo Contendere Plea.

(1)   Advising and Questioning the Defendant.

Before the court accepts a plea of guilty or nolo contendere, the defendant may be placed under oath, and the court must address the defendant personally in open court. During this address, the court must inform the defendant of, and determine that the defendant understands, the following:

(A) the government's right, in a prosecution for perjury or false statement, to use against the defendant any statement that the defendant gives under oath;

(B) the right to plead not guilty, or having already so pleaded, to persist in that plea;

(C) the right to a jury trial;

(D) the right to be represented by counsel—and if necessary have the court appoint counsel—at trial and at every other stage of the proceeding;

(E) the right at trial to confront and cross-examine adverse witnesses, to be protected from compelled self-incrimination, to testify and present evidence, and to compel the attendance of witnesses;

(F) the defendant's waiver of these trial rights if the court accepts a plea of guilty or nolo contendere;

(G) the nature of each charge to which the defendant is pleading;

(H) any maximum possible penalty, including imprisonment, fine, and term of supervised release;

(I) any mandatory minimum penalty;

(J) any applicable forfeiture;

(K) the court's authority to order restitution;

(L) the court's obligation to impose a special assessment;

(M) in determining a sentence, the court's obligation to calculate the applicable sentencing-guideline range and to consider that range, possible departures under the Sentencing Guidelines, and other sentencing factors under 18 U.S.C. §3553(a);

(N) the terms of any plea-agreement provision waiving the right to appeal or to collaterally attack the sentence.

(O) that, if convicted, a defendant who is not a United States citizen may be removed from the United States, denied citizenship, and denied admission to the United States in the future.

(2)   Ensuring That a Plea Is Voluntary.

Before accepting a plea of guilty or nolo contendere, the court must address the defendant personally in open court and determine that the plea is voluntary and did not result from force, threats, or promises (other than promises in a plea agreement).

(3)   Determining the Factual Basis for a Plea.

Before entering judgment on a guilty plea, the court must determine that there is a factual basis for the plea.

(c)   Plea Agreement Procedure.

(1)   In General.

An attorney for the government and the defendant's attorney, or the defendant when proceeding pro se, may discuss and reach a plea agreement. The court must not participate in these discussions. If the defendant pleads guilty or nolo contendere to either a charged offense or a lesser or related offense, the plea agreement may specify that an attorney for the government will:

(A) not bring, or will move to dismiss, other charges;

(B) recommend, or agree not to oppose the defendant's request, that a particular sentence or sentencing range is appropriate or that a particular provision of the Sentencing Guidelines, or policy statement, or sentencing factor does or does not apply (such a recommendation or request does not bind the court); or

(C) agree that a specific sentence or sentencing range is the appropriate disposition of the case, or that a particular provision of the Sentencing Guidelines, or policy statement, or sentencing factor does or does not apply (such a recommendation or request binds the court once the court accepts the plea agreement).

(2)   Disclosing a Plea Agreement.

The parties must disclose the plea agreement in open court when the plea is offered, unless the court for good cause allows the parties to disclose the plea agreement in camera.

(3) Judicial Consideration of a Plea Agreement.

(A) To the extent the plea agreement is of the type specified in Rule 11(c)(1)(A) or (C), the court may accept the agreement, reject it, or defer a decision until the court has reviewed the presentence report.

(B) To the extent the plea agreement is of the type specified in Rule 11(c)(1)(B), the court must advise the defendant that the defendant has no right to withdraw the plea if the court does not follow the recommendation or request.

(4) Accepting a Plea Agreement.

If the court accepts the plea agreement, it must inform the defendant that to the extent the plea agreement is of the type specified in Rule 11(c)(1)(A) or (C), the agreed disposition will be included in the judgment.

(5) Rejecting a Plea Agreement.

If the court rejects a plea agreement containing provisions of the type specified in Rule 11(c)(1)(A) or (C), the court must do the following on the record and in open court (or, for good cause, in camera):

(A) inform the parties that the court rejects the plea agreement;

(B) advise the defendant personally that the court is not required to follow the plea agreement and give the defendant an opportunity to withdraw the plea; and

(C) advise the defendant personally that if the plea is not withdrawn, the court may dispose of the case less favorably toward the defendant than the plea agreement contemplated.

(d) Withdrawing a Guilty or Nolo Contendere Plea.

A defendant may withdraw a plea of guilty or nolo contendere:

(1) before the court accepts the plea, for any reason or no reason; or

(2) after the court accepts the plea, but before it imposes sentence if:

(A) the court rejects a plea agreement under Rule 11(c)(5); or

(B) the defendant can show a fair and just reason for requesting the withdrawal.

(e)   Finality of a Guilty or Nolo Contendere Plea.

After the court imposes sentence, the defendant may not withdraw a plea of guilty or nolo contendere, and the plea may be set aside only on direct appeal or collateral attack.

(f)   Admissibility or Inadmissibility of a Plea, Plea Discussions, and Related Statements.

The admissibility or inadmissibility of a plea, a plea discussion, and any related statement is governed by Federal Rule of Evidence 410.

(g)   Recording the Proceedings.

The proceedings during which the defendant enters a plea must be recorded by a court reporter or by a suitable recording device. If there is a guilty plea or a nolo contendere plea, the record must include the inquiries and advice to the defendant required under Rule 11(b) and (c).

(h)   Harmless Error.

A variance from the requirements of this rule is harmless error if it does not affect substantial rights.

Rule 14.   Relief from Prejudicial Joinder

(a)   Relief.

If the joinder of offenses or defendants in an indictment, an information, or a consolidation for trial appears to prejudice a defendant or the government, the court may order separate trials of counts, sever the defendants' trials, or provide any other relief that justice requires.

(b)   Defendant's Statements.

Before ruling on a defendant's motion to sever, the court may order an attorney for the government to deliver to the court for in camera inspection any defendant's statement that the government intends to use as evidence.

Rule 16.   Discovery and Inspection

(a)   Government's Disclosure.

(1)   Information Subject to Disclosure.

(A) Defendant's Oral Statement. Upon a defendant's request, the government must disclose to the defendant the substance of any relevant oral statement made by the defendant, before or after arrest, in response to interrogation by a person the defendant knew was a government agent if the government intends to use the statement at trial.

(B) Defendant's Written or Recorded Statement. Upon a defendant's request, the government must disclose to the defendant, and make available for inspection, copying, or photographing, all of the following:

(i) any relevant written or recorded statement by the defendant if:

- the statement is within the government's possession, custody, or control; and
- the attorney for the government knows—or through due diligence could know—that the statement exists;

(ii) the portion of any written record containing the substance of any relevant oral statement made before or after arrest if the defendant made the statement in response to interrogation by a person the defendant knew was a government agent; and

(iii) the defendant's recorded testimony before a grand jury relating to the charged offense.

(C) Organizational Defendant. Upon a defendant's request, if the defendant is an organization, the government must disclose to the defendant any statement described in Rule 16(a)(1)(A) and (B) if the government contends that the person making the statement:

(i) was legally able to bind the defendant regarding the subject of the statement because of that person's position as the defendant's director, officer, employee, or agent; or

(ii) was personally involved in the alleged conduct constituting the offense and was legally able to bind the defendant regarding that conduct because of that person's position as the defendant's director, officer, employee, or agent.

(D) Defendant's Prior Record. Upon a defendant's request, the government must furnish the defendant with a copy of the defendant's prior criminal record that is within the government's possession, custody, or control if the attorney for the government knows—or through due diligence could know—that the record exists.

(E) Documents and Objects. Upon a defendant's request, the government must permit the defendant to inspect and to copy or photograph books, papers, documents, data, photographs, tangible objects, buildings or places, or copies or portions of any of these items, if the item is within the government's possession, custody, or control and:

(i) the item is material to preparing the defense;

(ii) the government intends to use the item in its case-in-chief at trial; or

(iii) the item was obtained from or belongs to the defendant.

(F) Reports of Examinations and Tests. Upon a defendant's request, the government must permit a defendant to inspect and to copy or photograph the results or reports of any physical or mental examination and of any scientific test or experiment if:

(i) the item is within the government's possession, custody, or control;

(ii) the attorney for the government knows—or through due diligence could know—that the item exists; and

(iii) the item is material to preparing the defense or the government intends to use the item in its case-in-chief at trial.

(G) Expert witnesses. At the defendant's request, the government must give to the defendant a written summary of any testimony that the government intends to use under Rules 702, 703, or 705 of the Federal Rules of Evidence during its case-in-chief at trial. If the government requests discovery under subdivision (b)(1)(C)(ii) and the defendant complies, the government must, at the defendant's request, give to the defendant a written summary of testimony that the government intends to use under Rules 702, 703, or 705 of the Federal Rules of Evidence as evidence at trial on the issue of the defendant's mental condition. The summary provided under this subparagraph must describe the witness's opinions, the bases and reasons for those opinions, and the witness's qualifications.

(2)   Information Not Subject to Disclosure.

Except as permitted by Rule 16(a)(1)(A)-(D), (F), and (G), this rule does not authorize the discovery or inspection of reports, memoranda, or other internal government documents made by an attorney for the government or other government agent in connection with investigating or prosecuting the case. Nor does this rule authorize the discovery or inspection of statements made by prospective government witnesses except as provided in 18 U.S.C. §3500.

(3)   Grand Jury Transcripts.

This rule does not apply to the discovery or inspection of a grand jury's recorded proceedings, except as provided in Rules 6, 12(h), 16(a)(1), and 26.2.

(b)   Defendant's Disclosure.

(1)   Information Subject to Disclosure.

(A) Documents and Objects. If a defendant requests disclosure under Rule 16(a)(1)(E) and the government complies, then the defendant must permit the government, upon request, to inspect and to copy or photograph books, papers, documents, data, photographs, tangible objects, buildings or places, or copies or portions of any of these items if:

(i) the item is within the defendant's possession, custody, or control; and

(ii) the defendant intends to use the item in the defendant's case-in-chief at trial.

(B) Reports of Examinations and Tests. If a defendant requests disclosure under Rule 16(a)(1)(F) and the government complies, the defendant must permit the government, upon request, to inspect and to copy or photograph the results or reports of any physical or mental examination and of any scientific test or experiment if:

(i) the item is within the defendant's possession, custody, or control; and

(ii) the defendant intends to use the item in the defendant's case-in-chief at trial, or intends to call the witness who prepared the report and the report relates to the witness's testimony.

(C) Expert Witnesses.—The defendant must, at the government's request, give to the government a written summary of any testimony that the defendant intends to use under Rules 702, 703, or 705 of the Federal Rules of Evidence as evidence at trial, if—

(i) the defendant requests disclosure under subdivision (a)(1)(G) and the government complies; or

(ii) the defendant has given notice under Rule 12.2(b) of an intent to present expert testimony on the defendant's mental condition.

This summary must describe the witness's opinions, the bases and reasons for those opinions, and the witness's qualifications.

(2)   Information Not Subject to Disclosure.

Except for scientific or medical reports, Rule 16(b)(1) does not authorize discovery or inspection of:

(A) reports, memoranda, or other documents made by the defendant, or the defendant's attorney or agent, during the case's investigation or defense; or

(B) a statement made to the defendant, or the defendant's attorney or agent, by:

(i) the defendant;

(ii) a government or defense witness; or

(iii) a prospective government or defense witness.

(c)   *Continuing Duty to Disclose.*

A party who discovers additional evidence or material before or during trial must promptly disclose its existence to the other party or the court if:

(1) the evidence or material is subject to discovery or inspection under this rule; and

(2) the other party previously requested, or the court ordered, its production.

(d)   *Regulating Discovery.*

(1)   Protective and Modifying Orders.

At any time the court may, for good cause, deny, restrict, or defer discovery or inspection, or grant other appropriate relief. The court may permit a party to show good cause by a written statement that the court will inspect ex parte. If relief is granted, the court must preserve the entire text of the party's statement under seal.

(2)   Failure to Comply.

If a party fails to comply with this rule, the court may:

(**A**) order that party to permit the discovery or inspection; specify its time, place, and manner; and prescribe other just terms and conditions;

(**B**) grant a continuance;

(**C**) prohibit that party from introducing the undisclosed evidence; or

(**D**) enter any other order that is just under the circumstances.

Rule 23.   Jury or Nonjury Trial

(a)   *Jury Trial.*

If the defendant is entitled to a jury trial, the trial must be by jury unless:

(**1**) the defendant waives a jury trial in writing;

(**2**) the government consents; and

(**3**) the court approves.

(b)   *Jury Size.*

(1)   In General.

A jury consists of 12 persons unless this rule provides otherwise.

(2)   Stipulation for a Smaller Jury.

At any time before the verdict, the parties may, with the court's approval, stipulate in writing that:

(**A**) the jury may consist of fewer than 12 persons; or

(B) a jury of fewer than 12 persons may return a verdict if the court finds it necessary to excuse a juror for good cause after the trial begins.

(3)   Court Order for a Jury of 11.

After the jury has retired to deliberate, the court may permit a jury of 11 persons to return a verdict, even without a stipulation by the parties, if the court finds good cause to excuse a juror.

(c)   Nonjury Trial.

In a case tried without a jury, the court must find the defendant guilty or not guilty. If a party requests before the finding of guilty or not guilty, the court must state its specific findings of fact in open court or in a written decision or opinion.

Rule 26.2.   Producing a Witness's Statement

(a)   Motion to Produce.

After a witness other than the defendant has testified on direct examination, the court, on motion of a party who did not call the witness, must order an attorney for the government or the defendant and the defendant's attorney to produce, for the examination and use of the moving party, any statement of the witness that is in their possession and that relates to the subject matter of the witness's testimony.

Rule 41.   Search and Seizure

(a)   Scope and Definitions.

(1)   Scope.

This rule does not modify any statute regulating search or seizure, or the issuance and execution of a search warrant in special circumstances.

(2)   Definitions.

The following definitions apply under this rule:

(A) "Property" includes documents, books, papers, any other tangible objects, and information.

(B) "Daytime" means the hours between 6:00 a.m. and 10:00 p.m. according to local time.

(C) "Federal law enforcement officer" means a government agent (other than an attorney for the government) who is engaged in enforcing the criminal laws and is within any category of officers authorized by the Attorney General to request a search warrant.

(D) "Domestic terrorism" and "international terrorism" have the meanings set out in 18 U.S.C. §2331.

(E) "Tracking device" has the meaning set out in 18 U.S.C. §3117(b).

(b)   Venue for a Warrant Application

At the request of a federal law enforcement officer or an attorney for the government:

(1) a magistrate judge with authority in the district—or if none is reasonably available, a judge of a state court of record in the district—has authority to issue a warrant to search for and seize a person or property located within the district;

(2) a magistrate judge with authority in the district has authority to issue a warrant for a person or property outside the district if the person or property is located within the district when the warrant is issued but might move or be moved outside the district before the warrant is executed;

(3) a magistrate judge—in an investigation of domestic terrorism or international terrorism—with authority in any district in which activities related to the terrorism may have occurred has authority to issue a warrant for a person or property within or outside that district; and

(4) a magistrate judge with authority in the district has authority to issue a warrant to install within the district a tracking device; the warrant may authorize use of the device to track the movement of a person or property located within the district, outside the district, or both; and

(5) a magistrate judge having authority in any district where activities related to the crime may have occurred, or in the District of Columbia, may issue a

warrant for property that is located outside the jurisdiction of any state or district, but within any of the following:

(A)   a United States territory, possession, or commonwealth;
(B)   the premises—no matter who owns them—of a United States diplomatic or consular mission in a foreign state, including any appurtenant building, part of a building, or land used for the mission's purposes; or
(C)   a residence and any appurtenant land owned or leased by the United States and used by United States personnel assigned to a United States diplomatic or consular mission in a foreign state.

(6) a magistrate with authority in any district where activities related to a crime may have occurred has authority to issue a warrant to use remote access to search electronic storage media and to seize or copy electronically stored information located within or outside that district if:

(A)   the district where the media or information is located has been concealed through technological means; or
(B)   in an investigation of a violation of 18 U.S.C. §1030(a)(5), the media are protected computers that have been damaged without authorization and are located in five or more districts.

(c)   Persons or Property Subject to Search or Seizure.

A warrant may be issued for any of the following:

(1) evidence of a crime;

(2) contraband, fruits of crime, or other items illegally possessed;

(3) property designed for use, intended for use, or used in committing a crime; or

(4) a person to be arrested or a person who is unlawfully restrained.

(d)   Obtaining a Warrant.

(1)   In General.

After receiving an affidavit or other information, a magistrate judge—or if authorized by Rule 41(b), a judge of a state court of record—must issue the warrant if there is probable cause to search for and seize a person or property or to install and use a tracking device.

(2)   Requesting a Warrant in the Presence of a Judge.

(A) In General. A magistrate judge may issue a warrant based on information communicated by telephone or other reliable electronic means.

(B) Recording Testimony. Upon learning that an applicant is requesting a warrant under Rule 41(d)(3)(A), a magistrate judge must:

(i) place under oath the applicant and any person on whose testimony the application is based; and

(ii) make a verbatim record of the conversation with a suitable recording device, if available, or by a court reporter, or in writing.

(C) Recording Testimony. Testimony taken in support of a warrant must be recorded by a court reporter or by a suitable recording device, and the judge must file the transcript or recording with the clerk, along with any affidavit.

(3)   Requesting a Warrant by Telephonic or Other Means.

In accordance with Rule 4.1, a magistrate judge may issue a warrant based on information communicated by telephone or other reliable electronic means.

(e)   Issuing the Warrant.

(1)   In General.

The magistrate judge or a judge of a state court of record must issue the warrant to an officer authorized to execute it.

(2)   Contents of the Warrant.

(A) Warrant to Search for and Seize a Person or Property. Except for a tracking-device warrant, the warrant must identify the person or property to be searched, identify any person or property to be seized, and designate the magistrate judge to whom it must be returned. The warrant must command the officer to:

(i) execute the warrant within a specified time no longer than 14 days;

(ii) execute the warrant during the daytime, unless the judge for good cause expressly authorizes execution at another time; and

(iii) return the warrant to the magistrate judge designated in the warrant.

(B) Warrant Seeking Electronically Stored Information. A warrant under Rule 41(e)(2)(A) may authorize the seizure of electronic storage media or the seizure or copying of electronically stored information. Unless otherwise specified, the warrant authorizes a later review of the media or information consistent with the warrant. The time for executing the warrant in Rule 4(e)(2)(A) and (f)(1)(A) refers to the seizure or on-site copying of the media or information, and not to any later off-site copying or review.

(C) Warrant for a Tracking Device. A tracking-device warrant must identify the person or property to be tracked, designate the magistrate judge to whom it must be returned, and specify a reasonable length of time that the device may be used. The time must not exceed 45 days from the date the warrant was issued. The court may, for good cause, grant one or more extensions for a reasonable period not to exceed 45 days each. The warrant must command the officer to:

(**i**) complete any installation authorized by the warrant within a specified time no longer than 10 calendar days;

(**ii**) perform any installation authorized by the warrant during the daytime, unless the judge for good cause expressly authorizes installation at another time; and

(**iii**) return the warrant to the judge designated in the warrant.

(f)   Executing and Returning the Warrant.

(1)   Warrant to Search for and Seize a Person or Property.

(A) Noting the Time. The officer executing the warrant must enter on it the exact date and time it was executed.

(B) Inventory. An officer present during the execution of the warrant must prepare and verify an inventory of any property seized. The officer must do so in the presence of another officer and the person from whom, or from whose premises, the property was taken. If either one is not present, the officer must prepare and verify the inventory in the presence of at least one other credible person. In a case involving the seizure of electronic storage media or the seizure or copying of electronically stored information, the inventory may be limited to describing the physical storage media that were seized or copied. The officer may retain a copy of the electronically stored information that was seized or copied.

(C) Receipt. The officer executing the warrant must give a copy of the warrant and a receipt for the property taken to the person from whom, or from whose premises, the property was taken or leave a copy of the warrant and receipt at the place where the officer took the property.

(D) Return. The officer executing the warrant must promptly return it—together with a copy of the inventory—to the magistrate judge designated on the warrant. The judge must, on request, give a copy of the inventory to the person from whom, or from whose premises, the property was taken and to the applicant for the warrant.

(2)   Warrant for a Tracking Device.

(A) Noting the Time. The officer executing a tracking-device warrant must enter on it the exact date and time the device was installed and the period during which it was used.

(B) Return. Within 10 calendar days after the use of the tracking device has ended, the officer executing the warrant must return it to the judge designated in the warrant.

(C) Service. Within 10 calendar days after the use of the tracking device has ended, the officer executing a tracking-device warrant must serve a copy of the warrant on the person who was tracked or whose property was tracked. Service may be accomplished by delivering a copy to the person who, or whose property, was tracked; or by leaving a copy at the person's residence or usual place of abode with an individual of suitable age and discretion who resides at that location and by mailing a copy to the person's last known address. Upon request of the government, the judge may delay notice as provided in Rule 41(f)(3).

(3)   Delayed Notice.

Upon the government's request, a magistrate judge—or if authorized by Rule 41(b), a judge of a state court of record—may delay any notice required by this rule if the delay is authorized by statute.

(g)   Motion to Return Property.

A person aggrieved by an unlawful search and seizure of property or by the deprivation of property may move for the property's return. The motion must be filed in the district where the property was seized. The court must receive evidence on any factual issue necessary to decide the motion. If it grants the motion, the court must return the property to the movant, but may impose reasonable conditions to protect access to the property and its use in later proceedings.

(h)   Motion to Suppress.

A defendant may move to suppress evidence in the court where the trial will occur, as Rule 12 provides.

(i)   Forwarding Papers to the Clerk.

The magistrate judge to whom the warrant is returned must attach to the warrant a copy of the return, of the inventory, and of all other related papers and must deliver them to the clerk in the district where the property was seized.

Excerpted Statutes

18 U.S.C.

§3142.   RELEASE OR DETENTION OF A DEFENDANT PENDING TRIAL

(a) **In general.**—Upon the appearance before a judicial officer of a person charged with an offense, the judicial officer shall issue an order that, pending trial, the person be—

(1) released on personal recognizance or upon execution of an unsecured appearance bond, under subsection (b) of this section;

(2) released on a condition or combination of conditions under subsection (c) of this section;

(3) temporarily detained to permit revocation of conditional release, deportation, or exclusion under subsection (d) of this section; or

(4) detained under subsection (e) of this section.

(b) **Release on personal recognizance or unsecured appearance bond.**—The judicial officer shall order the pretrial release of the person on personal recognizance, or upon execution of an unsecured appearance bond in an amount specified by the court, subject to the condition that the person not commit a Federal, State, or local crime during the period of release and subject to the condition that the person cooperate in the collection of a DNA sample from the person if the collection of such a sample is authorized pursuant to section 3 of the DNA Analysis Backlog Elimination Act of 2000 (42 U.S.C. §14135a), unless the judicial officer determines that such release will not reasonably assure the appearance of the person as required or will endanger the safety of any other person or the community.

(c) **Release on conditions.**—(1) If the judicial officer determines that the release described in subsection (b) of this section will not reasonably assure the appearance of the person as required or will endanger the safety of any other person or the community, such judicial officer shall order the pretrial release of the person—

(A) subject to the condition that the person not commit a Federal, State, or local crime during the period of release and subject to the condition that the person cooperate in the collection of a DNA sample from the person if the collection of such a sample is authorized pursuant to section 3 of the DNA Analysis Backlog Elimination Act of 2000 (42 U.S.C. §14135a); and

(B) subject to the least restrictive further condition, or combination of conditions, that such judicial officer determines will reasonably assure the appearance of the person as required and the safety of any other person and the community, which may include the condition that the person—

(i) remain in the custody of a designated person, who agrees to assume supervision and to report any violation of a release condition to the court, if the designated person is able reasonably to assure the judicial officer that the person will appear as required and will not pose a danger to the safety of any other person or the community;

(ii) maintain employment, or, if unemployed, actively seek employment;

(iii) maintain or commence an educational program;

(iv) abide by specified restrictions on personal associations, place of abode, or travel;

(v) avoid all contact with an alleged victim of the crime and with a potential witness who may testify concerning the offense;

(vi) report on a regular basis to a designated law enforcement agency, pretrial services agency, or other agency;

(vii) comply with a specified curfew;

(viii) refrain from possessing a firearm, destructive device, or other dangerous weapon;

(ix) refrain from excessive use of alcohol, or any use of a narcotic drug or other controlled substance, as defined in section 102 of the Controlled Substances Act (21 U.S.C. §802), without a prescription by a licensed medical practitioner;

(x) undergo available medical, psychological, or psychiatric treatment, including treatment for drug or alcohol dependency, and remain in a specified institution if required for that purpose;

(xi) execute an agreement to forfeit upon failing to appear as required, property of a sufficient unencumbered value, including money, as is reasonably necessary to assure the appearance of the person as required, and shall provide the court with proof of ownership and the value of the property along with information regarding existing encumbrances as the judicial office may require;

(xii) execute a bail bond with solvent sureties; who will execute an agreement to forfeit in such amount as is reasonably necessary to assure appearance of the person as required and shall provide the court with information regarding the value of the assets and liabilities of the surety if other than an approved surety and the nature and extent of encumbrances against the surety's property; such surety shall have a net worth which shall have sufficient unencumbered value to pay the amount of the bail bond;

(xiii) return to custody for specified hours following release for employment, schooling, or other limited purposes; and

(xiv) satisfy any other condition that is reasonably necessary to assure the appearance of the person as required and to assure the safety of any other person and the community.

In any case that involves a minor victim under section 1201, 1591, 2241, 2242, 2244(a)(1), 2245, 2251, 2251A, 2252(a)(1), 2252(a)(2), 2252(a)(3), 2252A(a)(1), 2252A(a)(2), 2252A(a)(3), 2252A(a)(4), 2260, 2421, 2422, 2423, or 2425 of this title, or a failure to register offense under section 2250 of this title, any release order shall contain, at a minimum, a condition of electronic monitoring and each of the conditions specified at subparagraphs (iv), (v), (vi), (vii), and (viii).

(2) The judicial officer may not impose a financial condition that results in the pretrial detention of the person.

(3) The judicial officer may at any time amend the order to impose additional or different conditions of release.

(d) **Temporary detention to permit revocation of conditional release, deportation, or exclusion.** — If the judicial officer determines that—

(1) such person—

(A) is, and was at the time the offense was committed, on—

(i) release pending trial for a felony under Federal, State, or local law;

(ii) release pending imposition or execution of sentence, appeal of sentence or conviction, or completion of sentence, for any offense under Federal, State, or local law; or

(iii) probation or parole for any offense under Federal, State, or local law; or

(B) is not a citizen of the United States or lawfully admitted for permanent residence, as defined in section 101(a)(20) of the Immigration and Nationality Act (8 U.S.C. §1101(a)(20)); and

(2) such person may flee or pose a danger to any other person or the community; such judicial officer shall order the detention of such person, for a period of not more than ten days, excluding Saturdays, Sundays, and holidays, and direct the attorney for the Government to notify the appropriate court, probation or parole official, or State or local law enforcement official, or the appropriate official of the Immigration and Naturalization Service. If the official fails or declines to take such person into custody during that period, such person shall be treated in accordance with the other provisions of this section, notwithstanding the applicability of other provisions of law governing release pending trial or deportation or exclusion proceedings. If

temporary detention is sought under paragraph (1)(B) of this subsection, such person has the burden of proving to the court such person's United States citizenship or lawful admission for permanent residence.

(e) **Detention.**—(1) If, after a hearing pursuant to the provisions of subsection (f) of this section, the judicial officer finds that no condition or combination of conditions will reasonably assure the appearance of the person as required and the safety of any other person and the community, such judicial officer shall order the detention of the person before trial.

(2) In a case described in subsection (f)(1) of this section, a rebuttable presumption arises that no condition or combination of conditions will reasonably assure the safety of any other person and the community if such judicial officer finds that—

(A) the person has been convicted of a Federal offense that is described in subsection (f)(1) of this section, or of a State or local offense that would have been an offense described in subsection (f)(1) of this section if a circumstance giving rise to Federal jurisdiction had existed;

(B) the offense described in subparagraph (A) was committed while the person was on release pending trial for a Federal, State, or local offense; and

(C) a period of not more than five years has elapsed since the date of conviction, or the release of the person from imprisonment, for the offense described in subparagraph (A), whichever is later.

(3) Subject to rebuttal by the person, it shall be presumed that no condition or combination of conditions will reasonably assure the appearance of the person as required and the safety of the community if the judicial officer finds that there is probable cause to believe that the person committed—

(A) an offense for which a maximum term of imprisonment of ten years or more is prescribed in the Controlled Substances Act (21 U.S.C. §801 et seq.), the Controlled Substances Import and Export Act (21 U.S.C. §951 et seq.), or chapter 705 of title 46;

(B) an offense under section 924(c), 956(a), or 2332b of this title;

(C) an offense listed in section 2332b(g)(5)(B) of title 18, United States Code, for which a maximum term of imprisonment of 10 years or more is prescribed;

(D) an offense under chapter 77 of this title for which a maximum term of imprisonment of 20 years or more is prescribed; or

(E) an offense involving a minor victim under section 1201, 1591, 2241, 2242, 2244(a)(1), 2245, 2251, 2251A, 2252(a)(1), 2252(a)(2), 2252(a)(3), 2252A(a)(1), 2252A(a)(2), 2252A(a)(3), 2252A(a)(4), 2260, 2421, 2422, 2423, or 2425 of this title.

(f) **Detention hearing.**—The judicial officer shall hold a hearing to determine whether any condition or combination of conditions set forth in subsection (c) of this section will reasonably assure the appearance of such person as required and the safety of any other person and the community—

(1) upon motion of the attorney for the Government, in a case that involves—

(A) a crime of violence, a violation of section 1591, or an offense listed in section 2332b(g)(5)(B) for which a maximum term of imprisonment of 10 years or more is prescribed;

(B) an offense for which the maximum sentence is life imprisonment or death;

(C) an offense for which a maximum term of imprisonment of ten years or more is prescribed in the Controlled Substances Act (21 U.S.C. §801 et seq.), the Controlled Substances Import and Export Act (21 U.S.C. §951 et seq.), or chapter 705 of title 46;

(D) any felony if such person has been convicted of two or more offenses described in subparagraphs (A) through (C) of this paragraph, or two or more State or local offenses that would have been offenses described in subparagraphs (A) through (C) of this paragraph if a circumstance giving rise to Federal jurisdiction had existed, or a combination of such offenses; or

(E) any felony that is not otherwise a crime of violence that involves a minor victim or that involves the possession or use of a firearm or destructive device (as those terms are defined in section 921), or any other dangerous weapon, or involves a failure to register under section 2250 of title 18, United States Code; or

(2) Upon motion of the attorney for the Government or upon the judicial officer's own motion, in a case that involves—

(A) a serious risk that such person will flee; or

(B) a serious risk that such person will obstruct or attempt to obstruct justice, or threaten, injure, or intimidate, or attempt to threaten, injure, or intimidate, a prospective witness or juror.

The hearing shall be held immediately upon the person's first appearance before the judicial officer unless that person, or the attorney for the Government, seeks a continuance. Except for good cause, a continuance on motion of such person may not exceed five days (not including any intermediate Saturday, Sunday, or legal holiday), and a continuance on motion of the attorney for the Government may not exceed three days (not including any intermediate Saturday, Sunday, or legal holiday). During a continuance, such person shall be detained, and the judicial officer, on motion of the attorney for the Government or sua sponte, may order that, while in custody, a person who appears to be a narcotics addict receive a medical examination to determine whether such person is an addict. At the hearing, such person has the right to be represented by counsel, and, if financially unable to obtain adequate representation, to have counsel appointed. The person shall be afforded an opportunity to testify, to present witnesses, to cross-examine witnesses who appear at the hearing, and to present information by proffer or otherwise. The rules concerning admissibility of evidence in criminal trials do not apply to the presentation and consideration of information at the hearing. The facts the judicial officer uses to support a finding pursuant to subsection (e) that no condition or combination of conditions will reasonably assure the safety of any other person and the community shall be supported by clear and convincing evidence. The person may be detained pending completion of the hearing. The hearing may be reopened, before or after a determination by the judicial officer, at any time before trial if the judicial officer finds that information exists that was not known to the movant at the time of the hearing and that has a material bearing on the issue whether there are conditions of release that will reasonably assure the appearance of such person as required and the safety of any other person and the community.

(g) **Factors to be considered.**—The judicial officer shall, in determining whether there are conditions of release that will reasonably assure the appearance of the person as required and the safety of any other person and the community, take into account the available information concerning—

(1) the nature and circumstances of the offense charged, including whether the offense is a crime of violence, a violation of section 1591, a Federal crime of terrorism, or involves a minor victim or a controlled substance, firearm, explosive, or destructive device;

(2) the weight of the evidence against the person;

(3) the history and characteristics of the person, including—

(A) the person's character, physical and mental condition, family ties, employment, financial resources, length of residence in the community, community ties, past conduct, history relating to drug or alcohol abuse, criminal history, and record concerning appearance at court proceedings; and

(B) whether, at the time of the current offense or arrest, the person was on probation, on parole, or on other release pending trial, sentencing, appeal, or completion of sentence for an offense under Federal, State, or local law; and

(4) the nature and seriousness of the danger to any person or the community that would be posed by the person's release. In considering the conditions of release described in subsection (c)(1)(B)(xi) or (c)(1)(B)(xii) of this section, the judicial officer may upon his own motion, or shall upon the motion of the Government, conduct an inquiry into the source of the property to be designated for potential forfeiture or offered as collateral to secure a bond, and shall decline to accept the designation, or the use as collateral, of property that, because of its source, will not reasonably assure the appearance of the person as required.

(h) **Contents of release order.**—In a release order issued under subsection (b) or (c) of this section, the judicial officer shall—

(1) include a written statement that sets forth all the conditions to which the release is subject, in a manner sufficiently clear and specific to serve as a guide for the person's conduct; and

(2) advise the person of—

    (A) the penalties for violating a condition of release, including the penalties for committing an offense while on pretrial release;

    (B) the consequences of violating a condition of release, including the immediate issuance of a warrant for the person's arrest; and

    (C) sections 1503 of this title (relating to intimidation of witnesses, jurors, and officers of the court), 1510 (relating to obstruction of criminal investigations), 1512 (tampering with a witness, victim, or an informant), and 1513 (retaliating against a witness, victim, or an informant).

(i) **Contents of detention order.**—In a detention order issued under subsection (e) of this section, the judicial officer shall—

    (1) include written findings of fact and a written statement of the reasons for the detention;

    (2) direct that the person be committed to the custody of the Attorney General for confinement in a corrections facility separate, to the extent practicable, from persons awaiting or serving sentences or being held in custody pending appeal;

    (3) direct that the person be afforded reasonable opportunity for private consultation with counsel; and

    (4) direct that, on order of a court of the United States or on request of an attorney for the Government, the person in charge of the corrections facility in which the person is confined deliver the person to a United States marshal for the purpose of an appearance in connection with a court proceeding.

The judicial officer may, by subsequent order, permit the temporary release of the person, in the custody of a United States marshal or another appropriate person, to the extent that the judicial officer determines such release to be necessary for preparation of the person's defense or for another compelling reason.

(j) **Presumption of innocence.**—Nothing in this section shall be construed as modifying or limiting the presumption of innocence.

§3144. RELEASE OR DETENTION OF A MATERIAL WITNESS

If it appears from an affidavit filed by a party that the testimony of a person is material in a criminal proceeding, and if it is shown that it may become impracticable to secure the presence of the person by subpoena, a judicial officer may order the arrest of the person and treat the person in accordance with the provisions of section 3142 of this title. No material witness may be detained because of inability to comply with any condition of release if the testimony of such witness can adequately be secured by deposition, and if further detention is not necessary to prevent a failure of justice. Release of a material witness may be delayed for a reasonable period of time until the deposition of the witness can be taken pursuant to the Federal Rules of Criminal Procedure.

§3161.   Time Limits and Exclusions

(a) In any case involving a defendant charged with an offense, the appropriate judicial officer, at the earliest practicable time, shall, after consultation with the counsel for the defendant and the attorney for the Government, set the case for trial on a day certain, or list it for trial on a weekly or other short-term trial calendar at a place within the judicial district, so as to assure a speedy trial.

(b) Any information or indictment charging an individual with the commission of an offense shall be filed within thirty days from the date on which such individual was arrested or served with a summons in connection with such charges. If an individual has been charged with a felony in a district in which no grand jury has been in session during such thirty-day period, the period of time for filing of the indictment shall be extended an additional thirty days.

(c)(1) In any case in which a plea of not guilty is entered, the trial of a defendant charged in an information or indictment with the commission of an offense shall commence within seventy days from the filing date (and making public) of the information or indictment, or from the date the defendant has appeared before a judicial officer of the court in which such charge is pending, whichever date last occurs. If a defendant consents in writing to be tried before a magistrate judge on a complaint, the trial shall commence within seventy days from the date of such consent.

(2) Unless the defendant consents in writing to the contrary, the trial shall not commence less than thirty days from the date on which the defendant first appears through counsel or expressly waives counsel and elects to proceed pro se.

(d)(1) If any indictment or information is dismissed upon motion of the defendant, or any charge contained in a complaint filed against an individual is dismissed or otherwise dropped, and thereafter a complaint is filed against such defendant or individual charging him with the same offense or an offense based on the same conduct or arising from the same criminal episode, or an information or indictment is filed charging such defendant with the same offense or an offense based on the same conduct or arising from the same criminal episode, the provisions of subsections (b) and (c) of this section shall be applicable with respect to such subsequent complaint, indictment, or information, as the case may be.

(2) If the defendant is to be tried upon an indictment or information dismissed by a trial court and reinstated following an appeal, the trial shall commence within seventy days from the date the action occasioning the trial becomes final, except that the court retrying the case may extend the period for trial not to exceed one hundred and eighty days from the date the action occasioning the trial becomes final if the unavailability of witnesses or other factors resulting from the passage of time shall make trial within seventy days impractical. The periods of delay enumerated in section 3161(h) are excluded in computing the time limitations specified in this section. The sanctions of section 3162 apply to this subsection.

(e) If the defendant is to be tried again following a declaration by the trial judge of a mistrial or following an order of such judge for a new trial, the trial shall commence within seventy days from the date the action occasioning the retrial becomes final. If the defendant is to be tried again following an appeal or a collateral attack, the trial shall commence within seventy days from the date the action occasioning the retrial becomes final, except that the court retrying the case may extend the period for retrial not to exceed one hundred and eighty days from the date the action occasioning the retrial becomes final if unavailability of witnesses or other factors resulting from passage of time shall make trial within seventy days impractical. The periods of delay enumerated in section 3161(h) are excluded in computing the time limitations specified in this section. The sanctions of section 3162 apply to this subsection.

(f) Notwithstanding the provisions of subsection (b) of this section, for the first twelve-calendar-month period following the effective date of this section as set forth in section 3163(a) of this chapter the time limit imposed with respect to the period between arrest and indictment by subsection (b) of this section shall be sixty days, for the second such twelve-month period such time limit shall be forty-five days and for the third such period such time limit shall be thirty-five days.

(g) Notwithstanding the provisions of subsection (c) of this section, for the first twelve-calendar-month period following the effective date of this section as set forth in section 3163(b) of this chapter, the time limit with respect to the period between arraignment and trial imposed by subsection (c) of this section shall be one hundred and eighty days, for the second such twelve-month period such time limit shall be one hundred and twenty days, and for the third such period such time limit with respect to the period between arraignment and trial shall be eighty days.

(h) The following periods of delay shall be excluded in computing the time within which an information or an indictment must be filed, or in computing the time within which the trial of any such offense must commence:

(1) Any period of delay resulting from other proceedings concerning the defendant, including but not limited to—

(A) delay resulting from any proceeding, including any examinations, to determine the mental competency or physical capacity of the defendant;

(B) delay resulting from trial with respect to other charges against the defendant;

(C) delay resulting from any interlocutory appeal;

(D) delay resulting from any pretrial motion, from the filing of the motion through the conclusion of the hearing on, or other prompt disposition of, such motion;

(E) delay resulting from any proceeding relating to the transfer of a case or the removal of any defendant from another district under the Federal Rules of Criminal Procedure;

(F) delay resulting from transportation of any defendant from another district, or to and from places of examination or hospitalization, except that any time consumed in excess of ten days from the date an order of removal or an order directing such transportation, and the defendant's arrival at the destination shall be presumed to be unreasonable;

(G) delay resulting from consideration by the court of a proposed plea agreement to be entered into by the defendant and the attorney for the Government; and

(H) delay reasonably attributable to any period, not to exceed thirty days, during which any proceeding concerning the defendant is actually under advisement by the court.

(2) Any period of delay during which prosecution is deferred by the attorney for the Government pursuant to written agreement with the defendant, with the approval of the court, for the purpose of allowing the defendant to demonstrate his good conduct.

(3)(A) Any period of delay resulting from the absence or unavailability of the defendant or an essential witness.

(B) For purposes of subparagraph (A) of this paragraph, a defendant or an essential witness shall be considered absent when his whereabouts are unknown and, in addition, he is attempting to avoid apprehension or prosecution or his whereabouts cannot be determined by due diligence. For purposes of such subparagraph, a defendant or an essential witness shall be considered unavailable whenever his whereabouts are known but his presence for trial cannot be obtained by due diligence or he resists appearing at or being returned for trial.

(4) Any period of delay resulting from the fact that the defendant is mentally incompetent or physically unable to stand trial.

(5) If the information or indictment is dismissed upon motion of the attorney for the Government and thereafter a charge is filed against the defendant for the same offense, or any offense required to be joined with that offense, any period of delay from the date the charge was dismissed to the date the time limitation would commence to run as to the subsequent charge had there been no previous charge.

(6) A reasonable period of delay when the defendant is joined for trial with a codefendant as to whom the time for trial has not run and no motion for severance has been granted.

(7)(A) Any period of delay resulting from a continuance granted by any judge on his own motion or at the request of the defendant or his counsel or at the request of the attorney for the Government, if the judge granted such continuance on the basis of his findings that the ends of justice served by taking such action outweigh the best interest of the public and the defendant in a speedy trial. No such period of delay resulting from a continuance granted by the court in accordance with this paragraph shall be excludable under this subsection unless the court sets forth, in the record of the case, either orally or in writing, its reasons for finding that the ends of justice served by the granting of such continuance outweigh the best interests of the public and the defendant in a speedy trial.

(**B**) The factors, among others, which a judge shall consider in determining whether to grant a continuance under subparagraph (A) of this paragraph in any case are as follows:

(**i**) Whether the failure to grant such a continuance in the proceeding would be likely to make a continuation of such proceeding impossible, or result in a miscarriage of justice.

(**ii**) Whether the case is so unusual or so complex, due to the number of defendants, the nature of the prosecution, or the existence of novel questions of fact or law, that it is unreasonable to expect adequate preparation for pretrial proceedings or for the trial itself within the time limits established by this section.

(**iii**) Whether, in a case in which arrest precedes indictment, delay in the filing of the indictment is caused because the arrest occurs at a time such that it is unreasonable to expect return and filing of the indictment within the period specified in section 3161(b), or because the facts upon which the grand jury must base its determination are unusual or complex.

(**iv**) Whether the failure to grant such a continuance in a case which, taken as a whole, is not so unusual or so complex as to fall within clause (ii), would deny the defendant reasonable time to obtain counsel, would unreasonably deny the defendant or the Government continuity of counsel, or would deny counsel for the defendant or the attorney for the Government the reasonable time necessary for effective preparation, taking into account the exercise of due diligence.

(**C**) No continuance under subparagraph (A) of this paragraph shall be granted because of general congestion of the court's calendar, or lack of diligent preparation or failure to obtain available witnesses on the part of the attorney for the Government.

(8) Any period of delay, not to exceed one year, ordered by a district court upon an application of a party and a finding by a preponderance of the evidence that an official request, as defined in section 3292 of this title, has been made for evidence of any such offense and that it reasonably appears, or reasonably appeared at the time the request was made, that such evidence is, or was, in such foreign country.

(i) If trial did not commence within the time limitation specified in section 3161 because the defendant had entered a plea of guilty or nolo contendere subsequently withdrawn to any or all charges in an indictment or information, the defendant shall be deemed indicted with respect to all charges therein contained within the meaning of section 3161, on the day the order permitting withdrawal of the plea becomes final.

(j)(1) If the attorney for the Government knows that a person charged with an offense is serving a term of imprisonment in any penal institution, he shall promptly—

   (A) undertake to obtain the presence of the prisoner for trial; or

   (B) cause a detainer to be filed with the person having custody of the prisoner and request him to so advise the prisoner and to advise the prisoner of his right to demand trial.

(2) If the person having custody of such prisoner receives a detainer, he shall promptly advise the prisoner of the charge and of the prisoner's right to demand trial. If at any time thereafter the prisoner informs the person having custody that he does demand trial, such person shall cause notice to that effect to be sent promptly to the attorney for the Government who caused the detainer to be filed.

(3) Upon receipt of such notice, the attorney for the Government shall promptly seek to obtain the presence of the prisoner for trial.

(4) When the person having custody of the prisoner receives from the attorney for the Government a properly supported request for temporary custody of such prisoner for trial, the prisoner shall be made available to that attorney for the Government (subject, in cases of interjurisdictional transfer, to any right of the prisoner to contest the legality of his delivery).

(k)(1) If the defendant is absent (as defined by subsection (h)(3)) on the day set for trial, and the defendant's subsequent appearance before the court on a bench warrant or other process or surrender to the court occurs more than 21 days after the day set for trial, the defendant shall be deemed to have first appeared before a judicial officer of the court in which the information or indictment is pending within the meaning of subsection (c) on the date of the defendant's subsequent appearance before the court.

(2) If the defendant is absent (as defined by subsection (h)(3)) on the day set for trial, and the defendant's subsequent appearance before the court on a bench warrant or other process or surrender to the court occurs not more than 21 days after the day set for trial, the time limit required by subsection (c), as extended by subsection (h), shall be further extended by 21 days.

28 U.S.C.

§2241. POWER TO GRANT WRIT

(a) Writs of habeas corpus may be granted by the Supreme Court, any justice thereof, the district courts and any circuit judge within their respective jurisdictions. The order of a circuit judge shall be entered in the records of the district court of the district wherein the restraint complained of is had.

(b) The Supreme Court, any justice thereof and any circuit judge may decline to entertain an application for a writ of habeas corpus and may transfer the application for hearing and determination to the district court having jurisdiction to entertain it.

(c) The writ of habeas corpus shall not extend to a prisoner unless

(1) He is in custody under or by color of the authority of the United States or is committed for trial before some court there of; or

(2) He is in custody for an act done or omitted in pursuance of an Act of Congress, or an order, process, judgment or decree of a court or judge of the United States; or

(3) He is in custody in violation of the constitution or laws or treaties of the United States; or

(4) He, being a citizen of a foreign state and domiciled therein is in custody for an act done or omitted under any alleged right, title, authority, privilege, protection, or exemption claimed under the commission, order or sanction of any foreign state, or under color thereof, the validity and effect of which depend upon the law of nations; or

(5) It is necessary to bring him into court to testify or for trial.

(d) Where an application for a writ of habeas corpus is made by a person in custody under the judgment and sentence of a court of a State which contains two or more Federal judicial districts, the application may be filed in the district court for the district wherein such person is in custody or in the district court for the district within which the State court was held which convicted and sentenced him and each of such district courts shall have concurrent jurisdiction to entertain the application. The district court for the district wherein such an application is filed in the exercise of its discretion and in furtherance of justice may transfer the application to the other district court for hearing and determination.

(e)(1) No court, justice, or judge shall have jurisdiction to hear or consider an application for a writ of habeas corpus filed by or on behalf of an alien detained by the United States who has been determined by the United States to have been properly detained as an enemy combatant or is awaiting such determination.

(2) Except as provided in paragraphs (2) and (3) of section 1005(e) of the Detainee Treatment Act of 2005 (10 U.S.C. §801 note), no court, justice, or judge shall have jurisdiction to hear or consider any other action against the United States or its agents relating to any aspect of the detention, transfer, treatment, trial, or conditions of confinement of an alien who is or was detained by the United States and has been determined by the United States to have been properly detained as an enemy combatant or is awaiting such determination.

§2242. APPLICATION

Application for a writ of habeas corpus shall be in writing signed and verified by the person for whose relief it is intended or by someone acting in his behalf.

It shall allege the facts concerning the applicant's commitment or detention, the name of the person who has custody over him and by virtue of what claim or authority, if known.

It may be amended or supplemented as provided in the rules of procedure applicable to civil actions.

If addressed to the Supreme Court, a justice thereof or a circuit judge it shall state the reasons for not making application to the district court of the district in which the applicant is held.

§2243.   ISSUANCE OF WRIT; RETURN; HEARING; DECISION

A court, justice or judge entertaining an application for a writ of habeas corpus shall forthwith award the writ or issue an order directing the respondent to show cause why the writ should not be granted, unless it appears from the application that the applicant or person detained is not entitled thereto.

The writ, or order to show cause shall be directed to the person having custody of the person detained. It shall be returned within three days unless for good cause additional time, not exceeding twenty days, is allowed.

The person to whom the writ or order is directed shall make a return certifying the true cause of the detention.

When the writ or order is returned a day shall be set for hearing, not more than five days after the return unless for good cause additional time is allowed.

Unless the application for the writ and the return present only issues of law the person to whom the writ is directed shall be required to produce at the hearing the body of the person detained.

The applicant or the person detained may, under oath, deny any of the facts set forth in the return or allege any other material facts.

The return and all suggestions made against it may be amended, by leave of court, before or after being filed.

The court shall summarily hear and determine the facts, and dispose of the matter as law and justice require.

§2244.   FINALITY OF DETERMINATION

(a) No circuit or district judge shall be required to entertain an application for a writ of habeas corpus to inquire into the detention of a person pursuant to a judgment of a court of the United States if it appears that the legality of such detention has been determined by a judge or court of the United States on a prior application for a writ of habeas corpus except as provided in section 2255.

(b)(1) A claim presented in a second or successive habeas corpus application under section 2254 that was presented in a prior application shall be dismissed.

(2) A claim presented in a second or successive habeas corpus application under section 2254 that was not presented in a prior application shall be dismissed unless—

(A) the applicant shows that the claim relies on a new rule of constitutional law, made retroactive to cases on collateral review by the Supreme Court, that was previously unavailable; or

(B)(i) the factual predicate for the claim could not have been discovered previously through the exercise of due diligence; and

(ii) the facts underlying the claim, if proven and viewed in light of the evidence as a whole, would be sufficient to establish by clear and convincing evidence that, but for constitutional error, no reasonable fact-finder would have found the applicant guilty of the underlying offense.

(3)(A) Before a second or successive application permitted by this section is filed in the district court, the applicant shall move in the appropriate court of appeals for an order authorizing the district court to consider the application.

(B) A motion in the court of appeals for an order authorizing the district court to consider a second or successive application shall be determined by a three-judge panel of the court of appeals.

(C) The court of appeals may authorize the filing of a second or successive application only if it determines that the application makes a prima facie showing that the application satisfies the requirements of this subsection.

(D) The court of appeals shall grant or deny the authorization to file a second or successive application not later than 30 days after the filing of the motion.

(E) The grant or denial of an authorization by a court of appeals to file a second or successive application shall not be appealable and shall not be the subject of a petition for rehearing or for a writ of certiorari.

(4) A district court shall dismiss any claim presented in a second or successive application that the court of appeals has authorized to be filed unless the applicant shows that the claim satisfies the requirements of this section.

(c) In a habeas corpus proceeding brought in behalf of a person in custody pursuant to the judgment of a State court, a prior judgment of the Supreme Court of the United States on an appeal or review by a writ of certiorari at the instance of the prisoner of the decision of such State court, shall be conclusive as to all issues of fact or law with respect to an asserted denial of a Federal right which constitutes ground for discharge in a habeas corpus proceeding, actually adjudicated by the Supreme Court therein, unless the applicant for the writ of habeas corpus shall plead and the court shall find the existence of a material and controlling fact which did not appear in the record of the proceeding in the Supreme Court and the court shall further find that the applicant for the writ of habeas corpus could not have caused such fact to appear in such record by the exercise of reasonable diligence.

(d)(1) A 1-year period of limitation shall apply to an application for a writ of habeas corpus by a person in custody pursuant to the judgment of a State court. The limitation period shall run from the latest of—

(A) the date on which the judgment became final by the conclusion of direct review or the expiration of the time for seeking such review;

(B) the date on which the impediment to filing an application created by State action in violation of the Constitution or laws of the United States is removed, if the applicant was prevented from filing by such State action;

(C) the date on which the constitutional right asserted was initially recognized by the Supreme Court, if the right has been newly recognized by the Supreme Court and made retroactively applicable to cases on collateral review; or

(D) the date on which the factual predicate of the claim or claims presented could have been discovered through the exercise of due diligence.

(2) The time during which a properly filed application for State post-conviction or other collateral review with respect to the pertinent judgment or claim is pending shall not be counted toward any period of limitation under this subsection.

§2245. Certificate of Trial Judge Admissible in Evidence

On the hearing of an application for a writ of habeas corpus to inquire into the legality of the detention of a person pursuant to a judgment the certificate of the judge who presided at the trial resulting in the judgment, setting forth the facts occurring at the trial, shall be admissible in evidence. Copies of the certificate shall be filed with the court in which the application is pending and in the court in which the trial took place.

§2246. Evidence; Depositions; Affidavits

On application for a writ of habeas corpus, evidence may be taken orally or by deposition, or, in the discretion of the judge, by affidavit. If affidavits are admitted any party shall have the right to propound written interrogatories to the affiants, or to file answering affidavits.

§2247. Documentary Evidence

On application for a writ of habeas corpus documentary evidence, transcripts of proceedings upon arraignment, plea and sentence and a transcript of the oral testimony introduced on any previous similar application by or in behalf of the same petitioner, shall be admissible in evidence.

§2248. RETURN OR ANSWER; CONCLUSIVENESS

The allegations of a return to the writ of habeas corpus or of an answer to an order to show cause in a habeas corpus proceeding, if not traversed, shall be accepted as true except to the extent that the judge finds from the evidence that they are not true.

§2249. CERTIFIED COPIES OF INDICTMENT, PLEA AND JUDGMENT; DUTY OF RESPONDENT

On application for a writ of habeas corpus to inquire into the detention of any person pursuant to a judgment of a court of the United States, the respondent shall promptly file with the court certified copies of the indictment, plea of petitioner and the judgment, or such of them as may be material to the questions raised, if the petitioner fails to attach them to his petition, and same shall be attached to the return to the writ, or to the answer to the order to show cause.

§2250. INDIGENT PETITIONER ENTITLED TO DOCUMENTS WITHOUT COST

If on any application for a writ of habeas corpus an order has been made permitting the petitioner to prosecute the application in forma pauperis, the clerk of any court of the United States shall furnish to the petitioner without cost certified copies of such documents or parts of the record on file in his office as may be required by order of the judge before whom the application is pending.

§2251. STAY OF STATE COURT PROCEEDINGS

A justice or judge of the United States before whom a habeas corpus proceeding is pending, may, before final judgment or after final judgment of discharge, or pending appeal, stay any proceeding against the person detained in any State court or by or under the authority of any State for any matter involved in the habeas corpus proceeding.

After the granting of such a stay, any such proceeding in any State court or by or under the authority of any State shall be void. If no stay is granted, any such proceeding shall be as valid as if no habeas corpus proceedings or appeal were pending.

§2252. NOTICE

Prior to the hearing of a habeas corpus proceeding in behalf of a person in custody of State officers or by virtue of State laws notice shall be served on the attorney general or other appropriate officer of such State as the justice or judge at the time of issuing the writ shall direct.

§2253.   APPEAL

(a) In a habeas corpus proceeding or a proceeding under section 2255 before a district judge, the final order shall be subject to review, on appeal, by the court of appeals for the circuit in which the proceeding is held.

(b) There shall be no right of appeal from a final order in a proceeding to test the validity of a warrant to remove to another district or place for commitment or trial a person charged with a criminal offense against the United States, or to test the validity of such person's detention pending removal proceedings.

(c)(1) Unless a circuit justice or judge issues a certificate of appealability, an appeal may not be taken to the court of appeals from—

(A) the final order in a habeas corpus proceeding in which the detention complained of arises out of process issued by a State court; or

(B) the final order in a proceeding under section 2255.

(2) A certificate of appealability may issue under paragraph (1) only if the applicant has made a substantial showing of the denial of a constitutional right.

(3) The certificate of appealability under paragraph (1) shall indicate which specific issue or issues satisfy the showing required by paragraph (2).

§2254.   STATE CUSTODY; REMEDIES IN STATE COURTS

(a) The Supreme Court, a Justice thereof, a circuit judge, or a district court shall entertain an application for a writ of habeas corpus in behalf of a person in custody pursuant to the judgment of a State court only on the ground that he is in custody in violation of the Constitution or laws or treaties of the United States.

(b)(1) An application for a writ of habeas corpus on behalf of a person in custody pursuant to the judgment of a State court shall not be granted unless it appears that—

(A) the applicant has exhausted the remedies available in the courts of the State; or

(B)(i) there is an absence of available State corrective process; or

(ii) circumstances exist that render such process ineffective to protect the rights of the applicant.

(2) An application for a writ of habeas corpus may be denied on the merits, notwithstanding the failure of the applicant to exhaust the remedies available in the courts of the State.

(3) A State shall not be deemed to have waived the exhaustion requirement or be estopped from reliance upon the requirement unless the State, through counsel, expressly waives the requirement.

(c) An applicant shall not be deemed to have exhausted the remedies available in the courts of the State, within the meaning of this section, if he has the right under the law of the State to raise, by any available procedure, the question presented.

(d) An application for a writ of habeas corpus on behalf of a person in custody pursuant to the judgment of a State court shall not be granted with respect to any claim that was adjudicated on the merits in State court proceedings unless the adjudication of the claim—

(1) resulted in a decision that was contrary to, or involved an unreasonable application of, clearly established Federal law, as determined by the Supreme Court of the United States; or

(2) resulted in a decision that was based on an unreasonable determination of the facts in light of the evidence presented in the State court proceeding.

(e)(1) In a proceeding instituted by an application for a writ of habeas corpus by a person in custody pursuant to the judgment of a State court, a determination of a factual issue made by a State court shall be presumed to be correct. The applicant shall have the burden of rebutting the presumption of correctness by clear and convincing evidence.

(2) If the applicant has failed to develop the factual basis of a claim in State court proceedings, the court shall not hold an evidentiary hearing on the claim unless the applicant shows that—

(A) the claim relies on—

(i) a new rule of constitutional law, made retroactive to cases on collateral review by the Supreme Court, that was previously unavailable; or

(ii) a factual predicate that could not have been previously discovered through the exercise of due diligence; and

(B) the facts underlying the claim would be sufficient to establish by clear and convincing evidence that but for constitutional error, no reasonable factfinder would have found the applicant guilty of the underlying offense.

(f) If the applicant challenges the sufficiency of the evidence adduced in such State court proceeding to support the State court's determination of a factual issue made therein, the applicant, if able, shall produce that part of the record pertinent to a determination of the sufficiency of the evidence to support such determination. If the applicant, because of indigency or other reason is unable to produce such part of the record, then the State shall produce such part of the record and the Federal court shall direct the State to do so by order directed to an appropriate State official. If the State cannot provide such pertinent part of the record, then the court shall determine under the existing facts and circumstances what weight shall be given to the State court's factual determination.

(g) A copy of the official records of the State court, duly certified by the clerk of such court to be a true and correct copy of a finding, judicial opinion, or other reliable written indicia showing such a factual determination by the State court shall be admissible in the Federal court proceeding.

(h) Except as provided in section 408 of the Controlled Substances Act, in all proceedings brought under this section, and any subsequent proceedings on review, the court may appoint counsel for an applicant who is or becomes financially unable to afford counsel, except as provided by a rule promulgated by the Supreme Court pursuant to statutory authority. Appointment of counsel under this section shall be governed by section 3006A of title 18.

(i) The ineffectiveness or incompetence of counsel during Federal or State collateral post-conviction proceedings shall not be a ground for relief in a proceeding arising under section 2254.

§2255. Federal Custody; Remedies on Motion Attacking Sentence

(a) A prisoner in custody under sentence of a court established by Act of Congress claiming the right to be released upon the ground that the sentence was imposed in violation of the Constitution or laws of the United States, or that the court was without jurisdiction to impose such sentence, or that the sentence was in excess of the maximum authorized by law, or is otherwise subject to collateral attack, may move the court which imposed the sentence to vacate, set aside or correct the sentence.

(b) Unless the motion and the files and records of the case conclusively show that the prisoner is entitled to no relief, the court shall cause notice thereof to be served upon the United States attorney, grant a prompt hearing thereon, determine the issues and make findings of fact and conclusions of law with respect thereto. If the court finds that the judgment was rendered without jurisdiction, or that the sentence imposed was not authorized by law or otherwise open to collateral attack, or that there has been such a denial or infringement of the constitutional rights of the prisoner as to render the judgment vulnerable to collateral attack, the court shall vacate and set the judgment aside and shall discharge the prisoner or resentence him or grant a new trial or correct the sentence as may appear appropriate.

(c) A court may entertain and determine such motion without requiring the production of the prisoner at the hearing.

(d) An appeal may be taken to the court of appeals from the order entered on the motion as from a final judgment on application for a writ of habeas corpus.

(e) An application for a writ of habeas corpus in behalf of a prisoner who is authorized to apply for relief by motion pursuant to this section, shall not be entertained if it appears that the applicant has failed to apply for relief, by motion, to the court which sentenced him, or that such court has denied him relief, unless it also appears that the remedy by motion is inadequate or ineffective to test the legality of his detention.

(f) A 1-year period of limitation shall apply to a motion under this section. The limitation period shall run from the latest of—

(1) the date on which the judgment of conviction becomes final;

(2) the date on which the impediment to making a motion created by governmental action in violation of the Constitution or laws of the United States is removed, if the movant was prevented from making a motion by such governmental action;

(3) the date on which the right asserted was initially recognized by the Supreme Court, if that right has been newly recognized by the Supreme Court and made retroactively applicable to cases on collateral review; or

(4) the date on which the facts supporting the claim or claims presented could have been discovered through the exercise of due diligence.

(g) Except as provided in section 408 of the Controlled Substances Act, in all proceedings brought under this section, and any subsequent proceedings on review, the court may appoint counsel, except as provided by a rule promulgated by the Supreme Court pursuant to statutory authority. Appointment of counsel under this section shall be governed by section 3006A of title 18.

(h) A second or successive motion must be certified as provided in section 2244 by a panel of the appropriate court of appeals to contain—

(1) newly discovered evidence that, if proven and viewed in light of the evidence as a whole, would be sufficient to establish by clear and convincing evidence that no reasonable factfinder would have found the movant guilty of the offense; or

(2) a new rule of constitutional law, made retroactive to cases on collateral review by the Supreme Court, that was previously unavailable.

§2261.   PRISONERS IN STATE CUSTODY SUBJECT TO CAPITAL SENTENCE; APPOINTMENT OF COUNSEL; REQUIREMENT OF RULE OF COURT OR STATUTE; PROCEDURES FOR APPOINTMENT

(a) This chapter shall apply to cases arising under section 2254 brought by prisoners in State custody who are subject to a capital sentence. It shall apply only if the provisions of subsections (b) and (c) are satisfied.

(b) **Counsel.**—This chapter is applicable if—

(1) the Attorney General of the United States certifies that a State has established a mechanism for providing counsel in postconviction proceedings as provided in section 2265; and

(2) counsel was appointed pursuant to that mechanism, petitioner validly waived counsel, petitioner retained counsel, or petitioner was found not to be indigent.

(c) Any mechanism for the appointment, compensation, and reimbursement of counsel as provided in subsection (b) must offer counsel to all State prisoners under capital sentence and must provide for the entry of an order by a court of record—

(1) appointing one or more counsels to represent the prisoner upon a finding that the prisoner is indigent and accepted the offer or is unable competently to decide whether to accept or reject the offer;

(2) finding, after a hearing if necessary, that the prisoner rejected the offer of counsel and made the decision with an understanding of its legal consequences; or

(3) denying the appointment of counsel upon a finding that the prisoner is not indigent.

(d) No counsel appointed pursuant to subsections (b) and (c) to represent a State prisoner under capital sentence shall have previously represented the prisoner at trial in the case for which the appointment is made unless the prisoner and counsel expressly request continued representation.

(e) The ineffectiveness or incompetence of counsel during State or Federal post-conviction proceedings in a capital case shall not be a ground for relief in a proceeding arising under section 2254. This limitation shall not preclude the appointment of different counsel, on the court's own motion or at the request of the prisoner, at any phase of State or Federal post-conviction proceedings on the basis of the ineffectiveness or incompetence of counsel in such proceedings.

§2262.   MANDATORY STAY OF EXECUTION; DURATION; LIMITS ON STAYS OF EXECUTION; SUCCESSIVE PETITIONS

(a) Upon the entry in the appropriate State court of record of an order under section 2261(c), a warrant or order setting an execution date for a State prisoner shall be stayed upon application to any court that would have jurisdiction over any proceedings filed under section 2254. The application shall recite that the State has invoked the post-conviction review procedures of this chapter and that the scheduled execution is subject to stay.

(b) A stay of execution granted pursuant to subsection (a) shall expire if—

(1) a State prisoner fails to file a habeas corpus application under section 2254 within the time required in section 2263;

(2) before a court of competent jurisdiction, in the presence of counsel, unless the prisoner has competently and knowingly waived such counsel, and after having been advised of the consequences, a State prisoner under capital sentence waives the right to pursue habeas corpus review under section 2254; or

(3) a State prisoner files a habeas corpus petition under section 2254 within the time required by section 2263 and fails to make a substantial showing of the denial of a Federal right or is denied relief in the district court or at any subsequent stage of review.

(c) If one of the conditions in subsection (b) has occurred, no Federal court thereafter shall have the authority to enter a stay of execution in the case, unless the court of appeals approves the filing of a second or successive application under section 2244 (b).

§2263. FILING OF HABEAS CORPUS APPLICATION; TIME REQUIREMENTS; TOLLING RULES

(a) Any application under this chapter for habeas corpus relief under section 2254 must be filed in the appropriate district court not later than 180 days after final State court affirmance of the conviction and sentence on direct review or the expiration of the time for seeking such review.

(b) The time requirements established by subsection (a) shall be tolled—

(1) from the date that a petition for certiorari is filed in the Supreme Court until the date of final disposition of the petition if a State prisoner files the petition to secure review by the Supreme Court of the affirmance of a capital sentence on direct review by the court of last resort of the State or other final State court decision on direct review;

(2) from the date on which the first petition for post-conviction review or other collateral relief is filed until the final State court disposition of such petition; and

(3) during an additional period not to exceed 30 days, if—

(A) a motion for an extension of time is filed in the Federal district court that would have jurisdiction over the case upon the filing of a habeas corpus application under section 2254; and

(B) a showing of good cause is made for the failure to file the habeas corpus application within the time period established by this section.

§2264. SCOPE OF FEDERAL REVIEW; DISTRICT COURT ADJUDICATIONS

(a) Whenever a State prisoner under capital sentence files a petition for habeas corpus relief to which this chapter applies, the district court shall only consider a claim or claims that have been raised and decided on the merits in the State courts, unless the failure to raise the claim properly is—

(1) the result of State action in violation of the Constitution or laws of the United States;

(2) the result of the Supreme Court's recognition of a new Federal right that is made retroactively applicable; or

(3) based on a factual predicate that could not have been discovered through the exercise of due diligence in time to present the claim for State or Federal post-conviction review.

(b) Following review subject to subsections (a), (d), and (e) of section 2254, the court shall rule on the claims properly before it.

§2265.   CERTIFICATION AND JUDICIAL REVIEW

(a) **Certification.**—

(1) **In general.**—If requested by an appropriate State official, the Attorney General of the United States shall determine—

(A) whether the State has established a mechanism for the appointment, compensation, and payment of reasonable litigation expenses of competent counsel in State postconviction proceedings brought by indigent prisoners who have been sentenced to death;

(B) the date on which the mechanism described in subparagraph (A) was established; and

(C) whether the State provides standards of competency for the appointment of counsel in proceedings described in subparagraph (A).

(2) **Effective date.**—The date the mechanism described in paragraph (1)(A) was established shall be the effective date of the certification under this subsection.

(3) **Only express requirements.**—There are no requirements for certification or for application of this chapter other than those expressly stated in this chapter.

(b) **Regulations.**—The Attorney General shall promulgate regulations to implement the certification procedure under subsection (a).

(c) **Review of certification.**—

(1) **In general.**—The determination by the Attorney General regarding whether to certify a State under this section is subject to review exclusively as provided under chapter 158 of this title.

(2) **Venue.**—The Court of Appeals for the District of Columbia Circuit shall have exclusive jurisdiction over matters under paragraph (1), subject to review by the Supreme Court under section 2350 of this title.

(3) **Standard of review.**—The determination by the Attorney General regarding whether to certify a State under this section shall be subject to de novo review.

§2266.   LIMITATION PERIODS FOR DETERMINING APPLICATIONS AND MOTIONS

(a) The adjudication of any application under section 2254 that is subject to this chapter, and the adjudication of any motion under section 2255 by a person under sentence of death, shall be given priority by the district court and by the court of appeals over all noncapital matters.

(b)(1)(A) A district court shall render a final determination and enter a final judgment on any application for a writ of habeas corpus brought under this chapter in a capital case not later than 450 days after the date on which the application is filed, or 60 days after the date on which the case is submitted for decision, whichever is earlier.

(B) A district court shall afford the parties at least 120 days in which to complete all actions, including the preparation of all pleadings and briefs, and if necessary, a hearing, prior to the submission of the case for decision.

(C)(i) A district court may delay for not more than one additional 30-day period beyond the period specified in subparagraph (A), the rendering of a determination of an application for a writ of habeas corpus if the court issues a written order making a finding, and stating the reasons for the finding, that the ends of justice that would be served by allowing the delay outweigh the best interests of the public and the applicant in a speedy disposition of the application.

(ii) The factors, among others, that a court shall consider in determining whether a delay in the disposition of an application is warranted are as follows:

(I) Whether the failure to allow the delay would be likely to result in a miscarriage of justice.

(II) Whether the case is so unusual or so complex, due to the number of defendants, the nature of the prosecution, or the existence of novel questions of fact or law, that it is unreasonable to expect adequate briefing within the time limitations established by subparagraph (A).

(III) Whether the failure to allow a delay in a case that, taken as a whole, is not so unusual or so complex as described in subclause (II), but would otherwise deny the applicant reasonable time to obtain counsel, would unreasonably deny the applicant or the government continuity of counsel, or would deny counsel for the applicant or the government the reasonable time necessary for effective preparation, taking into account the exercise of due diligence.

(iii) No delay in disposition shall be permissible because of general congestion of the court's calendar.

(iv) The court shall transmit a copy of any order issued under clause (i) to the Director of the Administrative Office of the United States Courts for inclusion in the report under paragraph (5).

(2) The time limitations under paragraph (1) shall apply to—

(A) an initial application for a writ of habeas corpus;

(B) any second or successive application for a writ of habeas corpus; and

(C) any redetermination of an application for a writ of habeas corpus following a remand by the court of appeals or the Supreme Court for further proceedings, in which case the limitation period shall run from the date the remand is ordered.

(3)(A) The time limitations under this section shall not be construed to entitle an applicant to a stay of execution, to which the applicant would otherwise not be entitled, for the purpose of litigating any application or appeal.

(B) No amendment to an application for a writ of habeas corpus under this chapter shall be permitted after the filing of the answer to the application, except on the grounds specified in section 2244 (b).

(4)(A) The failure of a court to meet or comply with a time limitation under this section shall not be a ground for granting relief from a judgment of conviction or sentence.

(B) The State may enforce a time limitation under this section by petitioning for a writ of mandamus to the court of appeals. The court of appeals shall act on the petition for a writ of mandamus not later than 30 days after the filing of the petition.

(5)(A) The Administrative Office of the United States Courts shall submit to Congress an annual report on the compliance by the district courts with the time limitations under this section.

(B) The report described in subparagraph (A) shall include copies of the orders submitted by the district courts under paragraph (1)(B)(iv).

(c)(1)(A) A court of appeals shall hear and render a final determination of any appeal of an order granting or denying, in whole or in part, an application brought under this chapter in a capital case not later than 120 days after the date on which the reply brief is filed, or if no reply brief is filed, not later than 120 days after the date on which the answering brief is filed.

(B)(i) A court of appeals shall decide whether to grant a petition for rehearing or other request for rehearing en banc not later than 30 days after the date on which the petition for rehearing is filed unless a responsive pleading is required, in which case the court shall decide whether to grant the petition not later than 30 days after the date on which the responsive pleading is filed.

(ii) If a petition for rehearing or rehearing en banc is granted, the court of appeals shall hear and render a final determination of the appeal not later than 120 days after the date on which the order granting rehearing or rehearing en banc is entered.

(2) The time limitations under paragraph (1) shall apply to—

(A) an initial application for a writ of habeas corpus;

(B) any second or successive application for a writ of habeas corpus; and

(C) any redetermination of an application for a writ of habeas corpus or related appeal following a remand by the court of appeals en banc or the Supreme Court for further proceedings, in which case the limitation period shall run from the date the remand is ordered.

(3) The time limitations under this section shall not be construed to entitle an applicant to a stay of execution, to which the applicant would otherwise not be entitled, for the purpose of litigating any application or appeal.

(4)(A) The failure of a court to meet or comply with a time limitation under this section shall not be a ground for granting relief from a judgment of conviction or sentence.

(B) The State may enforce a time limitation under this section by applying for a writ of mandamus to the Supreme Court.

(5) The Administrative Office of the United States Courts shall submit to Congress an annual report on the compliance by the courts of appeals with the time limitations under this section.